Cowherd Boys Nectar

Śrī Śrī
Preyo-Bhakti-Rasārṇava

The Nectar Ocean of Fraternal Devotion

Composed in Bengali poetry
with numerous Sanskrit quotations by

Śrī Nayanānanda Ṭhākura
1731 A.D.

Translation with Introductory Essays
and Appendixes by
Daśaratha-Suta Dāsa

Bookwrights Press
Charlottesville, Virginia

Text and cover design by Māyāpriyā Devī-Dasī
Śrīla Prabhupāda drawing by Kuladri Dāsa
Kurma Rūpa dāsa photo art by Māyāpriyā Devī-Dasī

Published by
Bookwrights Press
BookwrightsPress.com
editor@bookwrights.com
Previous edition published by Nectar Books
Printed in the United States of America
ISBN 978-1-880404-26-3

List of Paintings used in this book:

Front cover painting by Indischer Maler, c.1740. Museum of Fine Arts, Boston.

Back cover painting (top) from Basohli School, Kulu, circa 1790; and (bottom) from the Govinda Deccan School, Bikaner, c. 1820.

p. 23. Bizarre art, Artist unkown. circa 1920. Butter thieves.

p. 34. Los Angeles County Museum of Art. Artist unknown, Himachal Pradesh, circa 1760. Krishna and cowherds picnicking.

p. 36. V&A Museum. Painted by Chokha, Rajasthan, circa 1813. Painting depicts Krishna and the cowherd boys bringing the cows home in the evening, Godhuli, "The hour of Cowdust"

p. 62. Los Angeles County Museum of Art. Artist unknown, Gujarat, circa 1625. Krishna kills Trinavarta, while cowherd boys cheer.

p. 86. Painting by Mola Ram, circa 1790. Krishna holding Mount Govardhan.

p. 108. Smithsonian Freer and Sackler Gallery. Artist unknown, Guler/Kangra region, India, circa 1790.

p. 148. & 177 Painting from Basohli School, Kulu, circa 1790. Krishna and cowherds playing hide-and-seek.

p. 178. Los Angeles County Museum of Art. Artist unknown, Rajasthan, circa 1600. Krishna and Balarama conversing, with friends looking on.

p. 192. Los Angeles County Museum of Art. Artist unknown, Rajasthan, circa 1525. Krishna kills the crane, Bakasura.

p. 206. Los Angeles County Museum of Art. Artist unknown, Gujarat, circa 1625. Depicts Krishna and the cowherds receiving garlands in Mathura.

p. 215. Los Angeles County Museum of Art. Artist unknown, Rajasthan, circa 1750. Krishna and the cowherd boys at the edge of a forest.

Dedicated to our beloved spiritual master,
His Divine Grace A.C. Bhaktivedanta Swami Prabhupāda,
who brought the pure knowledge of Śrī Śrī Kṛṣṇa-Balarāma
and the cowherd boys to the dark and remote corners
of the suffering West; and who still guides us onward to
the eternal pasturelands.

We also dedicate this book to our gentle godbrother,
His Grace Kurma Rūpa dāsa (1948–2015),
a modernday caretaker and guardian of
Lord Kṛṣṇa's cows in Vraja dhama.

His work continues at CareforCows.com

Contents

Outline of *Śrī Śrī Preyo-Bhakti-Rasārṇava*

CHAPTER ONE
The Glories of Fraternal Devotional Service

CHAPTER TWO
Various Types of Cowherd Boys

CHAPTER THREE
The Ingredients of Transcendental Mellow

CHAPTER FOUR
Symptoms of the Cowherd Boys' Separation and Union

CHAPTER FIVE
Sudāma Sakhā's 64 Associates; The Glories of Kṛṣṇa and Balarāma

CHAPTER SIX
The Residences of Sudama and His Associates

CHAPTER SEVEN
Prātah-Kālīya-Sevā
Services Durning Morning Pastimes
(6:00–8:24 A.M.)

CHAPTER EIGHT
Pūrvāhna-Kālīya-Sevā
Services During Forenoon Pastimes
(8:24 A.M.–10:48 A.M.)

CHAPTER NINE
Madhyāhna-Kālīya-Sevā and Aparāhna-Kālīya-Sevā
Services During Midday and Afternoon Pastimes
(10:48 A.M.–3:36 P.M., 3:36 P.M.–6:00 P.M.)

CHAPTER TEN
Sāyāhna-Kālīya-Sevā and Rātri-Kālīya-Sevā
Services During Dusk and Evening Pastimes
(6:00 P.M.–8:24 P.M., 8:24 P.M.–10:48 P.M.)

Preface

Many might see this book and exclaim, "Wow! Cowherd boys!" They may be advised, however, that this volume introduces an intimate portrayal of transcendental life in Goloka Vṛndāvana. As a sacred and esoteric topic it should not be broadcast very openly, but honored by quiet personal study and appreciation. The technical science of *sakhyā-rasā* and confidential practice of *sakhyā-rasā-bhajan* are herein presented only as a research and study project. This information is not the last word in regard to the exalted fraternal mellow, but is merely another part of the puzzle to be added to the ever-growing spiritual understanding of international Gauḍīya Vaiṣṇavas.

Also, some may say, "I've never heard of this book or its author." As you will see in the introductory essays, everything has been exhaustively researched and clearly explained with full support from the revealed scriptures. Indeed, although it is a very rare and obscure composition, this book fills an important gap in the presently available Gauḍīya Vaiṣṇava *siddhānta*. Most of the Six Gosvāmīs and their successors wrote almost exclusively on *madhura-rasa;* a few modern devotees give certain interpretations to this fact. However, those *sādhakas* who are actually inclined toward the devotional feelings of other *rasas* have not found much for their *bhajan*. We noted this lack and have endeavored to supply it by providing this brief glimpse into the amazing world of Śrī Śrī Kṛṣṇa-Balarāma and the ecstatic cowherd boys.

Within the text at hand (Chapter One) we find the following statement, including a quote from Śrīla Rūpa Gosvāmī's *Bhakti-rasāmṛta-sindhu* that verifies the lofty status of *rāgānugā-bhakti-sādhana,* and specifically the *sādhana* of the *sakhya-rasa:*

duṣkaratvena virale dve sakhyātma-nivedane
kesāṁcid eva dhirānāṁ labhete sādhanārhatām

The tasting and relishing of the mellows of the cowherd boys (*sakhya-rasa-āsvādana*) is very difficult to attain. Indeed, the scriptures state that not only is it difficult, but it is very rarely attained.

[NOTE: Regarding two items of *sādhana* from the listing of sixty-four – #48 *sakhya* and #49 *ātma-nivedana* – Śrīla Rūpa Gosvāmī declares:] Devotional service in fraternal love and devotional service in total self-surrender are two processes that are very rarely seen due to the difficulty involved in their realization. Indeed, these are attained only by a few sober and exalted souls who have earned the right to act on such levels of *sādhana.* (*B.r.s* 1.2.198)]

Therefore, as a matter of issuing a healthy and cautious warning, the translator urges mature readers never to attempt any of the devotional worship procedures outlined herein without first receiving the merciful blessings and learned guidance of the *sādhus,* the *śāstras*, and especially Śrī Guru. Perhaps the safest position of all would be to first examine these topics in order to gain an increased understanding, and then remain bowing repeatedly at a reverential distance.

Hari Bol!

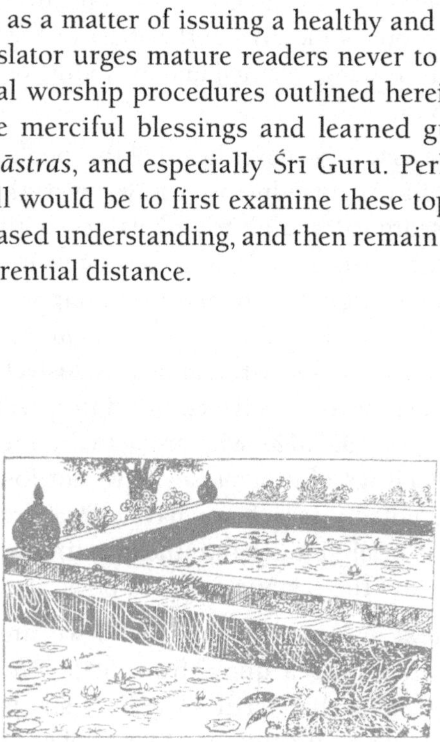

The Nectar Ocean of Fraternal Devotion

By the grace of the supremely merciful Śrī Śrī Nitāi-Gaurāṅga-sundara, this book about *sakhya-bhāva-aṣṭa-kāliya-līlā-smarana* (remembrance of eightfold daily pastimes in the mood of fraternal devotion) is published. The work is presented as an aid to *līlā-smarana* for the *sādhakas* taking shelter of the *sakhya-rasa* (*sakhya-rasāśrayi-bhaktas*). The source for this information is the unique book called *Śrī Śrī Preyo-Bhakti-Rasārṇava*, or *The Nectar Ocean of Fraternal Devotion*, composed in 1731 A.D. by Śrī Nayanānanda Ṭhākura. The word *preyo* is used in the *Bhakti-rasāmṛta-sindhu* as a synonym for *sakhya* (fraternity). The word *bhakti* means devotion, and *rasārṇava* means the ocean (*arṇava*) of transcendental mellows (*rasa*). Nayanānanda was a resident of Maṅgala-dihi village, and hailed from the disciplic branch of the famous Śrī Parṇī Gopāl, who was the direct disciple of Lord Nityānanda's personal associate known as Śrī Sundarānanda Gopāl. Sundarānanda is celebrated as the incarnation of Sudāma, one of the *dvādaśa-gopāls* (twelve principal cowherd boys), who are eternal associates of Lord Balarāma. These dear boyfriends incarnate on earth in order to sport with Balarāma when He descends as Lord Nityānanda Prabhu during the performance of Gaurāṅga-*līlā*. This is described in the Śrī *Caitanya-caritāmṛta, Ādi-līlā,* Chapter 11 (texts 13–48).

Since Ṭhākura Nayanānanda, the author of the book at hand, is in the disciplic succession of Sundarānanda (Sudāma Sakhā), his composition naturally follows in the footsteps of Sudāma. Therefore we find that the ecstatic descriptions of a day in the life of the cowherd boys of Vraja are centered mostly on the activities of Sudāma as well as the *sevā* rendered unto him by his personal friends and servants. Thus it is useful mostly for the *sādhakas* practicing *bhajan* with the specific intent of joining Śrī Sudāma's eternal group. Contemplating all this in the broader sense, we can know that those who wish to follow other specific cowherd boys must accordingly remember and serve their respective *sakhā* group-leader (*yūtheśvara*). Thus many more books could be compiled from the revealed scriptures specifically for the *bhajan* practiced by the devotees of Śrīdāma, Subala, and so forth.

The narrations of a day in the life of the cowherd boys herein (found in Chapters Seven through Ten) are highly nectarean. Still, they appear to be somewhat brief, giving a general outline of their fun-filled activities. Maybe later another volume will be compiled from the more expansive *līlā*-books written by the Gosvāmīs, and divided into eight periods of the day for a more organized profile. Thus we could pull segments from Jīva Gosvāmī's *Gopāla Campū,* Kavi-karṇapūra's *Ānanda Vṛndāvana Campū,* Kṛṣṇadāsa Kavirāja Gosvāmī's *Govinda-līlāmṛta,* Viśvanātha Chakravartī's *Kṛṣṇa Bhāvanāmṛta*, and so on, piecing them together to provide an expansive narration of a day in the life of the cowherd boys.

For glorious descriptions of fraternal love of God, please also be sure to see the superexcellent summary study of *Bhakti-rasāmṛta-sindhu* called *The Nectar of Devotion,* translated by His Divine Grace A. C. Bhaktivedānta Swami Prabhupāda. Especially noteworthy are the two chapters on fraternal love: Chapter 41 "Fraternal Devotion" and Chapter 42 "Fraternal Loving Affairs." There are also many other nice references to the cowherd boys, their beauty and mood throughout *The Nectar of Devotion;* you can have fun looking them up in the Index under "Friends of Kṛṣṇa," also "Fraternal love for Kṛṣṇa" (friendship), and "cows."

A brief note on our presentation of *Cowherd Boys Nectar.* The original work, *Preyo-Bhakti-Rasārṇava,* is written in Bengali couplets (called *pāyār*), with profuse quotations of Sanskrit verses. Included in Śrī Nayanānanda's text are seven Bengali songs, which we preserved in Roman transliteration for the readers to sing, plus we have included as many Sanskrit verses as possible. Regarding diacritic markings, we decided on a half-diacritic, half-phonetic approach. The full diacritic system, although accepted by the scholarly community worldwide, was not incorporated because we find that many readers still mispronounce the words marked with them anyway. Therefore, within the text we have used semi-phonetic spellings. In Sanskrit and Bengali verses quoted, full diacritics are present. We also added the larger type titles that you find throughout the translation. It just seems to make the flow of topics more accessible to the reader, plus it serves well in the outline in the front of the book – you can quickly find and easily zip to certain sections at will. We have labored very carefully to translate every word of every line of this book with painstaking scrutiny in extracting the literal meaning as well as the philosophical intentions of the author. Since we have endeavored to retain the very personal diction and quaint flow of the original Bengali poetry, therefore some sections may read rather awkwardly as far as modern English standards are concerned. May the kind reader indulge us for imperfectly mapping out this sublime pastureland excursion. Happy Cowherding!

Daśaratha-Suta dāsa
Murāri Sevaka Farm
Lord Balarāma's Rāsa-Yātrā
April 25, 1994

Introduction

The Worship of the Cowherd Boys

The process of worshiping Lords Kṛṣṇa and Balarāma and Their cowherd boyfriends is described very scientifically by the Vaiṣṇava *ācāryas* in their writings. Many of their quotes appear in the next essay as part of this introductory matter. The basic principle to be revered is: one attains the *darśana* and *sevā* of Śrī Śrī Rādhā-Govinda by engaging in Rādhā-Govinda's *līlā-smarana* while contemplating one's *siddha-svarūpa* as given in the disciplic succession by Śrī Guru. Śrīpād Rūpa Gosvāmī, who has revealed the path of this type of *bhajan*, and also the disciplic successors following have composed many books on the topic of *aṣṭa-kāliya-smarana* that assist in the *bhajan* following in the footsteps of the Vrajavāsīs. These descendants have elaborated on additional details related to the path of this type of *sādhana*. Śrīpād Rūpa Gosvāmī composed a small work of eleven verses (called *Ekādaṣa Ślokaḥ*) and gave it to Śrīla Kṛṣṇadāsa Kavirāja Gosvāmī for expansion. This is related in *Śrī Bhakti-ratnākāra* (1.818-819) thus:

vaiṣṇava icchāya ekādaśa śloka kailo
kṛṣṇa-dāsa kavirāja vistārite dilo
aṣṭa-kāla līlā tāte ati rasāyana
bhāgyavanta-jana se kore āsvādana

According to the wishes of the devotees, Śrīla Rūpa Gosvāmī composed eleven ślokas about Rādhā and Kṛṣṇa's pastimes. Later he gave the verses to Kṛṣṇadāsa Kavirāja to expand. The descriptions of eight-fold *līlās* contained therein are very nectarean, and they are relished by the fortunate souls.

Consequently, Śrīla Kṛṣṇadasa Kavirāja Gosvāmī has portrayed the Lord's indescribable pastimes in an expansive way by composing the 2,500-verse epic *Śrī Govinda-līlāmṛta*. After this, many other books were written that are also very useful for *aṣṭa-kāliya-līlā-smarana*, such as Kavi Karnapura's *Śrī Kṛṣṇāhnika-kaumudī*, Viśvanātha Chakravartī's *Śrī Kṛṣṇa-bhāvanāmṛta* and *Śrī Sankalpa Kalpadruma*, Śrī Gopāl Guru Gosvāmī's *Gaura-govinda-arcana-smarana-paddhati*, and Śrī Dhyāna-Chandra Gosvāmi's *Gaura-govinda-arcana-smarana-paddhati*, etc.

Most of these voluminous literatures are helpful only to the *sādhakas* who are taking shelter of the conjugal mellow (*madhura-rasāśrayī*). There are, however, very few literatures suitable for the remembrance of the *sādhakas* taking shelter of the fraternal mellow (*sakhya-rasāśrayī*). Therefore Śrī Nayanānanda Ṭhākura has provided a great benefit for the *sādhakas* who are attracted to the fraternal mellow by composing this book named *Preyo-Bhakti-Rasārṇava*. We had thought at first that it was not possible to publish the entire book at this time; the only copy of the original text we found in India contained just the Sixth through Tenth chapters. This is the portion specifically delineating *sakhya-bhāva-aṣṭa-kāliya-līlā-smarana*. But somehow by the merciful wishes of the devotees, a complete text was located, and we have finally completed the entire work. Our labor in this regard will be worthwhile if it proves helpful for the *līlā-smarana* and the appreciation of fraternal mellows by the *sādhakas* who are *sakhya-rasāśrayi*.

May the good-hearted readers forgive our all-pervading mistakes and be satisfied by tasting even a drop of the *Vraja-līlā-rasa* of Vraja-rāja-nandana Śrī Kṛṣṇa.

Summary of *Preyo-Bhakti-Rasārṇava*

This book is fully in concordance with Śrīla Rūpa Gosvāmī's *Śrī Śrī Bhakti-rasāmṛta-sindhu,* but with the specific feature of delineating the science of devotion as executed in the *sakhya-rasa,* the mellow of fraternal love. The **first through fourth chapters** outline the philosophy of *bhakti* according to Śrī Rūpa, giving profuse quotations from *Bhakti-rasāmṛta-sindhu.* Additionally, these sections describe the different types of *sakhās* (cowherd boys), their individual features, mode of dress, and service; *uddīpana* (stimulants), *vayasa* (age), *bhūśana* (ornaments); the ecstasies known as *sāttvika, vyabhichārī, sthāyī* and so forth; *ayoga* and *yoga* (separation and meeting). The **fifth and sixth chapters** give lists of Sudāma's 8 principal boyfriends, plus each of their 8 friends, thus totalling 64 *upa-sakhās;* a description of Sudāma's residence, and descriptions of Vṛṣabhānu-pur (Barṣāṇā) and Nandīśvar. The **seventh through tenth chapters** give narrations of the daily sports and personal *sevā* of the cowherd boys throughout the periods of the day and night known as *prātah* (morning), *pūrvāhṇa* (forenoon), *madhyāhna* (mid-day), *aparāhṇa* (afternoon), *sāyām* (twilight), and *rātri* (night).

60 *Daṇḍas* of the Day

You will note that the daily schedule of Lord Kṛṣṇa and the cowherd boys in this work is divided into units of measurement called *daṇḍa* (24 minutes each); 30 of these make up the day, beginning from about sunrise, and 30 the night, beginning from about sunset. In the daily schedule following Kṛṣṇa and the *gopīs* in the *madhura-rasa,* all 60 *daṇḍas* of the day and night are utilized for non-stop service to the Divine Couple. Practically no one – the Lord, His consort, nor any of the maidservants – get much rest at all. Just a few little naps here and there; the balance of time is spent in continuous and robust *līlās.* However, a day in the life of the cowherd boys in the *sakhya-rasa* is quite different in that they also sport throughout the 30 *daṇḍas* of the daytime, but only up to the tenth *daṇḍa* of the night (about 9:30–10 P.M.). This makes for a fun-filled daily routine of only 40 *daṇḍas*. Thus the cowherd boys actually do take rest, but they dream all the while of playing with Kṛṣṇa and Balarāma out in the pastures. [See chart of *daṇḍas* in the Appendixes.]

Different Names of Kṛṣṇa and Balarāma

Throughout the text of *Preyo-Bhakti-Rasārṇava* we find many different names of Kṛṣṇa, Balarāma and their friends. Since these were used in the original Bengali text, we have simply repeated them in our translation. Thus Kṛṣṇa is intimately addressed as **Kānāi, Kānu, Kṛṣṇa, Gokula-chandra, Śyāma, Gopa Kānta, Nata-bara, Rāya, Yādava Rāya, Guṇa-nidhī, Nanda-suta, Nanda-nandana, Nanda-lāl, Nanda-dulāl, Bhagavān, Hari** and so forth. Balarāma is most often referred to as Rāma, although occasionally we find Him addressed as **Śrī Rāma, Haladhar, Balabhadra, Rohinī-nandana** and **Rohinī-kumār.** Together Kṛṣṇa and Balarāma are referred to several times as **Yugala Kiśor** (the youthful pair). Regarding the name Rāma, it is stated in the *Śrīmad-Bhāgavatam*, 10.8.12: *ayaṁ hi rohiṇī-putro, ramayan suhṛdo guṇaiḥ, ākhyāsyate rāma iti.* "This son of Rohiṇi gives pleasure to His dear ones by His attributes; therefore He should be called Rāma." There are also many ways of addressing Mother Yaśodā that we have kept intact such as **Yaśomatī, Yaśodā Rāṇī, Nanda Rāṇī, Rāṇī**, and simply **Mā**.

The Process of Worship in the *Sakhya-Rasa*

Śrī Ṭhākura Nayanānanda, in *Preyo-Bhakti-Rasārṇava*, charmingly describes the mellow-sweetness of the Vraja-*līlā* of Śrī Kṛṣṇa, Who is Vraja-rāja-nandana Murali-manohar (the delightful son of the king of Vraja and the enchanting flute player). Other than following in the footsteps of the Vrajavāsīs in the transcendentally covetous mood of *rāgātmikā-bhakti*, there is no way to attain Nava-kiśor Naṭabara Śrī Kṛṣṇa. This process is clearly outlined in *Caitanya-caritāmṛta, Madhya-līlā* 22.152–166. To understand something of transcendental mellow, one should study this section very carefully, and take particular note of the Bengali words of the verses and their word-for-word equivalents. This passage stresses the difference between internal and external worship, a theme that recurs throughout the narrations of *Preyo-Bhakti-Rasārṇava.* The keynotes of this *siddhānta* are found in the above-mentioned *Caitanya-caritāmṛta* verses 156–157 thus:

> *bāhya, antara – ihāra dui to' sādhana*
> *'bāhye' sādhaka-dehe kore śravaṇa-kīrtana*
>
> *'mane' nija-siddha-deha koriyā bhāvana*
> *rātri-dine kore vraje kṛṣṇera sevana*

> There are two methods by which one executes the process of *rāgānugā-bhakti* – external and internal. Externally, in the body of a practitioner (*sādhaka-deha*) the devotee remains engaged in hearing and chanting the Lord's glories. Internally, within the mind, the devotee contemplates the perfect spiritual body (*siddha-deha*) and renders service unto Lord Kṛṣṇa in Vraja throughout the entire night and day.

In the next verse (158) of *Caitanya-caritāmṛta,* this process of living simultaneously in two different worlds is also stated very clearly by a Sanskrit verse quoted from Śrīla Rūpa Gosvāmī's *Bhakti-rasāmṛta-sindhu* (1.2.295) thus:

> *sevā sādhaka-rupena siddha-rūpena cātra hi*
> *tad-bhāva-lipsunā kāryā vraja-lokānusārataḥ*

> Service should be rendered by following in the footsteps of the residents of Vraja, being desirous of attaining their same mood. Such service is executed in two distinct ways at the same time – in the external form of a *sādhaka* (practitioner) and the internal form of a *siddha* (perfected being).

This verse from *Bhakti-rasāmṛta-sindhu* is also quoted by Śrīla Bhaktisiddhānta Sarasvatī Gosvāmī in his commentary on Śrī Rūpa's *Upadeśāmṛta,* verse eight. Here is an important excerpt from Bhaktisiddhānta's Sarasvatī's notes:

> ". . . *rāgānugā-bhakti*, or spontaneous devotional service, can be executed in the *śānta-rasa* when one aspires to be like Kṛṣṇa's cows or the stick or flute in the hand of Kṛṣṇa, or the flowers around Kṛṣṇa's neck. In the *dāsya-rasa* one follows in the footsteps of servants like Citraka, Patraka or Raktaka. In the friendly *sakhya-rasa* one can become a friend like Baladeva, Śrīdāma or Sudāma. In the *vātsalya-rasa,* characterized by parental affection, one can become like Nanda Mahārāja and Yaśodā, and in the *madhurya-rasa,* characterized by conjugal love, one can become like Śrīmati Rādhārāṇī or Her lady friends such as Lalitā and Her serving maids (*mañjarīs*) like Rūpa and Rati. This is the essence of all instruction in the matter of devotional service."

This is a very significant passage, for it clearly dispels the somehow widespread myth that all followers of Śrīla Rūpa Gosvāmī must eventually enter only the highest mellow, namely the *madhura-rasa*. From the factual conclusions of the previous *ācāryas* we see that one can aspire to be practically ANYTHING in Kṛṣṇa-*loka*; the transcendental realm is totally unlimited, and so there are absolutely unlimited ways in which we can participate in the Lord's service therein. On the pure spiritual platform, there is no "higher" or "lower." All beings share transcendental equality in serving their Lord to the very best of their capacity and taste.

Furthermore, the moods of those who approach Lord Kṛṣṇa in these different kinds of Vraja relationships are clearly described by Śrī Kṛṣṇa Himself in the *Caitanya-caritāmṛta, Ādi-līlā* 4.21–22, and 24–26:

> *mora putra, mora sakhā, mora prāṇa-pati*
> *ei-bhāve yei more kare śuddha-bhakti*

āpanāke baḍa māne, āmāre sama-hīna
sei bhāve ha-i āmi tāhāra adhīna

"Those who cherish pure loving devotion unto Me, believing: 'Kṛṣṇa is my helpless son' or 'Kṛṣṇa is my best friend' or 'Kṛṣṇa is my beloved paramour' – when they regard themselves as great and think Me to be their equal or inferior – then according to that mood of theirs I willingly become subordinate to them."

mātā more putra-bhāve korena bandhana
ati-hīna-jñāne kore lālana pālana

sakhā śuddha-sakhye kare, skandhe ārohaṇa
tumi kon baḍo loka, – tumi āmi sama

priyā jadi māna kori' karoye bhartsana
veda-stuti haite hare sei mora mana

"Mother Yaśodā fully considers Me to be her young son, and therefore feels free to bind Me when I'm naughty. Regarding Me to be utterly helpless, she endeavors to nourish Me with food and protect Me from harm.

"My cowherd boyfriends climb upon My shoulders out of pure friendship, and they address me boldly, 'You think you're so big? You and I are equal!'

"When My beloved consort gets into a pouting huff and chastises Me, then those words steal away my mind far more than the recitations of reverent Vedic hymns."

Thus the special characteristic feature of the Vrajavāsīs' *bhāva* is the expression of these various kinds of exalted loving moods toward their beloved Kṛṣṇa. There is one single path for attaining the most rarely-attained service of Śrī Śrī Rādhā-Kṛṣṇa, who are the most worshipful treasures of the Vraja *gopas* and *gopīs*. And that is *sādhana-bhajan* performed under the *sad-guru's* direction that follows in the footsteps of the followers of the Vraja *gopas* and *gopīs*. These topics are discussed by Narottama Dās Ṭhākura thus in Śrī *Prema-bhakti-candrikā*, section 5:

jūgala-caraṇa sebi niranṭara ei bhābi
aṇūrāge thākiba sadāya
sādhane bhābiba jāhā siddha-dehe pāba tāhā
rāga pathera ei se upāya

Serving the feet of the Divine Couple, and incessantly meditating upon this service, I will always remain as their affectionate follower. That upon which I meditate while performing my regulated *sādhana* practice – I will attain the same within my spiritual body (*siddha-deha*). This is the method for executing the path of spontaneous devotion (*rāga-patha*).

sādhane je dhana cāi siddha-dehe tāhā pāi
pakwa pakwa mātra se bicāra
pākile se prema-bhakti apakwe sādhana rīti
bhakati-lakṣaṇa-tattva sāra

That treasure I cherish while executing my *sādhana* I will obtain in my spiritual body. The thing to be considered is whether the fruits of devotion are ripe or unripe. The ripened fruits are tasted in the form of *prema-bhakti* (devotional service performed in loving ecstasy), while the unripe condition represents the external process of *sādhana-bhakti* (devotional service performed by regulated activities). These are the symptoms of devotion, which is the essence of all truths.

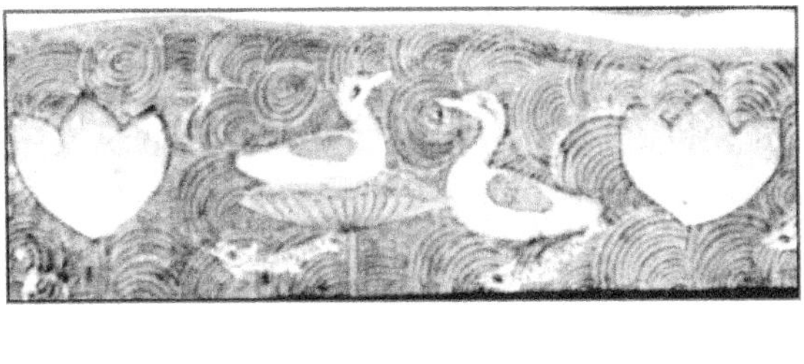

History of *Sakhya-rasa-bhakti* in Maṅgala-dihi Village, West Bengal

We have researched all available information on the Gauḍīya Vaiṣṇava lineage in the village of Maṅgala-dihi. Famous as *sakhya-rasa-upāsakas* (worshipers in the mood of fraternal love), this lineage and its various prominent *ācāryas* as well as descriptions of their writings have been outlined below.

Sundarānanda Ṭhākura

The *Śrīpāt* or holy place where Sundarānanda Prabhu appeared is the village of Haladā Maheśpur in the district of Jeshore (Jashohara), which is now in Bangladesh. His old residential house still exists there. Being a boyish cowherd at heart, he remained as a *naiṣṭika-brahmachārī*, never marrying. Therefore he had no direct descendants except for his disciples. However, there are still descendants of his other family members living in the village of Maṅgala-dihi in the district of Birbhūm. In that same village is a temple of Lord Balarāma (since almost everyone is a follower of the *sakhya-rasa*), and the deity there named Śrī Śrī Baladeva Jiu is regularly worshiped. Every year on the full moon day in the month of *Māgha* (January–February), the anniversary of Sundarānanda's disappearance is celebrated in Maheśpur, and people from the neighboring areas gather together to observe this festival.

The glories of Śrī Sundarānanda and his disciplic branch are stated in the *Caitanya-caritāmṛta* as follows, *Ādi-līlā* 11.23:

sundarānanda – nityānandera śākhā, bhṛtya marma
yāṅra saṅge nityānanda kare vraja-narma

Sundarānanda represents a major branch of Lord Nityānanda's disciplic tree, and is His intimate servant. In Sundarānanda's company, Nityānanda Prabhu makes jokes in the mood of Vraja.

It is also stated in the *Caitanya-bhāgavat, Antya-līlā 5.728*:

prema-rasa-samudra – sundarānanda nāma
nityānanda-svarūpera pārṣada-pradhāna

"The devotee named Sundarānanda is an ocean of love of God and the chief eternal associate of Śrī Nityānanda Svarūpa."

Sundarānanda of Gaurānga-*līlā* is celebrated to be an incarnation of the cowherd boy named Sudāma of Kṛṣṇa-*līlā*. This is confirmed in the *Gaura-gaṇoddeśa-dīpikā* (text 127) as follows: *purā sudāma nāmāsīd adya ṭhākkura-sundaraḥ* – "Whose name was formerly Sudāma has now become Sundara Ṭhākura."

Sudāma is the son of Ratna-bhānu, one of the three younger brothers of Mahārāja Vṛṣabhānu. Thus he is the cousin of Śrīmatī Rādhārani. Sudāma's sister is the famous Śrī Rūpa Mañjarī, personal attendant of Śrī Lalitā Sakhī and intimate maidservant of Śrī Rādhikā.

Once Sundarānanda was so absorbed in the divine madness of *prema* that he grabbed hold of a crocodile and pulled it out of the water. It is mentioned in the book *Vaiṣṇava-vandanā* that on another occasion he caused *kadamba* flowers to bloom out of the branches of a lime tree. Sundarānanda's chief disciple was Parṇī Gopāl (also known as Pānuyā Gopāl).

Parṇī Gopal

The village of Maṅgala-dihi is five *krośa* (about ten miles) south-east of the modern town of Siudi in Birbhūm district. Śrīman Mahāprabhu's *pārśada* (eternal associate) named Śrī Sundarānanda

Gopāl had a principal disciple named Śrī Parṇī (Pānuyā) Gopāl, who was the founding father of the Ṭhākura lineage at Maṅgala-dihi Pānuyā's father was named Mansukha. Although his given name was Gopāl Chandra, because he used to sell *pān* (betel leaves and nuts) he became known as Pānuyā Ṭhākura. Parṇī also means the same thing, dealer of betel. Somehow this was his engagement even though Vaiṣṇavas usually don't have anything to do with the intoxicating betel products. But Gopāl used to engage all the money he earned from such business in the service of the deity, and he even took the articles like bowls, trays and so forth that were used for peddling *pān* and utilized them in the deity's personal *sevā*.

Once there was a Vaiṣṇava *sannyāsī* named Śrī Dhruva Gosvāmī living in the forest of Kāmyavan in Vraja. Due to the atrocities committed by Muslims, he fled to Bengal with twelve deities of Kṛṣṇa as a young cowherd boy, and took shelter in the village of Bhāṇḍīravan. Soon after his arrival, something extremely terrible happened before his very eyes upon a raised platform normally used for *Dola-yatra* (the festival of rocking the deities of Rādhā and Kṛṣṇa on a swing); this calamity, described as follows, made him also flee from that place.

Close by the village of Bhāṇḍīravan in Bengal is the town of Khatangā. Once the ruler of that town discovered that a young widow in his family was having an illicit love affair with the *brāhmaṇa* who was cooking in her house. The king consequently ordered that the *brāhmaṇa's* head be cut in half. Hearing of this order, the *brāhmaṇa* had no recourse other than to run away from that town, and he took shelter at the āśrama of Śrī Dhruva Gosvāmī at Bhāṇḍīravan. The Gosvāmī assured him that no harm would come to him. A few days later the king's men arrived, grabbed hold of the *brāhmaṇa* and mercilessly slaughtered him in an extremely cruel manner. After this, Dhruva Gosvāmī only wanted to leave that place and go elsewhere, so he took his twelve deities and traveled to the bank of the Mayūrākṣi river. But it was the month of Caitra

(March–April), and both banks of the river were overflooded as a result of the profuse monsoon rainfall. The Gosvāmī managed to situate eleven of the deities one by one on boats, but the twelfth deity seemed to be unwilling to go anywhere else and assumed the form of immovable Viśvambhara. This induced Dhruva Gosvāmī to turn the deity over to the care of some poor beggar *brāhmaṇa* that happened to be nearby. He accepted the gift of this Gopāl, and the Gosvāmī then departed.

The poor *brāhmaṇa* clutched this Gopāl *mūrti* to his breast and went to the town of Noyā-dihi. Leaving the deity in the home of Śrī Nanda Dulāl Ghoāl, he left. Many days later a rich and charitable *brāhmaṇa* named Rāmanāth Bhāduri had a temple constructed at Bhāṇḍīravan, and together with the Ghoṣāl family they brought the deity of Śrī Gopāljī and installed Him there.

Meanwhile, Śrī Dhruva Gosvāmī returned to Maṅgala-dihi and stayed in the home of a *paṇḍit* there. In the course of conversation, he heard about a very devout and pious Vaiṣṇava named Gopāl, the son of a local man known as Mansukha. He sent a messenger to fetch Gopāl, who came and heard the *sannyāsī* narrate the wonderful story of the deity Śrī Śrī Śyāma-Chāndra. After thus becoming aquainted, Gopāl and Dhruva Gosvāmī became bound together by the rope of friendship. The *sannyāsī-ṭhākura* was enchanted with the transcendental qualities of Gopāl, and temporarily left his deities of Śrī Syāma-Chānda and Śrī Balarāma in Gopāl's home so he could freely travel for the *darśana* of Lord Jagannātha in Puri. Thus Gopāl along with his wife Lakṣmī-priyā and his sister Mādhavi-lata became immersed in the supreme bliss of serving Śrī Śyāma-Chānda all throughout the day and night. But when Dhruva Gosvāmī returned four years later and took the deities away, all of them became deeply distressed, being afflicted with miserable suffering in separation from the deity. However, the *sannyāsī* could not go very far away from the village, for the *Śrī Vigraha* had become bound by the ropes of loving *prema* offered by Pānuyā Gopāl and family. Thus the deity again assumed the form of immovable

Viśvambhara and would not go any further. Moreover, He ordered the *sannyāsī* in a dream to bring Him back to Maṅgala-dihi. This story is related in the book *Śrī Syāma-chandrodaya* composed by Śrī Jagadānanda in the poetic Bengali meter called *tripadi*.

It is said that this Pānuyā Ṭhākura would travel daily to the town of Panchakota to sell *pān*, then go to Kātoyā to bathe in the Gangā, thereafter returning to Maṅgala-dihi to continue engaging in service to his worshipful Lord. Indeed, he carried Bhagavān with him in his load of *pan*-selling supplies.

Once Pānuyā Thākura saw a tiger dragging off a cow, and he saved the cow by personally pulling it out of the tiger's mouth. Not only that, but he then initiated the tiger with *dikṣā* by giving it Kṛṣṇa-mantra. Another time, at the village of Ghoṣatikuri, he transformed the impure foodstuffs of the accomplished Muslim *fakir* Shāh Ābdulla into flowers.

It can be accepted that Parṇī Gopāl lived during the same time as Śrīman Mahāprabhu, since he is the direct disciple of Śrī Sundarānanda Gopāl. Ṭhākura Sundarānanda gave initiation to Parṇī Gopāl at a landing *ghāt* on the bank of the Puriyā Puṣkariṇī river, in a grove of *kadamba* trees. At that time, at that very place, a grand festival (*mahotsava*) commenced that lasted for twelve days. In honor of this event, even to this day on the celebration of Nandotsava (the day after Śrī Kṛṣṇa Janmāṣṭami) many people assemble and hold a festival at the top of this landing by bathing in the Puriyā and feasting on *chirā* (flat rice), *dadhi* (yogurt), sweets and other delicacies. Thus enjoying *prasād* they attain complete fulfillment.

The main festival days observed throughout the year at Maṅgala-dihi are: the Rāsotsava of the deity named Śrī Vinoda-Rāya; Śrī Pānuyā Gopāl's *Tirodhāna-utsava* (disappearance day) on the *Aśvinī Śuklā-saptami* (seventh day of the bright fortnight in the month of *Āśvina* (September–October); the *Diwāli-utsava* on the new-moon day in the month of *Kārtika* (October–November); and there is the *Nandotsava* festival on the bank of the Puriyā river, as described above.

Parṇī Gopāl's Descendants

Parṇī Gopāl had no offspring, but one *brāhmaṇa* disciple named Kāśināth from Gadagade village had five sons – Ananta, Kiśor, Hari-Caraṇ, Lakṣmaṇ and Kānu-Rāma – and Gopāl accepted them as adopted sons and gave them initiation. After the disappearance of Pānuyā, these boys took charge of his property as well as the *sevā* of his deity. It is said that Śrī Vinoda-Rāya is Pānuyā Ṭhākura's *kula-devatā* (family deity). The descendants of Ananta moved along with the deity of Śrī Balarāma and settled in Khayarāśāla. Kiśor's only daughter named Hīrā-Mani had descendants engaged in the service of Śrī Madana-gopāl. Hari-Caran had no sons, so the sons of Lakṣmaṇ and Kānu-Rāma took charge of the *sevā* of Śrī Śrī Syāma-Chānda.

Kānu-rāma's son named Gopāl-caran had two sons named Gokulānanda and Nayanānanda. The elder Gokulānanda (or Gokula-candra) was *parama premika* (absorbed in divine love) and an expert singer. He was especially successful in composing ecstatic songs (*kīrtan padas*), so much so that after displaying his art before the ruler of Kāśipur he was graciously awarded with tax-free proprietorship of the two villages named Gosvāmī-dihi and Motābega. The income from these properties was engaged only for the *sevā* of Śrī Śyāma-Chānda. Gokulānanda had a son named Jagadānanda who was not only a competent Sanskrit scholar, but also wrote many Bengali songs of *kirtan-padāvali*. He also penned the famous *Śyāma-chandrodaya*, which will eventually be outlined below.

Gokulānanda's younger brother Nayanānanda is the author of the present translation, *Preyo-Bhakti-Rasārṇava*, which includes several of Gokulānanda's songs.

Nayanānanda Thākura

He was the third descendant of Pānuyā Gopāl's disciplic succession in the village of Maṅgala-dihi in the district of Birbhūm. On the basis of Śrīla Rūpa Gosvāmī's Śrī Śrī *Bhakti-rasāmṛta-sindhu*, he composed two books in Bengali poetry – *Śrī Śrī Kṛṣṇa-*

bhakti-rasa-kadamba in 1652 *Śaka* era (1730 A.D.), and *Śrī Śrī Preyo-Bhakti-Rasārṇava* in 1653 *Śaka* (1731 A.D.). Writing these two famous books that systematically reveal the process of *bhajan* in the *sakhya-rasa,* he thereby brought perpetual glory to the village of Maṅgala-dihi. Indeed this town is gratified by holding Nayanānanda within its heart. Besides these compositions, he also wrote many songs for singing in *kīrtan.* Nayanānanda's nephew (the son of his elder brother Gokulānanda) was the famous and influential poet Jagadānanda Ṭhākura, who is mentioned later.

Outline of Nayanānanda's *Kṛṣṇa-bhakti-rasa-kadamba*

Complete in 18 chapters of Bengali couplets, this work outlines the *siddhānta* and methods of executing *Kṛṣṇa-bhakti* as presented by Śrīla Rūpa Gosvāmī in his *Bhakti-rasāmṛta-sindhu.* Throughout the composition we see Nayanānanda's predisposition for the *sakhya-rasa,* and many of his explanations and enthusiastic suggestions to the *sādhaka* are offered in that light.

The divisions of the book are: (1) *mangalācaraṇa* (auspicious invocation); (2) establishment of Śrī Kṛṣṇa *sādhana* as the topmost process of devotion; (3) how everyone is qualified to perform Kṛṣṇa *pūjā* at all times; examples of *bhakta-vātsalya* (Kṛṣṇa's quality of affection for His own devotees); other than Śrī Hari, there is no other goal; three kinds of *Purāṇas* according to the three modes of nature (*sāttvika, rajasika* and *tamasikā),* criticism of those who are Śrī Kṛṣṇa-*vimukha* (averse to Lord Kṛṣṇa); criticism of those who are *viśayī* (sense-gratifiers); the superexcellence of *bhakti;*

sakāmā and *niṣkāma-bhakti* (devotion tinged with desires, and devotion free of desires). [The **fourth through seventeenth** chapters systematically present the most important Sanskrit verses from every chapter of *Bhakti-rasāmṛta-sindhu,* complete with Bengali versifications, translations and explanations thus:] (4) symptoms of *sādhana-bhakti;* topics of *vaidhī* and rāga; effects of *bhakti* such as *kleśa-ghni* (how it destroys all miseries) and so forth; qualifications of one practicing *vaidhī-bhakti;* topics of *uttama, madhyama* and *kaniṣṭha;* topics of *saguṇa* and *nirguṇa* (devotion mixed with material qualities, devotion free from all material influences); how all classes of men are eligible for *bhakti;* (5) the 64 branches of *bhakti;* discussions of each one; (6) *sevāparādha* (offenses against devotional service); *nāma-māhātmya* (glories of the holy names); *nāmāparādha* (offenses against chanting the holy names); descriptions of *hari-nāma;* (7) *rāgānugā-sādhana* (practice of spontaneous devotional service); topics of *sādhaka-siddha-deha* (the two bodies – external body of a practitioner and internal perfect spiritual body); types of devotional desire such as *kāmānugā, sambandhānugā* and so forth; *prakaṭāprakaṭa-līlā* (the Lord's manifest and unmanifest pastimes); (8) topics of *bhāva-bhakti* (devotion in ecstatic love); *bhāvānkura-lakṣaṇa,* (symptoms of the seed of ecstasy sprouting); *prema-bhakti-lakṣaṇa* (symptoms of devotion in pure love of God); (9) symptoms of *vibhāva; alambana* and so forth; Kṛṣṇa's 64 qualities; four kinds of *nāyaka* (heroes) headed by *dhirodātta*; the eighteen faults; the perfection of a *bhakti-sādhaka; uddīpana* and so forth; Kṛṣṇa's different ages such as *kaumāra* and so forth; His *rupa-saundarya* (beautiful form) and so forth; details of His flutes, buffalo horn bugle and so forth; (10) *anubhāva* and *sāttvikā* ecstasies; (11) *vyabhichārī-bhāva, bhāva-śābalya* and so forth, *gariṣṭha-laghiṣṭha* and so forth; (12) *sthāyi-bhāva, kevalā, saṣkulā* and so forth; types of *rati* beginning with *dāsya* [NOTE: the eleventh and twelfth chapter are incomplete, as the only ancient manuscript is disintegrating]; (13) *śānta-bhakti-rasa, prīta-bhakti-rasa,* types of *yoga* and *ayoga* (meeting and separation); (14) *sakhya-bhakti-rasa;* (15) *vātsalya-bhakti-rasa;* (16) *madhura-bhakti-rasa;* (17) topics about Śrī Rādhikā's associates; *uddīpana* (stimulants) in the *madhura-rasa; anubhāva; sādhāramī, samañjasā* and so forth; symptoms of *rati*; topics of *rati* and *prema; śṛṅgāra-bheda* (types of decorations); *vipralambha; sambhoga; daśa-daśā* (the ten conditions of separation); *sapta-gauṇa-rasa* (seven secondary mellows) beginning with *hāsa* (laughing); **(18) Conclusion** – herein the author reviews the contents of the book and describes his worshipable predecessors and so forth.

Jagadānanda Ṭhākura

The famous and influential poet Jagadānanda Ṭhākura was Nayanānanda's nephew (the son of Nayanānanda's elder brother Gokulānanda). Jagadānanda was the fourth descendant of Pānuyā Gopāl's disciplic succession in the village of Maṅgala-dihi in the district of Birbhūm. He composed the famous work *Śrī Śyāma-chandrodaya* ("The Rising Moon of the Deity Śrī Śyāma") in Bengali poetry, as well as many *kīrtan-padas* (songs). Thus he brilliantly illuminated the Ṭhākura lineage of Maṅgala-dihi.

Outline of Jagadananda's Śyāma-*chandrodaya*

Written exclusively in *tripādī* meter, this composition narrates the stories about the service rendered by Pānuyā Gopāl to the deity named Śrī Syāma-candra, who was originally served by Śrī Dhruva Gosvāmī. The two opening Sanskrit verses run thus:

mandire varttate yasya śyāma-sundara-vigrahaḥ
parṇa-vikreya-dravyeṇa pūjā yena kṛtā purā

yavanānnaṁ kṛtaṁ puṣpaṁ vyāghre mantra-pradāyakaṁ
taṁ natvā parṇī-gopālaṁ kriyate pustakaṁ mayā

Whose deity of Śyāma-sundara
is present within the temple;
Who previously served Him with articles
used for selling betel leaves;
Who turned the food grains of the Muslims into flowers,
and initiated a tiger by giving mantra;

After first bowing to that Parṇī Gopāl,
I engage in writing this book.

As previously described, Dhruva Gosvāmī, the resident of the forest of Kāmyavan in Vraja, once came to live in Bengal, but due to the terroristic activities of Muslims he had to flee and take shelter in the town of Bhāṇḍīravan. Eventually he came to the village of Maṅgala-dihi and made friends with the greatly devoted and pious soul named Pānuyā Gopāl. Temporarily leaving his two deities of Śrī Śyāma-Chānda and Śrī Balarāma in Gopāl's house, the *sannyāsī* left to go on pilgrimage. Returning four years later he attempted to remove his deities, but Śyāma-Chānda had already become attracted to the excellent service rendered by Gopāl along with his wife and sister. Therefore the deity assumed the form of Viśvambhara and became so heavy that He could not be moved very far away from town. That night He gave Dhruva Goswāmī a divine command in a dream to bring Him back to Maṅgala-dihi. All these topics are discussed in the book *Śyāma-chandrodaya*. It is a shame that most of the original manuscript of this book has disintegrated due to age, leaving only the first chapter readable.

Dvārakānāth Thākura

The grandson of Jagadānanda Ṭhākura named Dvārakānāth was the sixth descendant of Pānuyā Gopāl's disciplic succession in the village of Maṅgala-dihi. Dvārakānāth Ṭhākura composed the famous Sanskrit drama named *Śrī-govinda-vallabha-nātaka*, which follows the style set by Jayadeva's *Gītā Govinda* and Rāmānanda Rāya's *Jagannātha-vallabha-nātaka*. However, the specialty of Dvārakānāth's book is that it describes the pastimes performed in Vraja on the occasion of *Śrī Gopāṣṭamī* (ceremony of worshiping the cows, which occurs seven days after the day of observing *Govardhana-pūjā*). This work of 10 Acts is narrated in simple and beautiful language, being a mixture of Sanskrit songs, verses, prose and stage directions. Although by and by there are descriptions of the mellows of *vātsalya* and *ujjvala-rasa*, still it is obvious that the author's focus is primarily the *sakhya-rasa*. Dvārakānāth states in the text (1.4) that the composition was undertaken on the order of his paternal grandfather Śrī Jagadānanda Ṭhākura.

All these compositions by the great souls of Maṅgala-dihi are thus quite unique in the *Gauḍīya-sampradāya* for proving the validity of worshiping Lord Kṛṣṇa in the divine mood of fraternal love. All the descendants of the Ṭhākura's lineage in Maṅgala-dihi are *upāsakas* (worshipers) in the *sakhya-bhāva*. That is very clearly revealed in every one of their books. Their conclusions are fully supported by the standard Vaiṣṇava authorities, and thus such empowered authors have opened up a whole world of sublime devotion that is now available for the many souls who are attracted with such taste to the all-merciful Lord.

Śrī Śrī
Preyo-Bhakti-Rasārṇava

The Nectar Ocean of Fraternal Devotion

by

Śrī Nayanānanda Ṭhākura

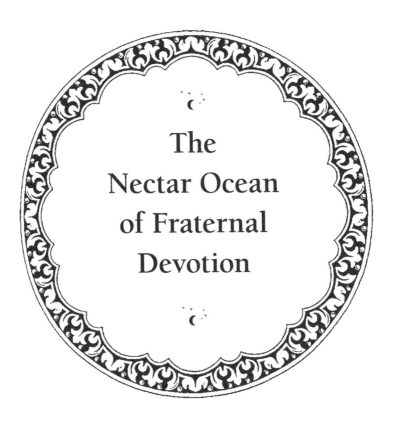

CHAPTER ONE

The Glories of Fraternal Devotional Service

Mangalācaraṇa – Auspicious Invocation

praṇamya paramānandaṁ
rāmeṇa vana-mālinam
pratanyate mayā yatnāt
preyo-bhakti-rasārṇavaḥ

Offering obeisances unto
the Personification of supreme bliss
He is accompanied by Rāma,
and wearing a forest-flower garland
It is undertaken by me, with great care and diligence
the book called *Preyo-Bhakti-Rasārṇava*.

pratapta-kāñcanābhaṁ taṁ
kambu-grīvaṁ śacī-sutam
nyagrodha-mandalākāraṁ
sāvadhūtaṁ namāmy aham

He Whose complexion is like molten gold
Whose neck is like a conchshell,
the Son of mother Śaci
Whose plump form measures
a fathom in circumference
Who is accompanied by the Madman,
I bow to Him.

vande śrī-sundarānandaṁ
sābhirāmaṁ kṛpāspadam
tathā śrī-parṇī-gopālaṁ
sa-gaṇaṁ sundara-priyam

I glorify Śrī Sundarānanda who,
along with Abhirām,
is the object of the Lord's mercy
Then I glorify Śrī Parṇī Gopāla and his associates
who are all dear disciples of Sundarānanda.

All glories, all glories to Rāma and Kṛṣṇa, the delightful sons of the King of Vraja, whose feet are worshiped by Lord Śiva, Brahmā, demigods and humans! All glories, all glories to the Lords, Prabhu Nitāi-Caitanya! By incarnating in the Kali-yuga they have rendered that age most fortunate. All glories, all glories to Śrīdāma, Sudāma and the other cowherd boys! All glories to the dear boyfriends and girlfriends of Lord Kṛṣṇa, and to Giri-Govardhana! All glories, all glories to the Vrajavāsīs and to the bank of the Yamunā River! All glories to the twelve forests of Vraja and to Dhīra Samīra! All glories to Śrī Advaita-candra who is overwhelmed with *Gaura-premānanda*! All glories to Gadādhara, Abhirām and Śrī Sundarānanda! The very dear disciple of Sundara is Pānuyā Gopāla. I bow to that merciful Ṭhākura who is our *kula-nātha* (the founding father of Maṅgala-dihi village).

The Glories of *Kṛṣṇa-Bhakti*

My dear mind, please worship Rāma and Kṛṣṇa, and meditate on Vṛndāvana. Remember the divine attributes of the sportive pastimes Kṛṣṇa performs in Vraja. Please worship Hari, renouncing mundane sense gratification in favor of performing devotional service. Keeping the company of *sādhus*, you will experience *premānanda* (love-bliss) and *mahā-sukha* (grand happiness). Whether one is a *yati* (renunciate), *dharmī* (follower of religious principles), *karmī* (one absorbed in fruitive gain), *siddha* (a perfected mystic), or any other type of person – one should relentlessly give up the paths of *yoga-yāga-jñāna* (mystic practices, performance of Vedic sacrifices, and intellectual knowledge). Abandoning lust, anger, greed, bewilderment and such, one should relinquish all attachment for *catur-varga* (the four goals of human life, namely *dharma, artha, kāma* and *mokṣa*), as well as all hopes for attaining the heavenly planets. All conceptions of sin or virtue, religiosity or irreligiosity, material ambitions – totally reject these things and just worship Govinda. Whoever worships Lord Hari while adhering to the rules of mystic *yoga*, Vedic sacrifices (*yāga*), performance of good *karma*, scholarly knowledge (*jñāna*), austerities (*tapasya*), giving charity (*dāna*) – that person will never become very satisfied by acting in these ways without *bhakti-bhāva*, the mood of devotion. Bhagavān has confirmed this Himself to Uddhava in the *Śrīmad-Bhāgavatam* as follows (11.14.20):

na sādhayati māṁ yogo na sāṁkhyaṁ dharma uddhava
na svādhyāyas tapas tyāgo yathā bhaktir mamorjitā

> "Not by performing *yoga*, nor by cultivating Sāṅkhya philosophy, nor by pious work, O Uddhava, nor by Vedic study, nor austerity, nor renunciation – no one brings Me under their control except by the superior practice of devotional service."

Those whose minds remain fixated on analytical Sānkhya philosophy, *yoga, jñāna, karma,* or *dharma* – none of them are equal to those who are absorbed in the mood of *Kṛṣṇa-bhakti*. But those who reject *bhakti* and attempt worship according to the rules of *jñāna* with the aim of attaining liberation do not get the mercy; indeed, all they earn is the troublesome botheration of mundane misery (*Bhāg.* 10.14.4). Two types of persons engage in this *Kṛṣṇa-bhakti:* some are *sakāma* (devotees with material desires) and others are *niṣkāma* (devotees without material desires). Those persons who aspire for life in the heavenly planets or for liberation from the material world altogether are *kāmi bhaktas,* and they continually come and go in the repeated cycle of birth and death. The *niṣkāma bhaktas* always remain under the shelter of Kṛṣṇa. [one line of original Bengali text missing]. Therefore render service by the performance of *niṣkāma bhakti,* for indeed even amongst the demigoddesses and gods there is no one equal to the devotees of this calibre. Who has this kind of devotion? In response, please listen to the words of the learned *muni:* The symptom of *bhakti* is the worshipful service rendered unto Śrī Kṛṣṇa (*Kṛṣṇa-sevā paricharyā*). The normal activities performed while focusing on Kṛṣṇa as the only objective are hearing, chanting and so forth with faith.

surarṣe vihitā śāstre harim uddiśya yā kriyā
saiva bhaktir iti proktā tayā bhaktiḥ parā bhavet

> "O sage amongst the gods! It is stated in the scriptures that those activities aiming at Lord Hari are verily defined as *bhakti.* And by the performance of such devotional service, one becomes transcendentally situated." (*Pañca-rātra*)

The *Śrīla Bhāgavat* lists some of the characteristics of *bhakti:* Those services which are rendered naturally (*svābhāvikī*) unto Lord Vāsudeva, in the form of hearing and chanting and so forth, with the totality of dedication focused on the personality of Śrī Kṛṣṇa, which are devoid of motives, and rendered incessantly – are called *bhāgavatī-bhakti* (*Bhāg.* 3.25.32). Here I will briefly outline the codes for *parama-bhakti,* the topmost process of devotion. These symptoms are seen in the devotee who renders service with all of their senses. One whose activities are bereft of desires for *bhukti* (material sense gratification) and *mukti* (liberation from *māya*) continuously renders favorable *Kṛṣṇa-sevā* as their chief occupational duty. In this way one cultivates a spotless mentality fixed in Kṛṣṇa. Thus I have spoken of the devotion of the *uttama bhakta.* This is described in the *Bhakti-rasāmṛta-sindhu* (1.1.11) as *anyābhilāṣitā-śūnyam* – devoid of any other desires. This *Kṛṣṇa-bhakti* is divided into three categories as (1) *sādhana-bhakti* (devotional service in practice), (2) *bhāva-bhakti* (ecstatic devotional service), and (3) *prema-bhakti* (devotional service in pure love of God). (*B.r.s.* 1.2.1).

(1)
Sādhana-Bhakti
Devotional Service in Practice

When one endeavors in various services by engaging the bodily senses in cleaning the temple of the Lord, collecting flowers and other items for His *sevā* – such activities performed within the range of one's abilities are called *sādhana-bhakti*. Now listen attentively as a doubt in this connection is dispelled. We understand that after *sādhana-bhakti* is first established, then *bhāva-bhakti* arises; thus we consider that *bhāva-bhakti* is the first stage of the third stage known as *prema*. Endeavors (*sādhana*) performed with the physical senses are characterized by the temporality of the perishable mortal body, and therefore the scriptural statement *nitya-siddhasya bhāvasya* – "the ecstatic mood of *bhāva* is eternally perfect" – removes any doubts about the performance of eternal devotional service. *Bhāva* is purely *nitya-siddha*, and can never be categorized as *sādhya* or that which can be attained by actions. Upon its manifestation within the heart, it is merely referred to as *sādhana* (that which is practiced by actions) (*B.r.s.* 1.2.2). This *sādhana-bhakti* is described as having two principal divisions, *vaidhī-bhakti sādhana* and *rāgānugā-bhakti sādhana*.

Vaidhī-Bhakti Sādhana
Regulated Devotional Service

The symptoms of the performance of *vaidhī* are: In the absence of the attainment of *rāga* (spontaneous affection for the Lord) one executes devotional activities according to the regulations advised in the scriptures; worshiping the Lord in knowledge of His Paramātmā feature, being aware that if Kṛṣṇa is not served then one may go to hell; and *bhajan* is performed out of fear of the dualistic conceptions of *pāpa* (sinful activity) and *punya* (virtuous activity) – these are the characteristics of performing regulated devotional service (*B.r.s.* 1.2.6). There are three types of *adhikārī* persons qualified to render such service in different capacities: *uttama* (elevated devotees), *madhyama* (intermediate devotees), and *kaniṣṭha* (neophyte devotees). One who is equally merciful to all living beings, who is steady in gain and loss, and who is expert in knowledge of scriptural statements is known as an *uttama bhakta*. One who is engaged in *Kṛṣṇa-pūjā*, who respects the Vaiṣṇavas performing devotional service, who is the follower of those who follow the predecessors, who is equal to those who are similar, who is averse to those who are averse, and who has uniform faith in the scriptures is known only as a *madhyama bhakta*. One who does not know the statements of scripture, who has weak faith, who worships Kṛṣṇa but not the devotees, and who does not serve the devotees but only Bhagavān is known only as a *kaniṣṭha bhakta*.

Other *Purāṇas* describe the symptoms of the *bhaktas* as being ten-fold, headed by absence of anger, renunciation and so forth:

akrodha-vairāgya-jitendriyatvaṁ
kṣamā dayā sarva-jana-priyatvam
nirlobha-dānaṁ bhaya-śoka-hīnaṁ
bhaktasya cihnaṁ daśa-lakṣaṇam ca

"Absence of anger (*akrodha*), renunciation (*vairāgya*), mastery over the senses (*jitendriyatva*), forgiveness (*ksamā*), compassion (*dayā*), being dear to everyone (*sarva-jana-priyatva*), absence of greed (*nirlobha*), giving freely in charity (*dāna*), being unfettered by fear (*bhaya-hīna*), and being free from lamentation (*śoka-hīna*) – these ten symptoms are the mark of the true devotee."

Devotees from the lowest *cāndāla* caste up to the learned and gentle *brāhmaṇas* are qualified as particular types of *adhikārī* according to their level of unmotivated worship of the Lord. Some serve the Lord seeking relief from distress (*ārtha*), others are inquisitive about the Absolute Truth (*jijñāsu*), some are desirous of wealth (*arthārtī*), and others are wise (*jñānī*). These are the attributes of four kinds of devotees, and these are illustrated respectively by the lives of Gajendra, Śaunaka, Dhruva and the Kumāras. But even though aspirants may approach the Lord with these motives, upon worshiping Him they quickly attain pure devotion.

Catuḥ-saṣthī bhakti-anga
The Sixty-Four Items of Devotional Service

There are many branches of *sādhana bhakti*, and these are known by the following sixty-four divisions headed by acceptance of the shelter of a bona-fide spiritual master (*B.r.s.* 1.2.74-92):

(1) *adau srī-guru-caraṇaśraya* – in the beginning, accepting shelter at the lotus feet of a self-effulgent spiritual master.

(2) *kṛṣṇa-dīkṣānuśikṣaṇa* – becoming initiated by the *guru* into Kṛṣṇa's service and receiving spiritual instructions from him.

(3) *viśvāsa-sahakāre śrī-guru-sevā* – attending the divine master with faith and confidence.

(4) *sādhu-vartmānuvarttana* – following in the footsteps of saintly persons.

(5) *sad-dharma-jijñāsā* – inquiring about eternal religious principles.

(6) *kṛṣṇārthe bhoga-tyāga* – renouncing material sense gratification for Kṛṣṇa's purposes.

(7) *dvārakā-gaṅgā-tire vāsa* – residing in a sacred place like Dvārakā or the bank of the river Gaṅgā.

(8) *yāvad-arthānuvarttitā* – accepting only what is necessary for basic survival.

(9) *śrī-hari-vāsara-sammāna* – honoring the day of Hari-vāsara (Ekādaśī).

(10) *aśvattha dhātrī ādira gaurava* – offering respect to sacred trees like the *aśvattha* (fig), the *dhātrī* and others.

(11) *abhakta-saṅga-tyāga* – giving up the company of non-devotees.

(12) *bahu-śiṣya-karma-tyāga* – giving up attempts to make many disciples.

(13) *eka-kāle bahu-karma-tyāga* – giving up trying to do too many different things at the same time.

(14) *abhakti-grantha-pātha-tyāga* – giving up reading nondevotional books [NOTE: *B.r.s.* here states that one should not study too many books].

(15) *vyavahāre kārpaṇya-tyāga* – giving up miserliness in ordinary dealings.

(16) *śoka-roṣādira-tyāga* – giving up lamentation and anger.

(17) *devatā-nindā-tyāga* – giving up disrespecting the demigods.

(18) *sarva-bhūte udvega-tyāga* – giving up causing anxiety to any living being.

(19) *sevāparādha-nāmāparādha-tyāga* – giving up offenses in serving the Deity as well as offenses in chanting the holy name.

(20) *kṛṣṇa-kṛṣṇa-bhakta-nindā-śravaṇa-tyāga* – giving up listening to blasphemy of Lord Kṛṣṇa or His devotees.

(21) *vaiṣṇava-chihna śaṅkha-chakra-tilakādi-dhāraṇa* – decorating the body with the distinguishing marks of a Vaiṣṇava, namely *tilaka* in the shape of the conchshell, disc, and so forth.

(22) *nāmākṣara-dhāraṇa* – decorating the body with the syllables of the Lord's holy names.

(23) *nirmālya-dhāraṇa* – accepting the flowers and flower garland remnants that were offered to the Deity.

(24) *agre tāṇḍava* – dancing before the Deity.

(25) *daṇḍavat praṇāma* – bowing down flat like a rod before the Deity.

(26) *darśane abhyutthāna* – standing up to receive the Deity when He appears.

(27) *paścād-gamana* – following behind the Deity when He is borne out for a procession.

(28) *sthāne gati* – regularly going to the residence (temple) of the Deity.

(29) *sthāna-parikramā* – circumambulating the temple of the Deity.

(30) *arcanā* – worshiping the Deity in the temple.

(31) *paricharyā* – rendering personal service to the Deity.

(32) *gītā* – singing songs in glorification of the Lord.

(33) *saṅkīrtana* – loud congregational chanting of the Lord's holy names.

(34) *japa* – soft personal chanting of the Lord's holy names.

(35) *vijñāpana* – offering prayers of submission.

(36) *stava-pātha* – reciting notable hymns of praise.

(37) *naivedya-prasāda-grahaṇa* – accepting food remnants offered to the Lord.

(38) *charaṇodaka-pāna* – drinking the water that has washed the Lord's lotus feet.

(39) *dhūpa-mālyādi-saurabha-grahaṇa* – smelling the incense, flowers and other scents offered to the Deity.

(40) *śrī-mūrti-sparśana* – touching the body of the Deity.

(41) *tad-darśana* – visiting the Deity by seeing Him with great devotion.

(42) *ārātrika-darśana, mahotsava-darśana* – seeing the daily ārati ceremony, and observing the special festivals in the Lord's honor.

(43) *nāmādi-śravaṇa* – hearing of the Lord's features headed by His holy names (His *nāma, rūpa, guṇa, līlā, dhāma* and so forth).

(44) *krpāpekṣaṇa* – expecting the mercy of the Lord.

(45) *smṛti* – remembering the Deity.

(46) *dhyāna* – meditating on the Deity's form.

(47) *dāsya* – rendering voluntary service unto the Deity.

(48) *sakhya* – regarding the Lord as a friend.

(49) *ātma-nivedana* – surrendering of one's entire self unto the Lord.

(50) *nija-priya-vastu-upaharaṇa* – offering a personally dear item unto the Deity.

(51) *kṛṣṇārthe-akhila-ceṣṭā* – performing all of one's activities only for Kṛṣṇa's purposes.

(52) *kṛṣṇe sadā śaraṇāpatti* – continuously remaining as a soul surrendered unto Kṛṣṇa.

(53) *tulasī-sevā* – serving the Tulasī tree.

(54) *śrī-bhāgavatādi-śāstra-sevā* – rendering service to the scriptures headed by *Śrīmad-Bhāgavatam* and others.

(55) *mathurā-sevā* – serving a sacred place like Mathurā.

(56) *vaiṣṇava-sevā* – offering service to the devotees.

(57) *sāmarthya thākile vaiṣṇava-gana-saha mahotsava* – participating in the Lord's festivals in the company of Vaiṣṇavas according to one's means.

(58) *kārttika-vrata* – honoring special services and vows during the month of Kārttika.

(59) *janma-yātrādi* – observing festivals celebrating the Lord's activities like Kṛṣṇa Janmāṣṭami and others.

(60) *śrī-mūrti-sevā* – serving the Deity with great care and devotion.

(61) *bhakta-saha śrīmad-bhāgavatārthāsvādana* – tasting and relishing the meaning of *Śrīmad-Bhāgavatam* in the company of the devotees.

(62) *sajātiyāśaya-bhakta-saṅga* – associating with devotees of similar mentality and aspiration.

(63) *nāma-saṅkīrtana* – chanting the holy names of the Lord.

(64) *śrī-mathurā-vāsa* – residing in the jurisdiction of Śrī Mathurā.

Thus the process of *sādhana-bhakti* systematically involves these sixty-four items of devotional service. Now, according to the concise words of Prahlāda Mahārāja, the process of devotion is said to involve nine branches (*navānga-bhakti*) as follows: hearing (*śravana*), chanting (*kīrtana*), remembrance of Kṛṣṇa (*smarana*), serving His lotus feet (*pāda-sevana*), worshiping Him (*arcanā*), offering prayers to Murāri (*vandana*), acting as His servant (*dāsya*), becoming His friend (*sakhya*), and surrendering one's soul unto Kṛṣṇa (*ātma-nivedana*). Some devotees focus their endeavors on just one of these nine items, while others regularly perform many of them. Thus I have briefly spoken of the techniques of *sādhana-bhakti*. I mentioned that *sādhana-bhakti* is of two types. First I have concisely described *vaidhī-bhakti* (devotional service rendered according to rules and regulations), and now I will speak of the second division known as *rāga-bhakti* (devotional service rendered according to spontaneous affection).

Rāga-Bhakti Sādhana
Spontaneous Devotional Service

Those who perform worship on the *vaidhi mārga* (service by the rules) do so in knowledge of Sarveśvara, the Absolute Lord of all. Ultimately they proceed toward Lord Viṣṇu due to the gradual process of their *sādhana* practices. These devotees never get a taste of transcendental sweetness (*mādhurya*), for it is difficult and rare to actually worship Nanda-suta in Vraja. However, since Śrī Nanda-nandana in Vraja is subservient to *prema*, it not difficult for the *rāgānugā* devotees to worship Him. If you have the desire to attain the feet of Vrajendra-nandana, then just practice devotion according to the *rāgānugā-mārga*. One who worships Murāri by following the path of *rāgānugā* will sport in His company after becoming a *sahacarī* (female companion). (*B.r.s.* 1.2.281)

While speaking of *rāgānugā*, I will first tell about the temperament of *rāgātmikā*. In Vraja, the *gopas* and *gopīs* are eternally fixed in the spontaneous mood known *rāgātmikā niṣṭhā* (devotional conviction in pure loving affection). The cowherd boys and girls are said to be the nature of *rāgātmikā*, and aspiring devotees who follow in their footsteps by cultivating similiar moods are called *rāgānugā* (literally "followers of spontaneous affection")

(*B.r.s.* 1.2.270). That mood which is characterized by a natural longing in love (*prema-tṛṣṇa*) focused only on Lord Kṛṣṇa, and which takes the form of supremely overwhelmed absorption (*paramāviṣṭatā rūpa*) is known by the name of *rāga*. And when that *rāga* remains continuously fixed among the devotees in the form of the spontaneous moods of *vatsalya* and so forth, then it is called *rāgātmikā niṣṭhā*. When one performs devotional service to the Lord which is fixed in an identical way to that of an eternal *rāgātmikā* personality, then this is said to be *svārasikī rāga* (affection according to one's own natural mellow) (*B.r.s.* 1.2.272).

Furthermore, *rāgātmikā* affection is considered to be of two types – *kāmātmikā* (according to amorous desire) and *sambandhātmikā* (according to family relationship). Then you should see that those in *kāmātmikā* (*kāma-rūpā*) have two different mentalities – some devotees are happy in facilitating Kṛṣṇa's pleasure, while others are [seemingly] concerned with their own pleasure. Those who become happy while catering to Kṛṣṇa's satisfaction are headed by Śrīmatī Rādhārāṇī. Whenever the word *kāma* (lust or personal desire) is mentioned in reference to these eternal associates, it should be understood to be a form of *prema* (pure love) (*B.r.s.* 1.2.285). The other type of [apparently selfish] *kāma-rūpā* devotion known as *sambhogecchā* (desirous of personal enjoyment with Kṛṣṇa) is favored by the girl Kubjā and others, and they enjoy His company in the city of Mathurā Purī and other places (*B.r.s.* 1.2.287).

The devotional mood known as *sambandha-rūpā* (affection according to family relationships) is favored by Govinda's fathers and mothers, as well as by those of the Vṛṣṇī and Yadu dynasties. Nanda-gopa as well as the cowherd boys fully embrace the mood of *sambandha* (as a personal relation to Kṛṣṇa), and thus it is indicated that their mood is one of pure, exclusive *prema*. (*B.r.s.* 1.2.289). In Vraja, the *gopas* and *gopīs* possess unadulterated *rāgātmikā niṣṭhā* – and one whose mind becomes covetous of imbibing their moods is called *rāgānugā*.

Becoming the follower of those eternal associates of the Lord, such a devotee faithfully listens to recitations of the irresistible sweetness found in Śrī Kṛṣṇa's Vraja-*līlā*. No longer relying on the injunctions of the scriptures, the devotee's mind becomes greedy to taste the nectar of Kṛṣṇa's divine pastimes. That person becomes qualified (*adhikārī*) by dint of their *sādhana*, and it is said that they know nothing at all about the difference between *vidhi* (appropriate external regulations) or *avidhi* (unregulated behavior) (*B.r.s.* 1.2.291). Becoming captivated by hearing about Kṛṣṇa's *līlā-mādhurī*, the devotee develops a state of great agitation by tasting those sweet pastimes. Such a person is qualified by dint of their *sādhana*, and they pay not even the slightest attention to the actions scripture holds as favorable for devotional practice or not. As long as one is in the embodied stage of life and ecstatic *bhāva* has not arisen, one remains a *vaidhī-bhakti-adhikārī*. During that period of devotional practice, one behaves according to the standard rules and regulations of the *vaidhī* path, being dependent on the reasoning which is characteristic of that way of life. But when *bhāva-bhakti* arises throughout the body, then one becomes freed from all such external conditions (*B.r.s.* 1.2.293). Thus is a brief description of the two types of *sādhana-bhakti* known as *vaidhī* and *rāga*.

(2)
Bhāva-Bhakti
Ecstatic Devotional Service

That spiritual potency whose special feature is that it is the original form of pure goodness (*śuddha-sattva-svarūpātmā*) is known as the *hlādinī-śakti* of Bhagavān, who is Himself of the nature of *śuddha-sattva.* Ecstatic emotion (*bhāva*), which is a product of the identity of *śuddha-sattva,* is the first stage of *prema,* which in turn melts the heart according to the development of taste (*ruci*). Without the awakening of *prema* the heart cannot be made to melt. Thus it is said that *bhāva* is the first sign that precedes *prema,* and it is compared to the beams of light heralding the rising sun of divine love. This is described in the *Bhakti-rasāmṛta-sindhu* (1.3.1). Please pay heed to the signs of the sprouting of *bhāva,* according to the authority of the scriptures:

kṣāntir avyartha-kālatvaṁ viraktir māna-śūnyatā
āśā-bandhaḥ samutkaṇṭhā nāma-gāne sadā ruciḥ

āsaktis tad-guṇākhyāne prītis tad-vasati-sthale
ity-ādayo 'nubhāvāḥ syur jāta-bhāvāṅkure jane

A devotee whose heart bears the sprouting of ecstatic emotion (*bhāva*) shows the following nine characteristic symptoms: *kṣānti* – tolerance and perseverance; *avyartha-kālatva* – making sure that time is not wasted in activities other than the Lord's service; *virakti* – detachment from material allurements; *māna-śūnyatā* – being devoid of expectations of respect from others; *āśā-bandha* – always hopeful of receiving the mercy of the Lord; *samutkaṇṭhā* – very eager in rendering devotional service; *nāma-gāne sadā-ruci* – having perpetual taste for singing the holy names; *tat-guṇākhyāne āsakti* – attachment to describing the transcendental qualities of the Lord; *tat-vasati-sthale prīti* – affection for residing in a holy place where the Lord's pastimes are performed. (*B.r.s.* 1.3.25–26)

(3)
Prema-Bhakti
Devotional Service in Pure Love

For one whose body bears the symptoms of the sprouting of *bhāva,* even the great happiness of attaining realization of Brahman becomes completely insignificant. Since *bhāva* is the preliminary stage of love of Godhead, after this ecstatic mood fixed on Kṛṣṇa thickens then one experiences the awakening of the great treasure that is *prema.* Thus the phenomenon known as *bhāva-bhakti* is the intrinsic product of pure goodness (*śuddha-sattva),* which is borne of the Lord's original pleasure-potency called *hlādinī.* This *bhāva* or ecstatic mood focused on Kṛṣṇa bears feelings of exclusive possessiveness, and the inherent symptom of *prema* is that it automatically bestows *puruṣārtha* or the ultimate goal of human life. The natural symptom of *bhāva* is that it thickens the soul with condensed humors of pure divine love. Bhīṣma, Uddhava, and others have described the nature of this *prema* (*B.r.s.* 1.4.1). There are many opinions as to the ways by which *prema-sādhana* may be performed; in that regard I will narrate the orderly process according to the injunction of the scriptures:

ādau śraddhā tataḥ sādhu-saṅgo 'tha bhajana-kriyā
tato 'nartha-nivṛttiḥ syāt tato niṣṭhā rucis tataḥ

athāsaktis tato bhāvas tataḥ premābhyudañcati
sādhakānām ayaṁ premṇaḥ prādurbhāve bhavet kramaḥ

The successive order in which pure divine love awakens in the heart of the *sādhaka* devotees is as follows: first of all there is *śraddhā* (faith), then *sādhu-saṅga* (association with saintly persons), then *bhajana-kriyā* (activities of worship), then *anartha-nivṛtti* (extinguishing of unwanted habits), then *niṣṭhā* (steadiness), then *ruci* (taste), then *āsakti* (attachment), then *bhāva* (ecstatic emotion), which finally gives rise to *prema* (transcendental love). (*B.r.s.* 1.4.15–16)

When this grand love for Kṛṣṇa takes birth within one's heart, the devotee performs such astounding deeds that even greatly learned persons cannot understand them (*B.r.s.* 1.4.17). This *prema* increases gradually and progressively as one tastes it, developing in sequence from *prema* (love) to *sneha* (personal affection), then *māna* (pouting, jealous anger), *praṇaya* (intimate love), and *rāga* (infatuated attachment). Thereafter comes *bhāva* (ecstatic emotion), which blossoms even further [in certain personalities] to the point of *mahābhāva* (grand ecstasy). All these increase as one tastes the *viṣaya* (the object) [of worship, namely Śrī Kṛṣṇa]. Thus I have truly spoken of this topic. In this way I have described the different symptoms of *bhāva* and *prema*, briefly praising their attributes.

Taking on the mood of *rāgānugā*, just serve Lord Hari in devotion by becoming the follower (*anugatā*) of your own favorite *rāgātmikā* personality (eternally liberated associate full of spontaneous love). Totally renouncing all external duties and practices such as *tantra* (occult rituals), *yantra* (worship of mystic diagrams), *yajña* (Vedic sacrifices) and *karma* (pious works), please worship Nanda-suta in Vraja until the end of your life. Vrajendra-nandana lives always in the town of Vraja-pur; just render service as the follower of one of His eternal *rāgātmikā* associates. You should know that you may live here or there, but by remembering Śrī Kṛṣṇa you will always dwell in Vṛndāvana. By following Kṛṣṇa's dear one who is your own worshipable ideal, you will become fixed in *kṛṣṇa-kathā* and thereby situated in Vraja.

> *kṛṣṇaṁ smaran janaṁ cāsya preṣṭhaṁ nija-samīhitam*
> *tat-tat-kathā-rataś cāsau kuryād vāsaṁ vraje sadā*

> A devotee should always reside in the transcendental realm of Vraja and engage in the daily remembrance of Śrī Kṛṣṇa and His beloved associates, especially the one that is accepted as one's own favorite ideal, and remain absorbed in discussing the *kathā* of Kṛṣṇa and His pastimes performed with such personalities. (*B.r.s.* 1.2.294)

Sādhaka-Deha and *Sīddha-Deha*

Please render *sevā* unto Kṛṣṇa in two bodies while pursuing entrance into Vraja. Kindly listen to this deliberation as I speak of the two different bodies. One is the *siddha-deha* (perfect spiritual body) and the other is the *sādhaka-deha* (practitioner's body). You have to become the follower of the Vrajavāsīs in both of these forms simultaneously. The physical *sādhaka-deha* takes birth from the father and mother, but you should understand that the *siddha-deha* is completely different from that. Know that a *siddha* is one who realizes a spiritual body according to their own internally-contemplated preference, and thereby resides in Vraja in the dress of a cowherd boy (*gopa*). In this way, just worship Nanda-suta in two bodies at the same time by becoming a follower of a favorite eternally-liberated Vrajavāsi. It is prescribed that you render *sevā* in the external *sādhaka-deha* by engaging in hearing, chanting, remembering, temple worship and so forth. And in the *siddha-deha* contemplated within the mind or heart (*mānasika*) you realize your form as a cowherd boy residing in Vraja, and accordingly follow in the footsteps of the residents of Vraja by emulating their mood. This is confirmed in the *Bhakti-rasāmṛta-sindhu* (1.2.295) as follows:

> *sevā sādhaka-rūpeṇa siddha-rūpeṇa cātra hi*
> *tad-bhāva-lipsunā kāryā vraja-lokānusārataḥ*

> Service should be rendered by following in the footsteps of the residents of Vraja, being desirous of attaining their same mood. Such service is performed in two distinct ways at the same time – in the external form of a *sādhaka* (practitioner) and the internal form of a *siddha* (perfected being).

I was at first unable to comprehend this verse, for a doubt had arisen. However, the commentator of *Bhakti-rasāmṛta-sindhu* has dispelled my doubt by his explanation of the meaning. He said that the residents of Vraja (*Vraja-loka*) are of two varieties, the personalities living in the eternal Vraja in the spiritual sky (*vrajastha*) and the great souls living in the visible worldly Vraja (*mahānta-gāna*). Even though the spiritually-realized *siddha mahāntas* are also in the category of *Vraja-loka* (residents of eternal Vraja), in the external *sādhaka-deha* they will render service as mentioned. According to the progressive difference in the terms *vrajānusāra* (following Vraja) and *lokānusāra* (following the residents), the word *loka* here refers to the *mahāntas*. The word *vraja* indicates all the Vrajavāsi cowherd *gopas* and *gopīs*. This I have understood by realizing the injunction of the scriptures:

"Living in Vraja in the *mānasika siddha-deha*, one should render service unto the assembly of *gopālas* by becoming their follower."

Ignorant persons cannot comprehend this secret of the scriptures, and they attempt to perform the activities of the *siddha-deha* while still on the *sādhaka* platform. Those who render *Kṛṣṇa-seva* by chanting *japa*, serving the Deity and so forth, but who try to behave with the *sādhaka-deha* like the residents of Vraja have no understanding of the appropriate mode of service (*sevā-dharma*), and they indeed earn the opposite result of certain downfall. Thus they bring down a crashing thunderbolt upon their own heads. The commentator of *Bhakti-rasāmṛta-sindhu* has clearly stated:

> *vraja-lokās tu dvi-vidhās tatra vraje ye gopā gopyaś ca, tathā tad-anugata-mahānubhāva-pravarāḥ mahāntaś ca vraja-lokau tayor anusārataḥ sevā kāryyā. siddhā-dehena gopa-gopīnām anusāratah, sādhaka-dehena mahāntānām anusārataḥ. evam ajñātvā kecit sva-śirasi mahā-vajra-nipātam manyate iti.*

> The residents of Vraja (*vraja-loka*) are of two types: (1) the *gopas* and *gopīs* [who are living eternally] in Vraja; and (2) their followers, the great souls (*mahāntas*) who are foremost in exalted transcendental realization, and who are engaged in rendering devotional service to the Lord that follows in the footsteps of the residents of Vraja. In their *siddha-dehas*, these *mahāntas* emulate the *gopas* and *gopīs*, and in their *sādhaka-dehas* they

emulate other great souls who came before them. It is considered that those who are ignorant of this truth cause a severe thunderbolt to crash down upon their own heads.

Therefore, dear readers, become the follower of your chosen *rāgātmikā* personality and worship Rāma and Kṛṣṇa in Vraja, realizing your *gopa-deha.* Fixing your intelligence in the *bhāva* that arises from your *guru,* remain in the cowherd boy's ecstatic mood of *sakhya-bhāva,* and in the company of the other cowherd boys please glorify Lord Hari in Vraja. You should endeavor to cultivate this *bhāva* that blossoms into the supremely rare *prema,* and you will certainly attain it. Incessantly adore Rāma and Kṛṣṇa in a non-duplicious manner (*akaitava*) in the company of the cowherd boys, who are full of the most confidential, secret *prema* of Vraja. Taking shelter of a prominent cowherd boy leader by becoming his comrade, worship Rāma and Kṛṣṇa as a member of that boy's particular group (*yūtha*).

sakhya-rūpaṁ saṁvidhāya sakhya-bhāvena sarvadā
pradhānānugato bhūtvā sakhyenāpi ca mānase

Fully accepting the form of a cowherd boy
Always in the ecstatic mood of fraternity
Becoming the follower of a prominent leader
Keeping intimate friendship within the mind.

The Exalted Nature of *Sakhya-Rasa Sādhana*

The tasting and relishing of the mellows of the cowherd boys (*sakhya-rasa-āsvādana*) is very difficult to attain. Indeed, the scriptures state that not only is it difficult, but it is very rarely attained.

duṣkaratvena virale dve sakhyātma-nivedane
keṣāṁcid eva dhīrāṇāṁ labhete sādhanārhatām

[NOTE: Regarding two items of *sadhana* from the previous listing of sixty-four – #48 *sakhya* and #49 *ātma-nivedana* – Śrīla Rūpa Gosvāmī declares]:

> Devotional service in fraternal love and devotional service in total self-surrender are two processes that are very rarely seen due to the difficulty involved in their realization. Indeed, these are attained only by a few sober and exalted souls who have earned the right to act on such levels of *sādhana.* (*B.r.s.* 1.2.198)

The pure mood of cowherd friendship never includes knowledge of the Lord's majestic spiritual opulences (*aiśvarya-jñāna*), but definitely functions only on the level of experiencing His divine sweetness (*mādhurya*). In this form of *sādhana* there is never any consideration of one person being greater or someone else being lesser, since pure spontaneous friendship cannot remain where such distinctions are made. For this reason, Śrī Kṛṣṇa has personally confirmed the greatness of the fraternal mood while speaking to Śrī Nārada Muni, as recorded in the *Nāradīya Purāṇa.* The *sakhya-rasa,* mellow of the cowherd boys, is the supreme mellow (*parama rasa*) and is very dear to Kṛṣṇa Himself. Indeed, Kṛṣṇa-Candra becomes subservient to those in the mood of *sakhya:*

sakhya-bhāvaḥ paraṁ bhāvo mama pritikaraḥ sadā
sakhyāt parataraṁ nānyat tasmāt sakhyena mām yaja

> The mood of *sakhya-bhāva* is supreme amongst all ecstatic emotions. It is the cause of My incessant pleasure. There is no higher consciousness than that of the cowherd boys. Therefore worship Me as a friend in the mood of *sakhya.*

My understanding is that the *sakhya-rasa* is more beloved than any other *rasa.* I consider this mellow so dear that it is even more dear than dearness itself.

dvayor apy eka-jātīya bhāva-mādhurya-bhāg asau
preyān kāmapi puṣṇāti rasaś citta-camatkṛtim

> Because the *preyo-bhakti-rasa* (*sakhya-rasa*) causes both Kṛṣṇa and His friends to simultaneously experience

the ecstatically sweet mood of being equals (*eka-jātīya*), therefore this mellow nourishes an indescribable astonishment of the heart.

prīte ca vatsale cāpi kṛṣṇa-tad-bhaktayoḥ punaḥ
dvayor anyo 'nya-bhāvasya bhinna-jātīyatā bhavet

Conversely, in the *prīta-bhakti-rasa* (*dāsya-rasa*) and the *vatsala-bhakti-rasa* (*vātsalya-rasa*), both Kṛṣṇa and the devotees will experience the mood of being of different status (*bhinna-jātīya*).

preyān eva bhavet preyān ataḥ sarva-raseṣv ayam
sakhya-saṁpṛkta-hṛdayaiḥ sadbhir evānubudhyate

For this reason, saintly persons whose hearts are endowed with the mellow of *sakhya-rasa* assuredly perceive that only this mood of the cowherd boys is the most beloved amongst all the other flavors of *rasa*. (*B.r.s.* 3.3.134–136)

[NOTE: Śrīla Rūpa Gosvāmī concludes his *B.r.s.* chapter on *Preyo-bhakti-Rasa*, or Fraternal Loving Affairs, with the preceding three verses. Only the third one was quoted in the text of *Preyo-Bhakti-Rasārṇava;* we have included the first two for further clarification.]

Even the *Gopīs* Praise the *Sakhya-Rasa*

Of all the amazing *līlās* performed by Śrī Kṛṣṇa during His incarnation, those pastimes enacted along with His cowherd boy-friends are the most enchanting.

caritaṁ kṛṣṇa-devasya sarvam evādbhutaṁ bhavet
gopāla-līlā tatrāpi sarvato 'ti-manoharā

"Of all the wonderful pastimes performed by Kṛṣṇa-Deva, His sports in the mode of *gopāla-līlā* are the most fascinating." (*Padma Purāṇa*)

Kṛṣṇa's pastimes with the *gopālas* are so captivating that even the *gopīs* sing songs about those *līlās* while imitating them. Therefore Kṛṣṇa-*līlā* is known as *śravana-maṅgala,* the bestower of auspiciousness when heard as recitations. The cowherd girls regularly make musical compositions about them. The statements of *Śrīmad-Bhāgavatam* like *iti veṇu-ravaṁ rājan* (10.21.6) indicate that the *gopīs* of Vraja became immersed in the mellows of *sakhya-rasa* and sang with abandon about the qualities of Kṛṣṇa. These cowherd damsels addressed their respective girlfriends while referring to themselves as less fortunate. They said, "The most praiseworthy thing for those who have eyes is the vision of Rāma and Kṛṣṇa sporting in the company of their cowherd boyfriends. Kṛṣṇa along with the *sakhās* have taken the calves and cows and are entering the forest of Vṛndāvana while filling the air with the sounds of their horns and flutes. Whoever continuously beholds the flute-adorned white-and-blue-lotus-faces of the two brothers Rāma and Kṛṣṇa, the sons of Vraja-rāja, is certainly glorious!" Thus spoke the *gopīkā* (*Bhāg.* 10.21.7).

Another *gopī* said, "O Sakhī! Please listen attentively! Today my eyes have seen Rāma and Kṛṣṇa going to the forest. In a greatly playful spirit Naṭabara Kṛṣṇa and Balarāma, the best of dancers, proceeded along while decorated with splendid mango buds, peacock feathers, fresh twigs, various flower garlands, and different kinds of valuable ornaments. These two brothers Rāma and Kṛṣṇa are thus the enchanters of the entire universe! Boldly prominent amidst the circle of their boyfriends, the two brothers herded their calves and cows here and there by playing on their flutes. Some were dancing, others were singing, while yet others were playing musical instruments or clapping their hands. In this way the two brothers enjoyed varieties of games in the company of their *sakhās*. Becoming fatigued by playing so vigorously, they were graced by drops of perspiration, and their moon-faces became drawn from the heat of the sun. The clouds in the sky noticed this condition of Kṛṣṇa and Balarāma and their boyfriends, and moved closer to form a shade-giving umbrella over their heads. Thus Kṛṣṇa sported along with his dear friends, and all these *sakhās* relished deep immersion in *premānanda* due to having obtained the personal association of Hari."

In this way the assembly of *gopīs* sang songs to each other glorifying the fortune of the cowherd boys. This famous passage of the *Śrīmad-Bhāgavatam*, known as *Venu-Gītā*, is narrated in the Tenth Canto, Chapter 21. Many varieties of pastimes were enjoyed in Gokula, and the *gopīs* sang about them, as described in various places in the Tenth Canto of the *Bhāgavatam*.

evaṁ vraja-striyo rājan kṛṣṇa-līlānugāyatīḥ
remire 'haḥsu tac-cittās tan-manaskā mahodayāḥ

(Śrī Śukadeva Gosvāmī said:) "O King, thus during the daytime the women of Vraja took pleasure in continuously singing about the pastimes of Kṛṣṇa, and those ladies' hearts and minds, absorbed in Him, were filled with great exultation." (*B.r.s.* 10.35.26)

All Vrajavāsīs Desire *Sakhya-Prema*

You should see that these residents of Vraja – whether men, women or anyone else living in the area – all desire to attain the mood of *sakhya* or personal friendship with Kṛṣṇa. The natural feature of *sakhya prema* is such that it is offered to Kṛṣṇa without any judgment, and also without any personal desire. Thus all the multitude of Vrajavāsīs aspire for the blessing of the mood of *sakhya*. For this reason Śrīla Vyāsadeva has described that the Vrajavāsīs are most fortunate. What can I possibly say about the glories of the residents of Vraja? Truly Vyāsadeva has proclaimed their excellence. So I say *Aho bhāgya*! *Aho bhāgya*! – How glorious! How glorious are the Vrajavāsīs! He who is *pūrṇa-brahma bhagavān*, the fullest embodiment of spiritual existence and the Supreme Personality of Godhead, is fully controlled by their love!

aho bhāgyam aho bhāgyaṁ nanda-gopa-vrajaukasām
yan-mitraṁ paramānandaṁ pūrṇaṁ brahma sanātanam

(Lord Brahmā prays:) "How greatly fortunate, how greatly fortunate are Nanda Mahārāja, the cowherd men and all the inhabitants of Vraja! There is no limit to their good fortune, because the Absolute Truth, the source of transcendental bliss, the eternal Supreme Brahman, has become their personal friend!" (*Bhāg.* 10.14.32)

During the time of sporting the *rāsa* dance, the *gopīs* also uttered statements glorifying the position of *sakhya* friendship, exclaiming, "O Kṛṣṇa! You are our Sakhā!"

vikhanasārtho viśva-guptaye
***sakha** udeyivān sātvatām kule*

"Because Lord Brahmā prayed for you to come and protect the universe, O friend, you have now appeared in the Sātvata dynasty." (*B.r.s.* 10.31.4)

Furthermore, the ultimate statement of Śrīmatī Rādhārāṇī Herself is recorded in the Tenth Canto, when Kṛṣṇa had first vanished from the company of the *gopīs,* and then from Her. She said, "*Hā* Nātha! O Rāmana! O Kānta! Where have you gone? Please show yourself, O Prāṇa-sakhā! I am your loyal maidservant!"

hā nātha ramaṇa preṣṭha kvāsi kvāsi mahā-bhuja
dāsyās te kṛpaṇāyā me sakhe darśaya sannidhim

"O master! O lover! O dearmost! Where are you? Where are you, O mighty-armed one? Please, **dearest friend**, show yourself to me, your wretched maidservant!" (*Bhāg.* 10.30.39)

The Ingredients of *Rasa*

Just worship Rāma and Kṛṣṇa in the mood of friendship by living perpetually in Vraja and becoming the follower of the chief cowherd boys. In the technical science of *rasa,* fraternal affection known as *sakhya-rati* has its place in the progressive relationship of mellows. One tastes the relishable *rasa* in conjunction with the associated ingredients (called *sāmagrī*). Next I write of the five types of affection (*pañca-rati*) headed by *śānta* (servitude), collectively called *sthāyi* or that which remains eternally constant. One should see that *rasa* itself consists of these flavors of affection variously combined with the four auxillary ingredients (*sāmagrī*), namely *vibhāva* (excitants and determinant persons), *anubhāva* (13 physical expressions of emotions), *sāttvika* (8 specially devastating ecstatic symptoms), and *vyabhicārī* (33 transitory assisting emotions) – *rasa* becomes balanced when befittingly accompanied by these ingredients. Just as *gur* (sugarcane juice) becomes more tasty by cooking it in different ways – for example by mixing it with camphor, fresh butter, and so forth, it becomes the preparation known as *amṛta-khanda* – similarly, the five kinds of *sthāyi rati* become *bhakti-rasa* when combined with the different ingredients of *rasa*. Please listen as I describe these in the following chapters.

vibhāvair anubhāvaiś ca sāttvikair vyabhicāribhiḥ
svādyatvaṁ hṛdi bhaktānām ānītā śravaṇādibhiḥ
eṣā kṛṣṇa-ratiḥ sthāyī bhāvo bhakti-raso bhavet

> By means of the items called *vibhāva, anubhāva, sāttvika* and *vyabhicārī*, cultivated along with hearing, remembering and so forth, the devotees achieve the relishable taste of *Kṛṣṇa-rati* in their hearts. This nourishes their respective moods of eternal *sthāyi-bhāva*. All these features combine to form what is called *bhakti-rasa*. (*B.r.s.* 2.1.5)

Those persons who have aspirations from their previous births for performing *sad-bhakti* (pure devotional service) verily attain the relishable taste of *bhakti-rasa*. My Lords are Śrī Caitanya and Śrī Nityānanda, Śrīyuta Sundarānanda and Śrī Parṇī Gopāla. Hoping at the feet of Gopāla Caraṇ Prabhu, this fallen Nayanānanda Dās has humbly described these topics.

Thus ends the first chapter of
Śrī Śrī Preyo-Bhakti-Rasārṇava

CHAPTER TWO

Various Types of Cowherd Boys

tvaṁ viśvarūpānuja-gaura-candraṁ
viśvambharaṁ sarva-guṇair upetam
pratapta-hemācala-gaura-dehaṁ
vande śacī-putra! jagan-nivāsam

You are the younger Brother of Viśvarūpa
the Golden Moon
The upholder of the universe
endowed with all good qualities
Of fair complexion like a golden mountain
I praise You, Son of Śacī,
the Abode of all creation!

Dvādaśa-Rati
The Twelve Affections

The twelve types of permanent affection (*sthāyi rati*) are classified as follows. The five primary divisions (*mukhya*) are: (1) *śānta* – neutrality, (2) *dāsya* – servitude, (3) *sakhya* – fraternity, (4) *vātsalya* – paternity, and (5) *priyatā* – conjugal love. And the seven secondary (*gauṇa*) divisions are: (6) *hāsya* – laughter, (7) *vismaya* – astonishment, (8) *utsāha* – enthusiasm, (9) *śoka* – lamentation, (10) *krodha* – anger, (11) *bhaya* – dread, and (12) *jugupsā* – ghastliness.

The Five Primary Affections

(1) *Śānta-Rati* (neutral affection)

The mood of śānta-*rati* is characterized by renunciation of sense-gratification, situation in one's own personal bliss (*nijānanda*), conception of Kṛṣṇa as the indwelling Supersoul (Paramātmā), a peaceful mentality, absence of pride and egoism, and being desireless for experiencing any of the other transcendental loving humors with the Lord.

(2) *Dāsya-Rati* (servitude affection)

The mood of *dāsya-rati* is characterized by a conception of Kṛṣṇa as the Lord and Master (Prabhu) and oneself as subordinate, with feelings of being very fallen and insignificant. This type of service attitude found in the relationship with Him as *sevya* (worshipable) and oneself as *sevaka* (servant), is also known as *prīta-bhakti*.

(3) *Sakhya-Rati* (friendly affection)

The mood of *sakhya-rati* is characterized by considering oneself equal to Kṛṣṇa, having great personal trust in Him, being fearless in dealing with Him on the same level, keeping constant loving companionship with Him, and having an attitude bereft of knowledge of His godly opulence (*aiśvarya*) due to the directive of familiar sweetness (*mādhurya*).

(4) *Vātsalya-Rati* (parental affection)

The mood of *vātsalya-rati* is characterized by feelings that Kṛṣṇa (as a mere boy) has to be protected, activities of caressing and nourishing Him with affection, genuinely selfless favor and preferential treatment, and showing extreme loving attachment, just as one does to one's own child.

Multiple Mixtures of Mellows – Saṣkulā-Rati

Furthermore, the three affections *dāsya, sakhya* and *vātsalya* can each manifest in two distinct ways – as *kevalā* (the pure state of the mellow, when only a single affection is favored), or as *saṣkulā* (the mixed state, when the primary mellow is blended with other humors) (*B.r.s.* 2.5.24). Some examples of the *kevalā* division are:

The servants residing eternally in Vṛndāvana headed by Rasāla accept nothing other than the *dāsya-rati*. The cowherd boys headed by Śrīdāma Sakhā never touch a mood other than pure *sakhya*, even in dreams. Nanda and Yaśomatī perpetually favor the mood of *vātsalya*, never considering any other humor such as viewing Kṛṣṇa's *aiśvarya* and so forth (*B.r.s.* 2.5.25). These unadulterated moods of *kevelā-rati* are eternally exhibited in Vṛndāvana, whereas the people of other towns view Kṛṣṇa with the mixed mellows known as *saṣkula-rati*. This is evident when the humors of *dāsya*, *sakhya* and *vātsalya* mix together in combinations of two and three. An example of such is seen in Uddhava, who sometimes considers Kṛṣṇa-candra to be his Prabhu, and at other times considers Him to be his friend. Bhīma and others sometimes view Kṛṣṇa as a friend and brother, while at other times they realize Him to be the Supreme Īśvara and experience apprehension of getting too close to Him. Kīrtidā's mother Mukharā and others exhibit the mood of *vātsalya* that is mixed with other humors. Thus is described the principle of *saṣkulā-rati* (*B.r.s.* 2.5.26).

(5) *Priyata-Rati* (conjugal affection)

The mood of *priyatā-rati* is characterized by the Divine Couple's activities of enjoying each other intimately and such, by which Kṛṣṇa and Śrīmatī's *prema* expands. Known as *priyatā-rati*, this humor is also called *madhura* (sweet) or *ujjvala* (brilliant).

Thus I have briefly described the five *mukhya* or primary forms of *sthāyi rati*; all of you please listen as I now speak of the seven *gauṇa* or secondary forms of *rati*. These auxiliary moods of affection – *hāsya* (laughter), *vismaya* (astonishment), *utsāha* (enthusiasm), *śoka* (lamentation), *krodha* (anger), *bhaya* (dread), and *jugupsā* (ghastliness) – are perpetually existent in a dormant state within the devotee's body, and this is why they are called "secondary" (or indirect). The five primary (or direct) *ratis* are seen to be actively displayed by respective devotees who are vessels for the occasional display of various secondary moods (*B.r.s.* 2.5.45). These five humors blend with the ingredients (*sāmagrī*) headed by *vibhāva*, forming the flow of actual *rasa* that progressively expands in relishable taste.

Vibhāva (Personalities and Ecstatic Stimulants)

The ingredient known as *vibhāva* enables *rasa* to be tasted; this principle involves two distinct items, namely *ālambana* (characters who are foundations of love, between whom love flows reciprocally), and *uddipana* (external factors which stimulate the awakening of love). These two items cause *rati* to appear and expand (*Agni Purāṇa; B.r.s.* 2.1.15). Furthermore, the principle of *ālambana* has two aspects – *viśayālambana* (objective foundation) and *āśrayālambana* (subjective foundation). These aspects are exhibited respectively by Kṛṣṇa and Kṛṣṇa's devotees. Kṛṣṇa is the *viṣaya* or object of the five mellows, and the devotees are the *āśraya* or subject, thereby comprising five types of *bhaktas* (*B.r.s.* 2.1.16). Vrajendra-nandana is the *nāyaka śiromaṇi* or crest-jewel of heroes, in whom all grand divine qualities perpetually reside. As *pūrṇa bhagavān* or the complete manifestation of the Supreme Personality of Godhead, He embodies 64 transcendental qualities, some of which are not exhibited by any other of His many *avatāras*. Thus I have spoken of the *ālambanas* of the *sakhya-rasa;* next I will delineate some details of *sakhya-rati*.

Śrī Kṛṣṇa, the Object of *Sakhya-Rati*

When two transcendental personalities see each other with love characterized by *sama-bhāva* (the mood of equality), then this is called *sakhya-rati*. The devotee exhibits an identity of equal self-esteem with Kṛṣṇa, as well as equal behavior. The relationship between the two bears an extremely trusting confidence that is not at all tinged with reverence. That mood in which the devotee will joke freely with Him, displaying pure love that is totally genuine, is known as *sakhya-rati* (*B.r.s.* 2.5.30). And when *sakhya-rati* mixes with the ingredients headed by *vibhāva*, then it is called *preyo-bhakti-rasa* (*B.r.s.* 3.3.1).

In the *sakhya-rasa* Kṛṣṇa is the *viśayālambana* (objective foundation) and the *sakhās* of the same age are the *āśrayālambana* (subjective foundation) (*B.r.s.* 3.3.2). In that regard Lord Hari as the *ālambana* is endowed with all transcendental qualities, and in Vraja-pur He exhibits His two-armed Bhagavān feature. Dark-complexioned like a fresh raincloud, or a brilliant sapphire, His hue is so beloved that it renders Him intensely fascinating. His face is radiant with gentle smiles, and His teeth are white as jasmine flower buds. His eyes, splendrously adorned by the outline of black cosmetics, beam with sidelong glances. His garment is so lustrous that it conquers the iridescence of the golden *ketakī* flower. Beautified with forest-flower garlands and forest mineral pigments He enchants the minds of even the great self-controlled sages. With lips graced by His flute as He returns from the pasturelands, He thus forcibly steals the minds of the *sakhās* by the lilting melodies of His flute (*B.r.s.* 3.3.4).

In this way Kṛṣṇa's bodily beauty as the *ālambana* foundation for *sakhya* affection in Vraja is described. Now please listen to the narration of His magnificence as exhibited in the towns of Mathurā and Dvārakā-pur. A complexion like fresh rainclouds, He holds the Pañcajanya conchshell as well as the disc, club and lotus, and He engages in various battles. His universe-enchanting *ālambana* feature there manifests in four-armed and two-armed forms, wearing yellow garments and adorned with the Kaustubha gem. Fully resplendent with all divine qualities, He is Svayam Bhagavān – the Supreme Personality of Godhead Himself (*B.r.s.* 3.3.5–7). Thus I speak of Kṛṣṇa's qualities in the mood of *sakhya*, please pay heed to these topics.

Śrī Kṛṣṇa's Boyfriends of the Same Age (*vayasya*)

Kṛṣṇa's boyfriends of the same age are characterized by similar forms, attire and qualities. Due to their pure unalloyed trust, they have no hesitation in boldly dealing with Him. This entire assembly of *vayasya* boys have personal confidence in Him that extends out from the core of their souls. They are absolutely fearless of Him and consider Him to be perfectly their equal (*B.r.s.*

3.3.8). These friends are seen in two places – some live in the villages of Vraja Puri, while others live in the cities of Mathurā Purī and Dvārakā Nagara. Those of Mathurā, Dvārakā and other towns are called *pura-sambandhīya* (relations of the city) and those *sakhās* living in the Vṛndāvana area are called *vraja-sambandhīya* (relations of Vraja). Some *pura-sambandhīya vayasyas* include Śrī Arjuna, Bhiṁasena, the daughter of Drupada (Draupadī), Śrīdāma Brāhmaṇa and others. Amongst these, Arjuna is the most dear to Kṛṣṇa. Please listen to his description according to the opinion of the scriptures (*B.r.s.* 3.3.14):

gāṇḍīva-pāṇiḥ kari-rāja-śuṇḍā-
ramyorur indīvara-sundarābhaḥ
rathāṅginā ratna-rathādhirohi
sa rohitākṣaḥ suta-rāma-rājīt

Who holds the bow Gāndiva in his hand
Whose thighs are charming like the trunk
of the king of elephants
Whose beautiful complexion is similar
to the best blue lotus
Who is seated upon a jewelled chariot
along with its driver Kṛṣṇa –
That Arjuna of reddish eyes
is radiating quite splendrously!

Lounging upon the same bedstead, engaged in confidential joking and laughter, Arjuna unhesitantly considers Kṛṣṇa his equal.

The boyfriends classified as *vraja-sambandhīya vayasyas* are always engaged in sporting with Śrī Kṛṣṇa, and if by chance they are separated from Him for even a moment, they experience that moment to be as long as millions of ages. These *sakhās* are the very life of Kṛṣṇa, indeed the wealth of His heart (*prāṇa-dhana*), and likewise they are also infused with life by their relationship with Kṛṣṇa (*B.r.s.* 3.3.16). The *vayasyas* of Vraja are uncountable. In hundreds of millions of millenniums they are never excluded from Śrī Kṛṣṇa's personal company. Who could possibly have the power to describe their beauty, dress, talents, activities or *svarūpa*?

They are portrayed thus in the *Govinda-vṛndāvanam* (1.149–150):

āyutāyuta-gopālāḥ sakhāyo rāma 'kṛṣṇayoḥ
teṣāṁ rūpaṁ svarūpaṅ ca guṇa-karmādayo 'pi ca
nahi varṇayituṁ śakyā kalpa-koṭi-śatair api

Rāma and Kṛṣṇa have tens of thousands, upon tens of thousands of cowherd boyfriends. Even if I had a billion millenniums to do it, I would not be able to describe all their forms, nature, qualities and activities.

Since the *sakhās* in Vraja are limitless in number, I will describe only the most prominent groups among them. Their attire is the same as Kṛṣṇa's, their age is the same as Kṛṣṇa's, and they are expert in creating a pleasant atmosphere by singing and playing music on buffalo horns, flutes and other instruments. Some have complexions like brilliant sapphires, some are golden, some silvery, some green like emeralds, some like crystal, and some like red lotuses. Residing in Vraja, they are adorned with variegated ornaments and engage in limitless pastimes for the pleasure of Śrī Kṛṣṇa (*B.r.s.* 3.3.17).

Friendship as Exhibited During *Govardhana-Dhāraṇā-Līlā*

The friendship that the *sakhās* share in the company of Kṛṣṇa is unfathomable. The *Purāṇas* glorify the events that occurred at the time of interrupting the *īndra-yajña*. When Kṛṣṇa caused the sacrifice to Lord Indra to be discontinued, He consequently held the hill named Giri Govardhana aloft on His left hand for an entire week. Seeing the huge mountain balanced upon Kṛṣṇa's hand, the assembly of *sakhās* experienced such a mood that they felt no distress for themselves but became very unhappy at Kṛṣṇa's [seeming] difficulty. This was only proper, since they loved Kṛṣṇa much more than themselves; this is the symptom of the *sakhās* who hold only Kṛṣṇa as their exclusive life-force. One son of a cowherd came before Kṛṣṇa and spoke with sweet supplication, revealing the anguish of his heart, "Listen, listen O Prāṇa-sakhā! O Nanda-nandan! You have been holding Giri Govardhan upon your hand for an entire week! This has caused great distress in the hearts of your dear cowherd boyfriends. They cannot bear to see your fatigue any longer. Just transfer the mountain from your hand to Śrīdāma's hand; doing this for even a moment will relieve your fatigue. If you won't give it to him, then at least take it with your right hand so we can give your left hand a massage. We cannot estimate how much your hand must hurt! This has caused all the *sakhās* to become extremely upset!" (*B.r.s.* 3.3.18). Who can describe the pure friendship that the *sakhās* feel for Kṛṣṇa? All these things are proclaimed throughout the *Agamas, Purāṇas* and *Tantras*.

Friendship as Exhibited During *Aghāsura-Vadha-Līlā*

The friendship that Kṛṣṇa shows to His *sakhās* is such that who could possibly describe it fully? Once the *māyāvādī* named Aghāsura, the servant of Kaṁsa, entered Vṛndāvana after taking the form of a huge serpent. His intention was to do harm to Kṛṣṇa, and he hid in a place that no one knew about. Opening his mouth wide, his upper lip touched the orb of the sky, and he cast his lower lip flat upon the ground.

Eventually Vrajendra-nandana came down that path in the company of His young cowherd boyfriends, playing merrily throughout the forest while tending their calves. Suddenly beholding the fascinating loftiness of the snake's jaws, the minds of those simple boys became enchanted. Someone said, "I have seen the amazing beauty of Govardhana Hill, but today I see something in Vṛndāvana that is supremely astonishing!" Making sounds by slapping their hands in their armpits and also by clapping their hands, shouting the cowherding exclamations "*Ābā! Ābā!*" the assembly of boys entered the giant snake's mouth while crying "*Jai! Jai!*" Seeing this, Aghāsura thought to himself, "That enemy of my brother is remaining at a distance. I will continue to wait here just to do Him harm." But Kṛṣṇa became alarmed at not seeing His comrades, and He looked for them with anxious eyes and spotted them entering the snake's mouth. Nanda-nandana thought to Himself, "This Aghāsura has swallowed my friends!" and He became very disturbed in their separation. Both His eyes swelled up with tears as He wept apprehensively and called out to them, "Śrīdāma! Sudāma! Dāma! *Bhāi, Bhāi!* O my brothers, O my brothers! Where is my dear Subal, Arjjuna and Vasudāma? Where is Labaṇga, Ujjvala and Śrī Kiṅkiṇī? O why have I come to this deep forest today without the company of Balarāma, who remained at home?"

After momentarily lamenting in this way and contemplating the situation, Lord Hari then entered into the mouth of Agha. Once inside, He began to expand in size until He forcibly emerged from the snake's split-open head. All the boys spilled out onto the forest path and were so glad to regain the company of Kṛṣṇa that they embraced Him in supreme bliss. Even though Kṛṣṇa killed Agha so dramatically and openly bestowed liberation upon him, still the cowherd boys did not consider Him to be the Supreme Lord (*B.r.s.* 3.3.20).

Four Principal Divisions of Cowherd Boys

Kṛṣṇa's *vayasyas* in Vraja are limitless in number, and they are divided into four principal and two secondary categories. The principal divisions are: (1) *suhṛt-sakhā* (friends of well-wishing heart), (2) *sakhā* (general friends), (3) *priya-sakhā* (confidential friends), and (4) *priya-narma-sakhā* (very intimate friends) (*B.r.s.* 3.3.21). The two secondary classifications are: (1) *vidūṣaka* (comical buffoons), and (2) *vīta* (sensual, artistic companions).

(1) *Suhṛt-Sakhā*

Those boys whose mood of friendship is mixed with the parental mellow of *vātsalya*, whose age is a little older than Kṛṣṇa, who are engaged in protecting Him from any possible harm, are called *suhṛt* (*B.r.s.* 3.3.22). Some boys from this category are Balabhadra, Mandalī-bhadra, Subhadra, Bhadra-vardhana, Gobhata, Yakṣa, Indrabhata, Bhadrānga, Vīra-bhadra, Mahāguṇa, Vijaya, and others (*B.r.s.* 3.3.23). Even though Balarāma is mentioned here as a boyfriend, it should be understood that He is nondifferent from Kṛṣṇa. He merely behaves as the best of the *suhṛt-sakhās* due to the trend of divine sweetness (*mādhurya*). Later on in this book I will systematically describe the meditation (*dhyāna*) and worship (*pūjā*) of Balabhadra [in Chapter Five]. Amongst the *suhṛt* boys there are two who are the foremost – Balabhadra and Mandalī-bhadra.

(2) *Sakhā*

Now to mention the characteristics of the *sakhās* – they are a little younger than Kṛṣṇa, they remain as if His little brothers, being endowed with a loving attachment to Him that is mixed with the mellow of servitude (*dāsya*), and they are thereby fixed in rendering personal services unto Him (*B.r.s.* 3.3.30). Some boys in this category are Deva-prastha, Viśāla, Vṛṣabha, Ojasvī, Varūthapa, Maranda, Kusumāpiḍa, Maṇi-bandha and Karandhama (*B.r.s.* 3.3.31). Amongst these boys, Deva-prastha is certainly the chief. Next please hear the description of the *priya-sakhās*.

(3) *Priya-Sakhā*

The *priya-sakhās* of Vraja are numberless, and amongst them all are twelve leaders (*yūtheśvara*) who are in charge of their own respective groups. Their dress, ornaments and age are similar to Kṛṣṇa's, and they always exhibit the disposition of being His equals in pure friendship. Their *sakhya-rati* or fraternal loving attachment is on the level of *kevalā* – totally unalloyed in innocent affection due to being entirely bereft of mixture with any other mellow (*B.r.s.* 3.3.36). These dear boyfriends enjoy playing sportive games in Kṛṣṇa's company like fist-fighting, stick-fighting and arm-wrestling. They jump about, display great pride, crash their sides against each other, smack their hands together, and perform other outrageously exciting amusements in an atmosphere of charming grace. According to the book *Gaṇoddeśa*, in this category of boys there are the following eleven: Śrīdāma, Sudāma, Vasudāma, Kiṅkiṇī, Stoka-Kṛṣṇa, Angśu, Bhadra-sena, Vilāsi, Puṇḍarīka, Vītankākṣa and Kalavinka. According to the *Rasāmṛta-sindhu*, Dāma is added to this list, totalling twelve cowherd boys (*dvādaśa-gopāla*) (*B.r.s.* 3.3.36–38).

The *Gopīs* Praise the Cowherd Boys' Friendship

The friendship exhibited by the *priya-sakhās* in the company of Kṛṣṇa is such that it was once described by the *gopīs* in the presence of Śrīmatī Rādhārānī thus:

> "What wonderful things we have beheld today on the bank of the river Yamunā! We saw Hari sporting in the afternoon along with His *priya-sakhās*. Some laughed, some danced, while others spoke in stuttering ways to make Kṛṣṇa smile. Uttering crooked statements they enjoyed joking and carousing. Thus the nature of the *priya-sakhās* is pure unadulterated friendship with Him. Sometimes they spread out their arms to block His path, and at other times they embrace Him lovingly with their limbs emptying with thrilled shivering." This is a very slight indication of the intimate dealings of the *priya-sakhās* (*B.r.s.* 3.3.39).

Friendship as Exhibited During *Gocaraṇa-Līlā*

It is a definite fact that Kṛṣṇa is the very life of the *sakhās*. Without the company of Kṛṣṇa, it is very doubtful that His beloved friends can even maintain their lives at all. Once Vrajendra-nandana took His *priya-sakhās* to the gardens on the bank of the river Yamunā and blissfully sported various games while tending the cows. Then He suddenly left their company on the plea of going to search for some cows that strayed from sight. Not beholding Kṛṣṇa there, Śrīdāma's mind became very alarmed and he exclaimed, "*kothā gelā bhāi ore!* Where has my brother gone? Oh, No!" He fell down to the ground and started rolling around due to losing Kṛṣṇa's companionship, and his limbs were thereby covered with dust. Getting up and frantically wandering here and there throughout the gardens, forests and groves on the bank of the Yamunā, he repeatedly called, "*Hā* Kṛṣṇa! *Hā* Priya!" in a loud voice. Seeing all this taking place, Bhagavān acted quickly and bestowed life upon His *sakhā* by playing His *muralī* flute. Hearing the sound of Kṛṣṇa's flute, the practically dead bodies of Śrīdāma and Sudāma became infused with life. Śrīdāma lifted his face upwards and cried, "Where is Kṛṣṇa?!" and then he finally saw Muralidhar standing before him. Addressing Him with a faltering voice Śrīdāma said, "*Ore bhāi!* O my dear brother, just look at our faces! Please come forward and embrace each and every boy! Leaving our assembly today, where have you gone? Not seeing you here, all of us have become like helpless orphans! But now it is our great fortune to have met you again! O brother, where in the forest had you gone alone? Without you, great havoc breaks loose! Each of us feel that our all-in-all – whether our wealth, relatives, cherished dreams, property, cows, friends, selves, and whatever we were doing – everything becomes totally disarranged if we lose sight of you for even a second!" Thus is the behavior of the *priya-sakhās;* if Kṛṣṇa leaves their sight for a moment they experience one *daṇḍa* (24 minutes) to pass like millions of *yugas* (*B.r.s.* 33.42).

Friendship as Exhibited During *Kāliya-Damana-Līlā*

Kṛṣṇa's dear friends always offer the totality of their souls only unto Him; for this reason the *priya-sakhās* are called "*Kṛṣṇa-prāṇa.*" In that regard, just see the descriptions in the Tenth Canto of the *Bhāgavatam*, how the *sakhās* offered their souls as well as their family members unto Kṛṣṇa. Just like during the pastime of chastising the serpent Kāliya, how the cowherd boys cried and despaired upon seeing Kṛṣṇa within the lake. Feeling Kṛṣṇa's separation the *sakhās'* minds reeled with the greatly emotional thoughts of, "What has happened?! What has happened?!" as they sobbed and wailed.

"Kṛṣṇa has entered the poisoned waters! Oh, how will this be resolved?!" Thus in Kṛṣṇa's separation they desired to simply die on the spot. At that time Śrīdāma fell to the ground and lost consciousness as tears resembling the gushing of the Yamunā river poured from his eyes. The beloved assembly of Kṛṣṇa's cowherd boyfriends have offered unto Govinda their souls, relatives, happiness, distress, personal friends, wives, wealth, families, and everything else that is dear to them. Truly Kṛṣṇa is their very *prāṇa* (life-force), just as water is the very life of the fish. As fish live within the water and suffer certain death without it, similarly the *sakhās* cannot hold onto their lives without Kṛṣṇa. All of their experiences of happiness or distress arise in the context of considering Kṛṣṇa to be their friend and equal; they could never imagine Him to be the Paramātmā or Supreme Being. Kṛṣṇa is their friend, Kṛṣṇa is their best pal, Kṛṣṇa is their life; without Kṛṣṇa the *sakhās* would just drop dead.

taṁ nāga-bhoga-parivītam adṛṣṭa-ceṣṭam
ālokya tat-priya-sakhāḥ paśupā bhṛśārtāḥ
kṛṣṇe 'rpitātma-suhṛd-artha-kalatra-kāmā
duḥkhānuśoka-bhaya-mūḍha-dhiyo nipetuḥ

When the boys of the cowherd community, who regarded Him as their dearmost friend, saw Him completely enveloped and motionless within the coils of the giant snake, they became greatly disturbed. They had offered Kṛṣṇa everything – their very selves, their families, their wealth, wives and all objects of desire. At the sight of Him in the clutches of the snake Kāliya, their intelligence became deranged by anguish, lamentation and fear, and thus they fell senselessly to the ground. (*Bhag.* 10.16.10)

Kṛṣṇa is Defeated in Sport at Bhāṇḍīravan

The cowherd boys continuously share affectionate love with Kṛṣṇa in the mood of pure intimate sweetness (*mādhurya*) and never perceive His divine opulence (*aiśvarya*), thereby entertaining the notion that He is God. Their whole consciousness is one of "You and I are equal. We have the same knowledge, same disposition, and play in the same manner." Just see the descriptions in the Tenth Canto of the *Bhāgavatam*.

At the base of the enormous banyan tree called Bhāṇḍira, Kṛṣṇa took His boyfriends and sported various playful pastimes as they allowed the cows to graze. Rāma and Kṛṣṇa separated their friends into two teams, with Śrīdāma, Vṛṣabha and others taking sides with Rāma, Subhadra, Maṇḍālī-bhadra and others sided with Kṛṣṇa on that day. The two brothers then made a wager on defeat in a contest of running as far as the Bhāndīra tree, and the losers would have to carry the winning team upon their shoulders.

During that particular game Rāma and His friends won, and since they were all playing as equals the members of the opposing team had to carry them. Balarāma-Chānda came forward to mount the shoulders of the defeated, but instead of climbing on Mandalī-bhadra He got up on the shoulders of the demon Pralamba. Upon the defeated Kṛṣṇa's shoulders rode the victorious Śrīdāma – I have never seen such a display of pure, unmotivated *prema*! Thus the boys carried their equal friends upon their shoulders at the base of the secluded Bhāṇḍīra tree.

Lord Kṛṣṇa, Who is never conquered by *samsāra,* who knows no defeat in any way whatsoever – becomes subservient to *prema* and thereby becomes totally defeated. In the mood of the purest mellow of divine friendship (*śuddha sakhya-rasa*) Śrīdāma rode upon His shoulders; this kind of causeless loving affection has never been seen anywhere else! (*Bhāg.* 10.18.23-24). How could I possibly describe the characteristics of genuine, non-duplicitous *prema*?

Kṛṣṇa even *shares* the half-eaten food remnants of the *sakhās* while they are dining together! As they are feasting in the forest, the cowherd boys habitually relish some food preparation according to their own taste, and finding it quite satisfying they happily place some into Kṛṣṇa's mouth so He can taste it also (*Bhāg.* 10.13.10). Thus He sports in the company of His *sakhās*. I have written only the briefest account of these topics, merely pointing in the general direction.

Four Leading Cowherd Boys

Amongst the assembly of *priya-sakhās*, four are outstanding. Their glory is recorded in the *Gautamīya Tantra* thus:

kintu dāma-sudāmādyā harer ati-priya matāḥ
gautamīyādiṣu proktaṁ tan-māhātmyam anuttamam

But the boys headed by Śrīdāma and Sudāma are especially dear to Lord Hari, according to the opinion of the sages headed by Gautama. Indeed, their glories are unsurpassed.

Kṛṣṇa is *tejaḥ-svarūpa*, the embodiment of divine effulgence. And these four friends of His are particularly described in the *Krama-Dīpikā:* Kṛṣṇa, the indwelling Supersoul, is surrounded by them like four coverings. Please observe and consider the following quote from the *Pūjā-prakaraṇa* (chapter on worship) in this *Tantra:*

dikṣv atha dāma-sudāmau vasudāmaḥ kiṅkiṇī ca sampūjyāḥ
tejo-rūpās tad-bahiraṅgāni ca keśaveṣu samabhiyajet

In the four directions are the fully worshipable Śrīdāma, Sudāma, Vasudāma and Kiṅkiṇī. One should worship Keśava, who is the personification of brilliance, along with these who are His external portions. (*Krama-Dīpikā* 4.28)

Thus Śrīdāma, Sudāma, Vasudāma and Kiṅkiṇī are the foremost among Kṛṣṇa's beloved boyfriends, being in full knowledge of all His secrets. They are equally aware of both types of Kṛṣṇa's *līlā* – those that are *agopya* (suitable for being revealed) as well as those that are *gopya* (appropriate to be concealed). Some pastimes are performed in the external realm while others are engaged within the internal sphere. All of the confidential Vraja-*līlās* like *vastra-haraṇa* (the stealing of the *gopīs*' clothes) are fully known to these four boys.

Friendship as Exhibited During *Gopī-Vastra-Haraṇa-Līlā*

One day the *gopīs* assembled together and traveled to the bank of the Yamunā in order to perform *pūjā* to Goddess Kātyāyani. Leaving their garments on the riverbank they immersed in the water and engaged in water-sports in a spirit of great prankish fun. Although situated elsewhere at the time, Yogeśvara Bhagavān (the Supreme Personality, Master of Mystics) could understand everything within Himself, and quickly came to that spot along with His confidential boyfriends. For the purpose of fulfilling the cherished desires of the *gopīkās,* He secretly stole all of their clothes. Collecting the garments with the help of His friends headed by Śrīdāma, He climbed up a *kadamba* tree and started laughing and joking along with them.

> *bhagavāṁs tad abhipretya kṛṣno yogeśvareśvaraḥ*
> *vayasyair āvṛtas tatra gatas tat-karma-siddhaye*

> Lord Kṛṣṇa, the Supreme Personality of Godhead and Master of all masters of mystic *yoga,* was aware of what the *gopīs* were doing, and thus He went there surrounded by His boyfriends in order to award the *gopīs* the perfection of their endeavor.

> *tāsāṁ vāsāṁsy upādāya nīpam āruhya satvaraḥ*
> *hasadbhiḥ prahasan bālaiḥ parihāsam uvāca ha*

> Taking the girls' garments, He quickly climbed to the top of a *kadamba* tree. Then, as He laughed loudly and His companions also laughed, He jokingly addressed the *gopīs.* (*Bhāg.* 10.22.9)

In the commentary on *Śrīmad-Bhāgavatam* called *Laghu-Toṣaṇī,* it is stated [by Śrīla Jīva Gosvāmī]:

> *'bhagavān tad-abhipretya' iti vayasyair iti bālair iti ca sakhībhir iti jñeyam, tair vṛtaḥ san āgaste ca param-antaraṅgā dāma-sudāma-vasudāma-kiṅkiṇayo jñeyaḥ tac choktaṁ gautamīye (10.82-83):*

dāma-su dāma-vasu dāma-kiṅkiṇī-gandha-puṣpakaiḥ
antaḥkaraṇa-rūpās te kṛṣṇasya parikirtitāḥ
ātmābhedena te pūjyā yathā kṛṣṇas tathaiva te

iti antaḥkaraṇa-rūpāḥ iti kramena buddhy-ahaṇkāra-citta-mano-rupā ity arthaḥ

In the verse beginning with the words *bhagavān tad-abhipretya* the use of *vayasyaiḥ* ("with the friends of the same age") indicates *bālaiḥ* ("with the boys") and also *sakhībhih* ("with His cowherd boyfriends"). Being surrounded by them, He arrived on the scene. It should be understood that these are His supremely intimate and internal friends Śrīdāma, Sudāma, Vasudāma and Kiṅkiṇī. That is also confirmed in the *Gautamīya Tantra* thus (10.82–83):

'The greatly famous Śrīdāma, Sudāma, Vasudāma and Kiṅkiṇī are the embodiments of Lord Kṛṣṇa's feature of *antaḥkaraṇa* (the indwelling Supersoul), being nondifferent from His very self, and therefore they are equally worshipable with scented flowers as is Kṛṣṇa. Thus being the personifications of His *antaḥkaraṇa* feature, they systematically represent His *buddhi* (intelligence), *ahaṅkāra* (egoism), *chitta* (heart), and *manaḥ* (mind).

This is the authoritative statement of the Gosvāmī. These four *sakhās* are not different in form than Kṛṣṇa Himself. Their dress and ornaments are impossible to describe in writing. The embodiment of Kṛṣṇa's intelligence is the *gopa* named Śrīdāma; and the embodiment of Kṛṣṇa's egoism is Sudāma; the embodiment of Kṛṣṇa's heart is Vasudāma; and the embodiment of Kṛṣṇa's mind is Kiṅkiṇī. There is no confidential pastime that Kṛṣṇa-candra secretly performs in Vraja that is not witnessed by these four boys. Truly one is never abandoned by one's own intelligence, ego, heart and mind; in all activities these accompany one, while always remaining in the background. All of Kṛṣṇa's *līlās* performed in Vraja throughout His three different ages – *bālya* (babyhood), *pauganda* (childhood) and *kiśor* (adolescence) – are never enacted without these particular boys. There is not a single thing about Kṛṣṇa that they are unaware of, from His relationships with parental *vātsalya* associates up to the extent of His dealings in amorous *śṛngār* sports.

Other boys of the next category of *sakhās* – the *priya-narma sakhās* (very intimate friends) – are accomplices in the *gopīs'* pastimes with Kṛṣṇa, and different members of this class will participate in different portions of the *līlā*. The *priya-narmas* headed by Subala, Arjjuna and others thus continually sport in the amusements enacted between the *gopas* and *gopīs*. However, the *priya-sakhās* can understand the internal intricacies of all these pastimes, but never reveal such secrets externally for fear of causing inharmony in the flow of mellows (*rasābhāsa*). Among the *priya-sakhās* the above-mentioned four boys embody the indwelling witness (*antaḥkaraṇa*), and they are completely full to overflowing with *Kṛṣṇānanda*.

Śrīdāma is the Chief

In the above-quoted Sanskrit *ślokas* listing the four most intimate boyfriends, the name "Dāma" should be understood to indicate Śrīdāma. Due to the particular meter being used in the *ślokas*, the respective authors merely abbreviated his name from Śrīdāma to Dāma. After duly considering the facts, I have thus concluded that when these four names are written together in the same place there is some figurative modification of the syllables in order to fit the meter. Thus the name of Dāma was used as a convention. According to the scriptures Śrīdāma is very, very dear to the Lord. This is evidenced in many places throughout the *śāstras* headed by the *Bhāgavatam*. The name of Rāma and Kṛṣṇa's beloved *sakhā* Śrīdāma is frequently written first, followed by the names of Subala, Stoka-Kṛṣṇa and others.

śrīdāmā nāma gopālo rāma-keśavayoḥ sakhā
subala-stokakṛṣṇādyā gopāḥ premṇedam abruvan

Once, some of the cowherd boys – Śrīdāma, the very close friend of Rāma and Keśava, along with Subala, Stoka-Kṛṣṇa and others – thus lovingly spoke. (*Bhāg.* 10.15.20)

It is also found in the *Varaha Purāṇa:*

śrīdāmā paścima 'dvāre sudāmā cottare tathā

The boy Śrīdāma is situated at the gate to the west, and Sudāma is situated at the gate to the north.

Everywhere it is seen that Śrīdāma is predominantly listed. In the *nyāya* philosophy of logic it is stated *evaṁ pradhānāpradhānayor madhye* and so forth – the most important of a group of items is listed first, followed by the lesser important. The personal beauty of Śrīdāma is described in the *Bhakti-rasāmṛta-sindhu* (3.3.41) thus:

vāsaḥ piṅgaṁ bibhrataṁ śṛṅga-pāniṁ
baddha-sparddhāṁ sauhṛdān mādhavena
tāmroṣṇīsaṁ śyāma-dāmābhirāmaṁ
śridāmānaṁ dāma-bhājaṁ bhajāmi

Who wears yellow garments,
holding a buffalo horn bugle
Who out of intimate affection
has the audacity to challenge Mādhava
Who wears a copper-colored turban
Whose charming complexion is blackish –
I worship that splendrously effulgent Śrīdāma.

Next, Sudama is described in the *Govinda-Vṛndāvanam* (1.159–160) thus:

rasiko nāgaro gauraḥ śarad-amburuhekṣanaḥ
agranthi-sarala-sthūla unmāda-nṛtya-sundaraḥ

mahā-rāsa-rasāhlāda pulaka-prema-vihvalaḥ
nānā-raṅga-rasopetaḥ sudāmā sa ca kīrtitaḥ

The cowherd boy celebrated as Sudāma is a relisher of confidential mellows, he is very heroic, his complexion is fair, and his eyes are like lotus flowers blooming in the autumn. He is detached from all ties, simple and straightforward, large, plump and strong, and he is beautified by wild and unrestrained dancing. He rejoices in the mellows of the *mahā-rāsa* dance, and is so overwhelmed with ecstatic love that his hairs stand on end. He is endowed with the mellows of various types of sport.

(4) *Priya-Narma-Sakhā*

The group of cowherd boys known as *priya-narma-sakhās* (most intimate friends) are a little younger than Kṛṣṇa, are in knowledge of His secrets, and render service unto Him in the mood of girlfriends (*sakhī-bhāva*). This category includes Subala, Arjjuna, Gandharva, Vasanta, Ujjvala, Kokila, Sananda and Vidagdha. The beauty of Subala is described in the *Govinda-vṛndāvanam* (1.153–154) thus:

gaurāṅgo nāda-gambhīro mahā-dambha-samanvitaḥ
rāsa-bhāvaḥ sadāmodaḥ paramānanda-kandaraḥ
kandarpa-koṭi-saundaryā nṛtya-līlā-viśāradaḥ
sāda prema-rasāhlādaḥ subalaḥ saṁprakīrtitaḥ

The cowherd boy celebrated as Subala has a fair complexion, a very deep voice, and a loud and boisterous nature. Always jovial, he is a source of supreme bliss for others. He is handsome like ten million Cupids, expert in dancing pastimes, and is continuously overwhelmed by the mellows of pure *prema*.

Two Secondary Divisions of Cowherd Boys

Thus I have very briefly described the group of cowherd boys known as *priya-narma*. This ends my listing of the four principal divisions of *sakhās* – (1) *suhṛt-sakhā* (friends of well-wishing heart),

(2) *sakhā* (general friends), (3) *priya-sakhā* (confidential friends), and (4) *priya-narma-sakhā* (very intimate friends). Now I speak of the two secondary divisions of *sakhās* – (1) *vidūśaka* (comical buffoons), and (2) *viṭa* (sensual, artistic companions).

(1) *Vidūśaka-Sakhā*

The *vidūśakas* or clowns tend to act up especially during times of eating in order to wrangle with Kṛṣṇa, and at other times they move their limbs with funny, distorted motions in order to create jokes and laughter.

> *vasantādy abhidho lolo bhojane kalahe priyaḥ*
> *vikṛtāṅga-vaco-veśair hāsyakārī vidūṣakaḥ*
> *vidagdha-mādhave khyāto yathāsau madhu-maṅgalaḥ*

> Vasanta and certain others boys, who become very greedy at the time of eating, who are fond of picking quarrels, who cause laughter by their twisted limbs, funny words and bizarre attire, are called *vidūśaka*. Just as in the drama *Vidagdha Mādhava Nātaka* the famous clown is the boy Madhu-maṅgala. (*Ujjvala Nīlamaṇi* 2.7)

Other *vidūśakas* are Puśpānka, Hāsānka and others.

(2) *Viṭa-Sakhā*

Those boys who are clever in details of fashion, who tend to be sensitive and cunning, who are in knowledge of a great many love-techniques as found in the *Kāma-śāstras*, are called *viṭa*.

> *veśopacāra-nipuno dhūrtto goṣṭhī-viśāradaḥ*
> *kāma-tantra-kalā-vedī viṭam ity abhidhīyate*

> Those who are expert in arranging clothing and ornaments, whose mentality is sensuous and sly, who are quite competent in social arrangements and counseling, who are knowledgeable of the amorous arts found in the *Kāma-tantras*, are called *viṭa*. (*Ujjvala Nīlamaṇi* 2.5)

kaḍāra-bhāratī-bandha-gandha-vedādayo viṭāḥ

The boys Kadāra, Bharatī-bandha, Gandha-veda and others are of the group of *viṭas*. (*Laghu-Rādhā-Kṛṣṇa-Gaṇoddeśa-Dīpikā* 73)

Sādhārana Vayasya (Ordinary Friends)

The general populace of Lord Kṛṣṇa's ordinary boyfriends in Vraja are uncountable; I will narrate something about those among them who are especially fixed in their loyal service attitude toward Him. Raktaka, Patraka, Patri, Madhu-kanthā, Madhu-vrata, Tāli, Māna-shālī, Mālā-dhara, Bhankura, Bhringāra and others are thus counted amongst the assembly of *sakhās* who act as servants. These boys render service unto Kṛṣṇa in the forest by carrying His walking stick, fighting stick, buffalo horn, flute and so forth. They remain close by His side during all His sports throughout the forest. Furthermore, there is Kalālāpa, Kalānkura, Keli-kalā, Prithukā, Komala, Phulla, Maṅgala, Kapila and other *sakhās* who are always rendering service close by. The boys headed by Suvilāsa and Rasālākṣa serve by preparing betel nuts (*tāmbūla*). Servants headed by Sārangada and Kuvalaya keep milk, water and sweets handy. In the forest, Prema-kanda, Mahā-gandha, and Sairindhra prepare decorations for bodily limbs out of various colorful mineral pigments that represent the splendor of the woodlands. Kusumollāsa, Sumanasa and others serve Kṛṣṇa by providing scented flower garlands. Many boys are qualified to attend His bodily needs such as Puṣpa-hāsa, Mahollāsa and others. Subandha, Karpūra, Kusuma and their group are especially capable in serving the lotus feet of Śrī Kṛṣṇa.

Thus I have very carefully written only of the most prominent amongst the *sakhās*, according to the descriptions found in *Bhakti-rasāmṛta-sindhu* and *Rādhā-Kṛṣṇa-Gaṇoddeśa-Dīpikā*. All these boys can again be classified into three divisions – (1) some among them are *nitya-priya* (eternally dear, or *nitya-siddha*), (2) some are *sura-vara* (the best among the demigods, elevated from *deva* status to the spiritual world); and (3) some are *sādhaka* (devotional practitioners who became perfected). All of these personalities render *sevā* unto Kṛṣṇa each in their own way – either by beloved words, smiles, jokes or other services – and in so many ways they give Him satisfaction and pleasure.

I have in this way spoken very briefly about the *āśrayālambana* (subjective foundation, or types of devotees that are receptacles of Kṛṣṇa's love). Now please hear of the *uddīpana* (stimulating) feature of *ālambana* as it is found in the *sakhya-rasa*. This book *Preyo-Bhakti-Rasārṇava* has been written while praying to the the two lotus feet of Śrī Caitanya, and bowing to Śrīla Nityānanda-Chānda, meditating exclusively on their feet as well as those of Abhirām and Sundarānanda Gopāl, and having great hope for the feet of Srī Parṇī Gopāl. Taking shelter of the feet of Gopāl Caraṇ, this Dās Nayanānanda has described all these things.

Thus ends the second chapter of
Śrī Śrī Preyo-Bhakti-Rasārṇava

CHAPTER THREE

The Ingredients of Transcendental Mellow

vrajendra-nandanaṁ vande
sa-rāmaṁ jalada-pmbham
śrīdāmādyaiḥ parivṛtaṁ
sakhya-prema-pariplutam

Obeisances unto Vrajendra-nandana
of raincloud-complexion, accompanied by Rāma
Surrounded by Śrīdāma and the others
Overflooded with the love of the cowherd boys.

All glories, all glories to Rāma, Kṛṣṇa and their assembly of *sakhās*! All glories, all glories to their beloved boyfriends (*priya*), beloved girlfriends (*priyā*), and to Śrīla Vṛndāvana!

O readers with the disposition of *sakhya-bhaktas*! Please listen with blissful minds. That which causes one to remember Śrī Kṛṣṇa is called *uddīpana* (stimulant). That thing which, upon viewing it or even hearing about it, awakens a connection with Kṛṣṇa is known in the scriptures as *uddīpana* (*B.r.s.* 2.1.301). Kṛṣṇa's age, dress, buffalo horn bugle, flute, conchshell and so forth; His qualities such as pleasing, funny, heroic and so forth; His dear devotees; His activities conducted while pretending to be a royal prince or appearing as various incarnations – all these things form the category of *uddīpana*. In this regard, please hear the statements of the scripture (*B.r.s.* 3.3.57).

Kṛṣṇa's Age (*vayaḥ*)

Śrī Kṛṣṇa's transcendental age is divided into 3 periods: *kaumāra* (babyhood), *pauganda* (childhood) and *kiśor* (adolescence). He spends the periods of *kaumāra, pauganda* and the beginning of *kiśor* in Vraja, sojourning to Mathurā at the end of *kiśor*. After that He comes into the age of *yauvana* (youth) (*B.r.s.* 3.3.58).

The period of *kaumāra* extends from Kṛṣṇa's birth up through 5 years of age; *pauganda* is 5 more years (age 6 through 10); and *kiśor* is from age 10 through 15 or 16. After spending the periods of *kaumāra, pauganda* and *kiśor* in Vraja, He departs for Mathurā at the end of *kiśor*. After that, Śrī Kṛṣṇa assumes the nature of youthful *yauvana* and sports His pastimes in Dvārāvatī while manifesting splendrous divine opulences (*B.r.s.* 2.1.309).

(1) *Kaumāra* (babyhood)

The period of Kṛṣṇa's *kaumāra* age is fully nourished by the parental *vātsalya-rati*, in which Nanda and the rest become very much satisfied. This *kaumāra* age can be further subdivided into three distinct periods – *ādya* (beginning), *madhya* (middle) and śeṣa (end).

The *ādya kaumāra* period extends up to the age of 1 year 8 months. Then the *madhya kaumāra* period extends up to the age of 3 years and 5 months. This interval gives rise to the highest expression of Kṛṣṇa's joking, dancing, adorable antics and so forth in the company of the *sakhās*. Then the *śeṣa kaumāra* period extends up to the age of 5 years, wherein He takes His calves to graze in the pasturelands along with His childhood boyfriends.

bibhrad veṇuṁ jaṭhara-paṭayoh śṛṅga-vetre ca kakṣe
vāme pāṇau masṛṇa-kavalaṁ tat-phalāny aṅgulīsu
tiṣṭhan madhye sva-parisuhṛdo hāsayan narmabhiḥ svaiḥ
svarge loke miṣati bubhuje yajña-bhug bāla-keliḥ

Kṛṣṇa sat with His flute tucked between His waist and the tight cloth on His right side, and with His horn bugle and cow-driving stick on His left. Holding in His hand a very nice preparation of yogurt and rice mixed with pieces of suitable fruit between His fingers, He sat like the whorl of a lotus flower, looking toward all His young cowherd boyfriends, personally joking with them and creating jubilant laughter among them as He ate. At that time, the denizens of the heavenly planets were watching and became struck with wonder at how the Personality of Godhead, who eats only in *yajña*, was now playfully eating with His childhood friends in the forest (*Bhāg.* 10.13.11)

(2) *Pauganda* (childhood)

After this comes Kṛṣṇa's *pauganda* age, also further subdivided into three periods – *ādya* (beginning), *madhya* (middle) and *śeṣa* (end).

The *ādya pauganda* period extends from the age of 5 years up to 6 years and 8 months, during which He performs varieties of sportive pastimes in the company of Śrīdāma and the rest. This interval is characterized by a reddish luster appearing in Kṛṣṇa's lips as well as in the palms of His hands. His neck develops circling lines like those on a conchshell, and His waist is very trim. The assembly of *sakhās* become completely enchanted to behold the vision of such a beautiful form. In the forest, the boys engage in numerous pastimes like fashioning flower-ornaments for each other and so forth. The following scene is described in the *Bhakti-rasāmṛta-sindhu* (3.3.66):

vṛndāraṇye samantāt surabhiṇi surabhī-vṛnda-rakṣā-vihārī
guñjā-hārī śikhaṇḍa-prakaṭita-mukuṭaḥ pīta-paṭṭāmbara-
śrīḥ karṇābhyāṁ karṇikāre dadhad alam urasā
phulla-mallīka-mālyaṁ
nṛtyan dor-yuddha-raṅge naṭa-vad iha sakhīn
nandayaty eṣa kṛṣṇaḥ

In the beautifully fragrant forest of Vṛndā
He sports merrily while tending His cows
that are scattered all around
He wears a garland of colorful *guñjā* berries,
and peacock feather in His crown
Hips adorned with exquisite yellow silken cloth
With *karṇikāra* flowers dangling from His ears
full-blown *mallikā* jasmine garland upon His chest
By dancing and playing arm-wrestling games
just like a dramatic actor –
this Kṛṣṇa is delighting the cowherd boys here!

Then the *madhya pauganda* period extends up to the age of 8 years and 4 months. Here Kṛṣṇa's bodily features become even more exquisite than before. He accepts full ornamentations like *venu* flute, buffalo horn bugle, golden armlets, fighting stick, walking stick, and cow-herding stick. This interval gives rise to the exciting games played with His friends underneath the huge Bhāṇḍiṛa banyan tree. At every opportunity He would endeavor to give pleasure to His *sakhās*. The activities of this period include the lifting of Govardhana Hill.

Thus I have described the features of *madhya pauganda*. The following is a depiction from the *Bhakti-rasāmṛta-sindhu* (3.3.70):

yaṣṭiṁ hasta-traya-parimitāṁ prāntayoḥ svarṇa-baddhāṁ
bibhran mālāṁ caṭula-camarī-cāru-cūḍojjvala-śrīḥ
baddhoṣṇīṣaḥ puraṭa-rucinā paṭṭa-pāśena pārśve
paśya krīḍan sukhayati sakhe! mitra-vṛndaṁ mukundaḥ

Carrying a walking stick three cubits in length (54")
bound with pure golden bands at both ends
Wearing a flower garland, His bouncing locks
are topped with a lovely, brilliantly opulent turban
secured at the sides with golden lace ties
Look, look O Sakhā! How Mukunda
delights His friends with such playful frolics!

Then the *śeṣa* portion of the *pauganda* period extends up to 10 years of age. Here Kṛṣṇa's physical movements become especially attractive. His curling and braided tresses fall down to His waist, and His face appears to be beaming from amongst the falls of such splendrous locks. His neck is like a conchshell, He wears a turban upon His head tilted to one side, and the *tilak* designs on His forehead are painted with dark musk paste. He moves His limbs gracefully while associating with His *sakhās* and thereby gives great delight to those boys. Reaching this *śeṣa pauganda* Kṛṣṇa appears just like an adolescent of *kiśor* endowment. He engages in activities such as praising the divine beauty of the *gopīs* and so forth. In the company of His confidential *narma sakhās* they indulge frequently in pastimes of whispering into each others' ears (*B.r.s.* 3.3.76). Thus I have described the three distinct subdivisions of the *pauganda* age. As illustrated in the *Bhakti-rasāmṛta-sindhu* (3.3.73):

agre-līlālaka-latikayālaṇkṛtaṁ bibhrad āsyaṁ
cañcad-veṇī-śikhara-śikhayā cumbita-śroṇi-bimbaḥ
uttuñgāṁsa-cchavir agha-haro raṅgam aṅga-śriyāva-
nyasyann eṣa priyasa-vayasāṁ gokulān nirjihīte

His head adorned with playfully scattered hair
completely surrounding His face
His hips kissed by the tip of His swinging braid
His raised and broadened shoulders
radiating pure youthful luster
The Destroyer of sins, by His own
vibrant and colorful bodily magnificence
gladdens His dear boyfriends while entering Gokula!

(3) *Kiśor* (adolescence)

The period of *kiśor* is also subdivided into intervals of *ādya*, *madhya* and *śeṣa*. First during *ādya kiśor*, Kṛṣṇa's already blackish complexion becomes intensely brilliant. Fine hairs upon His chest become slightly visible, and His eyes develop a luminous redness in their borders. In *madhya kiśor* His waist appears as trim as a lion's, and His chest spreads out broadly. From His ears dangle long earrings, and His cheeks sparkle. He is adorned with the *vaijayantī* flower garland, colorful mineral pigments, an elegant crown, jewelled necklaces, armlets, bracelets and more – truly an enchanting presentation! Skilled as the best of dancers, of the hue of rainclouds, He wears a peacock feather on His crown and walks with the gait of a maddened elephant. Placing His flute to His face and filling its holes with the nectar of His lips, Kṛṣṇa produces auspicious songs that give total bliss to His cowherd boyfriends. Rendering the earth of Vṛndāvana-bhūmi charming by His very footsteps, He personally enters the forest accompanied by His *sakhās* (*Bhāg.* 10.21.5).

During *madhya kiśor* the purely ravishing beauty of Lord Hari expands unlimitedly. The highly relishable sweetnesses of His divine bodily limbs are so intense that they bewilder the entire universe. His thighs become thicker, His arms fill out with muscles, His chest becomes broader still and His dark complexion appears exceptionally fascinating. His face continually beams with smiles and sidelong glances, and He plays world-mesmerizing songs upon His *muralī* flute. Wandering about in the forest with His cowherd boyfriends, they sport numerous athletic sports in great fun. During this period He also engages in grand amorous festivals in the secluded forest bowers, plus other pastimes headed by the *rasa* dance (*B.r.s.* 2.1.320).

During *śeṣa kiśor* the purely ravishing beauty of Lord Hari expands unlimitedly more than before. His limbs fully fill out and His entire body overflows with pure transcendental *rasa*. The flanks of His waist show three distinct folds of skin, and His attire displays limitless methods of ornamentation. Thus I have spoken of the magnificence of the end of His *kiśor* age (*B.r.s.* 2.1.327). The vision of Kṛṣṇa's youthful features thus appearing at the end of *kiśor* is described in the *rasa-śāstra* by the learned sages in this way (*B.r.s.* 2.1.330).

Kiśor is Kṛṣṇa's Eternal Age

It should be understood that Kṛṣṇa's *kiśor* age represents His true eternal form (*nitya-rūpa*). In this form He sports totally astonishing pastimes in the company of His *sakhās*. He showers the thirsty *chaṭāka*-birds of the *sakhās*' eyes with the rainfall of His nectar-smiles and sweet handsome figure. By this effect Śrīdāma becomes so full of bliss internally that it expresses outwardly all over his body as thrill-bumps and hairs standing erect (Śrī Kṛṣṇa and Śrīdāma are both of dark complexion – one like rainclouds and the other like a *tamāl* tree). They are both sitting clasped in a mutual embrace, the splendor of which is described as follows:

> *paśyotsikta-vali-trayī-vara-late vāsas taḍin mañjule*
> *pronmīlad vana-mālikā-parimala-stome tamāla-tviṣiḥ*
> *uksāty ambaka-cātakān smita-rasair dāmodarāmbhodhare*
> *śrīdāmā ramaṇīya-roma-kalikākīṇāṅga-śākhī babhau*

> Just see! That dark Dāmodara like a raincloud and that dark Śrīdāma like a *tamāl* tree are splendrously radiating! Their arms are wrapped around like pairs of excellent blossoming creepers, they are marked with three folds of skin on their bellies, and their garments are like entrancing lightning bolts. They dispense intense waves of fragrance from their forest-flower garlands. The Dāmodara monsoon-cloud is showering the rainfall of gentle *rasa*-laden smiles which saturate the *chaṭāka*-bird eyes of all the cowherd boys. And the body of that Śrīdāma, of dark *tamal*-tree complexion, appears to be studded with freshly blooming enchanting flower-buds in the form of his hairs standing on end! (*B.r.s.* 3.3.79)

Kṛṣṇa in His figure of *kiśor* is perpetually worshiped in Vraja, for all the devotees beginning with those in the mood of *dāsya* favor meditating upon Him in that age. Therefore dear readers please worship Kiśor Mohan in Vraja, taking shelter of either the mellow of *dāsya, sakhya, vātsalya,* or *madhurya.* Verily I have not written of the splendor He exhibits in His slightly older *yauvana* feature (after leaving Vraja); the devotees will please observe and consider the following statement of the scriptures:

prāyaḥ kiśora evāyaṁ sarva-bhakteṣu bhāsate
tena yauvana-śobhā 'sya neha kācit prapañcitā

> It is in this adolescent *kiśor* form that Śrī Kṛṣṇa mostly appears to all His devotees; for this reason the splendor of His *yauvana* age will not be described here. (*B.r.s.* 3.3.80).

Uddīpana (Ecstatic Stimulants)

Now I shall speak about how Kṛṣṇa's *rūpa* (bodily beauty) serves as an *uddīpana* (stimulant) by which the assembly of *sakhās* in Vraja are captivated. Once it was stated by Śrīdāma and the other *sakhās* to Kṛṣṇa that His limbs appear to be decorated even when they are not decorated with ornaments. Śrīdāma said. "Listen, Kṛṣṇa! *Ore bhāi!* O dear brother! There is no comparison anywhere to the attractiveness of your limbs! What use to you are so many fancy ornaments. Compared to the radiant effulgence of your transcendental features, these ornaments become totally insignificant! Indeed, your brilliant complexion has forcibly stolen the minds of all the cowherd boys!" Thus I have spoken this declaration of *rūpa-uddīpana,* stimulation of love by Kṛṣṇa's personal beauty (*B.r.s.* 3.3.81).

Śrīnga (buffalo horn bugle)

Arising in the morning, Rāma mounts a raised platform and vibrates his buffalo horn bugle, then shouts, "*Bhāi! Bhāi!* O brothers! O brothers!" Being awakened by this bugling, all the cowherd boys assemble together with minds blissfully united in remembrance of Kṛṣṇa (*B.r.s.* 3.3.82).

Veṇu (Kṛṣṇa's flute)

Once Kṛṣṇa went alone into the forest, and the *sakhās* became quite disturbed by His absence. To search Hari out they had gone to the gardens on the bank of the Yamunā River, when suddenly they heard the sound of His flute. Instantly becoming ecstatic upon hearing Kṛṣṇa's flute music, it was as if their dead bodies were gifted with the presence of a living soul. This incident is described in the *Bhakti-rasāmrta-sindhu* (3.3.83) thus:

suhṛdo! na hi yāta kātarā
harim anveṣtum itaḥ sutām raveḥ
kathayann amum atra vaiṇava-
dvani-dūtaḥ śikhare dhinoti naḥ

"O dear distressed boyfriends! Don't go to search for Hari on the bank of the Yamunā River (daughter of the sun)! The sound of Kṛṣṇa's flute coming from the peak of Govardhan Hill like a messenger has just announced Kṛṣṇa is here. This news has given us great delight!"

Śankha (Kṛṣṇa's conchshell)

Once Bhagavān was approaching the city of Hastināpur and from a distance vibrated His conchshell named Pāñcajanya. Hearing the sound of the Pāñcajanya, the sons of Pāndu (the Pandavas) along with their associates instantly became full of *kṛṣṇānanda*. In Vraja, all the pleasing statements shared between the *priya-narma-sakhā* Subala and the other boys are also *uddīpanas* or utterances that stimulate the awakening of Kṛṣṇa consciousness. Thus I have briefly outlined these items; now please listen to the codes of *anubhāva* (ecstatic symptoms) as they are found in the mood of *sakhya*.

Anubhāva (Subsequent Ecstatic Physical Expressions)

The principle of *anubhāva-rati* involves the awakening of ecstatic bodily reactions as the direct result of concentrating on

Kṛṣṇa within one's mental faculties. These meditations manifest externally in one's physical form as outrageous transformations such as dancing, singing, rolling on the ground, laughing and so forth (*B.r.s.* 2.1.1).

> *nṛtyaṁ viluṭhitaṁ gītaṁ krośanaṁ tanu-moṭanam*
> *huṅkāro jṛmbhaṇaṁ śvāsa-bhūmā lokānapekṣitā*
> *lālā-sravo 'ṭṭa-hāsaś ca ghūrṇā hikkā 'dayo 'pi ca*

> The 13 *anubhāvas* are: (1) *nṛtya* – dancing, (2) *vilunṭhana* – rolling upon the ground, (3) *gītā* – singing, (4) *krośana* – crying loudly (5) *tanu-moṭana* – stretching the body, (6) *huṇkāra* – loud shouting, (7) *jṛmbhaṇa* – yawning, (8) *śvāsa* – breathing heavily, (9) *lokānapekśana* – being unaware of the presence of others, (10) *lālā-srava* – drooling of saliva, (11) *aṭṭa-hāsa* – laughing loudly like a madman (12) *ghūrṇa* – wheeling of the head, and (13) *hikkā* – uncontrollable hiccups. (*B.r.s.* 2.1.2)

Thus I have narrated only the list of *anubhāva* symptoms. Now please hear about how the *anubhāvas* arise within the mellow of *sakhya*. The pleasurable pastimes of wrestling together, playing ball, gambling with dice, carrying each other upon the shoulders, twirling canes about, going places together, lounging upon the same bed, water-sports, joking, dancing, and singing in unison – all these playful activities conducted normally in the spirit of equality constitute ecstatic *anubhāvas* in the friendly mood of *sakhya* (*B.r.s.* 3.3.86–88).

The Moods of Various Classes of Cowherd Boys

Now please listen to the manners in which the six types of *sakhās* deal with Kṛṣṇa while in His personal company. Those of the *suhṛt sakhā* class are a little older than Kṛṣṇa, and thus are especially engaged in protecting Him. They advise Him in matters of favorable and unfavorable choices of action, and give protection to Him in the deep forests by judging what is good or bad in practical arrangements (*B.r.s.* 3.3.90).

Those of the general *sakhā* class like Viśāla, Vṛṣabha and others are a little younger than Kṛṣṇa. Please hear about the activities and behavior of this group. They prepare betel packets for Kṛṣṇa, smear sandalwood paste upon His limbs, adorn His hair and paint His *tilak*. These boys, who are fixed up in Kṛṣṇa's loyal *sevā*, decorate Him by fixing leaves and fresh twigs upon His person (*B.r.s.* 3.3.91).

Those of the more intimate *priya-sakhā* class are of the same age, same disposition and same mannerisms as Kṛṣṇa. Their mentality is: "I will conquer Kṛṣṇa in this fight!" They are so daring that they can forcibly snatch a flower right out of Kṛṣṇa's hand, and they are absolutely fearless while inducing Kṛṣṇa to decorate their own bodies. Performing various activities like hand-to-hand combat on an exactly equal level – such is the behavior of the *priya-sakhās* headed by Śrīdāma (*B.r.s.* 3.3.92).

Those of the most intimate *priya-narma-sakhā* class engage in dice-gambling. They tell Kṛṣṇa about the love of the *gopīkās* for Him, they go and tell the *gopīkās* about the love of Kṛṣṇa for them, and subsequently they return to Kṛṣṇa to whisper into His ear about the loving statements of the *gopīs* (*B.r.s.* 3.3.93–94).

The general class of cowherd boys known as *sādhārana-sakhās* in Vraja gain their own happiness simply by engaging in the personal *sevā* of Rāma and Kṛṣṇa. They tend cows according to the specific orders of Kṛṣṇa, they follow closely behind Him and they massage His limbs, fan Him and rub His back. They weave forest-flower garlands and offer them to various parts of Kṛṣṇa's body, and thereby receive the favor of His satisfaction. Bringing forest mineral pigments they adorn Kṛṣṇa in imaginative ways. Thus I have spoken to you of the activities of the *sādhārana sakhās* (*B.r.s.* 3.3.95).

Sāttvikā Bhāva (Existential Ecstasy)

Now I write of the form of existence known as *sāttvikā*. I see it described by the Gosvāmī in his book on *bhakti*. This condition is evident when a devotee's heart liquifies by being intensely affected with ecstatic emotions (*bhāva*) due to a direct relationship with Kṛṣṇa. Or, the ecstatic emotions can arise even when the devotee remains a little apart from Him in relationship. When the heart is thus affected it is considered to be the normal state of existence (*sattva*). Now the specific ecstatic emotions that affect the totality of such a state of existence are known by the name of *sāttvikā bhāva* (*B.r.s.* 2.3.1). The symptoms of this existential ecstasy are subdivided into 3 headings: *snigdha* (moist), *digdha* (burnt), and *rūkṣa* (dried-up) (*B.r.s.* 2.3.2).

1) *Snigdha Sāttvikā Bhāva* (moist existential ecstasy)

The exalted feature called *snigdha* is further subdivided into two distinct categories: *mukhya* (primary) and *gauṇa* (secondary). The ecstasies arising from Kṛṣṇa's direct relationship constitute *mukhya snigdha sāttvikā bhāva,* whereas those arising from living at a distance from Him constitute *gauṇa snigdha sāttvikā bhāva* (*B.r.s.* 2.3.3).

2) *Digdha Sāttvikā Bhāva* (burnt existential ecstasy)

When one's mind is attracted to Kṛṣṇa in any other way besides the five primary moods of *mukhya-rati* or the seven secondary moods of *gauṇa-rati,* then that is called *digdha sāttvikā bhāva.* Just see an example: Once when Mother Yaśodā saw a vision of the dead witch Pūtanā in a dream, her limbs began to tremble. Those moods in relation to Kṛṣṇa which are bereft of any of the normal forms of *rati* are called *digdha.* Now please listen as I speak of that known as *rūkṣa.*

3) *Rūkṣa Sāttvikā Bhāva* (dried-up existential ecstasy)

When *sāttvikā* ecstasies arise in the body of a person who is devoid of *rati* [i.e., a non-devotee] by hearing of the sweetness and wonder of *kṛṣṇa-līlā*, that is called *rūkṣa sāttvikā bhāva*. This also occurs when, by attentively hearing songs of Kṛṣṇa's pastimes, any of the symptoms headed by *romāñcha* (standing up of bodily hairs) manifests on the person of one who is normally desirous of material sense gratification, or of one desirous of liberation. Such visible bodily symptoms are known as *rūkṣa*.

Aṣṭa Sāttvikā Bhāva (The Eight Existential Ecstasies)

By hearing and chanting of Śrī Kṛṣṇa's pastimes and so forth, one's consciousness becomes intensely infused with the sheer power of the living force itself (*prāṇa*). This acute motion of one's own life-force gives rise to profound churning within, which in turn agitates the external body, which reacts with various physical transfigurations. These reactions manifest in the body according to how the vital force of life comes into contact with each of the five material elements: namely earth, water, fire, air and sky. The *jīva* soul is encased within the body made of these elements, accepting the body as its total existence; and sheltered within circulates the life-force that maintains the physical animation of the living being. When the *prāṇa* appears externally while in contact with one or more of the five elements within, then it produces the symptoms of the eight existential ecstasies (*aṣṭa sāttvikā bhāva*), headed by being stunned (*stambha*) and so forth (*B.r.s.* 2.3.16–17).

The *aṣṭa sāttvikā bhāvas* are: (1) *stambha* – becoming stunned, (2) *sveda* – perspiring, (3) *romāñcha* – standing up of hairs on the body, (4) *svara-bheda* – faltering of the voice, (5) *vepathu* – trembling, (6) *vaivarṇya* – changing of bodily color, (7) *aśru* – shedding tears, and (8) *pralaya* – devastation.

When the *prāṇa* contacts various material elements, a corresponding reaction is seen externally in the transfigured body, outlined as follows. When the vital force comes into contact with earth (*bhūmi*), then one becomes stunned. When the same force comes into contact with water (*jala*), there is the shedding of tears. When the life force comes into contact with fire (*teja*), then there is perspiring and changing of bodily color. When the force comes into contact with sky (*ākāśa*), there is complete devastation. When the force comes into contact with its own element of air (*vayu*), in any of the three different intensities – *manda* (gentle), *madhya* (intermediate) and *tīvra* (acute) – then there are the corresponding three reactions of standing of the hairs on the body, faltering of the voice and trembling (*B.r.s.* 2.3.18–19).

(1) *Stambha* (becoming stunned)

When the *prāṇa* contacts the element of earth, then one becomes stunned. This symptom is exhibited by cessation of movement, speechlessness, and feelings of emptiness. This *stambha* can be caused by jubilation (*harṣa*), fearfulness (*bhaya*), astonishment (*āścharya*), lamentation (*viṣāda*), and anger (*amarśa*).

An example of a devotee in the mood of *sakhya* becoming stunned is as follows. When the assembly of cowherd boys saw Kṛṣṇa jump into the poisoned waters of the Kāliya serpent's lake, they all became very disturbed. Śrīdāma exclaimed, "What has happened! What will happen!" All the other boys became so bewildered that they instantly stopped everything they were doing. In separation from Kṛṣṇa, Śrīdāma became completely still. His eyes simply stared and his arms fell motionless. Thus all of his senses became stunned and were bereft of consciousness due to the fright of Kṛṣṇa's dangerous predicament; all of Śrīdāma's boyfriends remained likewise (*B.r.s.* 3.3.97).

(2) *Sveda* (perspiring)

When the *prāṇa* contacts the element of fire, then one perspires excessively. This *sveda* can be caused by jubilation, fear, or anger (*B.r.s.* 2.3.28).

An example of one perspiring because of jubilation is as follows. Once the *rasa*-laden Kṛṣṇa took His friends Śrīdāma, Sudāma, Dāma, Subal and the rest to the bank of the Yamunā River, and He began to shower them all with the nectar-mellows of playful sports. Just as oysters produce pearls from raindrops that fall during the constellation of the Swāti star, similarly the oyster-like form of Śrīdāma produced pearl-like drops of perspiration during Kṛṣṇa's showering of nectar-mellow-sports (*krīdā-rasa-sudhā*). The drops of perspiration visible here and there upon his body appeared like strands of pearls, making his body quite splendrous by their intensified gleaming (*B.r.s.* 3.3.98).

(3) *Romāñcha* (standing up of hairs on the body)

When the *prāṇa* contacts its own element of air and intensifies, then the hairs of one's body stand erect. This *romāñca* can be caused by astonishment, enthusiasm, fear, or jubilation (*B.r.s.* 2.3.32).

An example of hairs standing up because of ecstatic enthusiasm (*utsāha*) is as follows. Once when Śrīdāma was involved in a game of mock fighting with Kṛṣṇa, he heard Kṛṣṇa blow His horn bugle to start the match. Śrīdāma was so eager to fight (feeling pure *kṛṣṇānanda*) that the hairs on his body immediately stood up (*B.r.s.* 2.3.35).

(4) *Svara-Bheda* (faltering of the voice)

When the *prāṇa* contacts its own element of air and intensifies even more, then one's body manifests the symptom of a faltering voice. This incomparable *svara-bheda* can be caused by lamentation, astonishment, anger, jubilation, or fear (*B.r.s.* 2.3.37).

An example of faltering voice is as follows. When Kṛṣṇa was fighting with the great ass-demon named Dhenuka, the assembly of *sakhās* were watching from behind with greatly anxious hearts. Śrīdāma was so worried the demon would harm Kṛṣṇa that his voice choked up until he was completely unable to speak.

Seeing Kṛṣṇa finally kill Dhenuka, the boys all became so joyous that they surrounded Him and spoke with faltering voices.

(7) *Aśru* (shedding tears)

When the *prāṇa* contacts the element of water, then tears flow from the eyes. This *aśru* can be caused by jubilation, anger, or lamentation. When the tears are generated from feelings of jubilation they are called *śīta* (cold); when they are generated from anger or lamentation they are called *uṣṇa* (hot).

Once all the cowherd boys were in the deep forest, grazing the cows within their respective groups. At that time, a forest fire suddenly broke out and spread all around, and the *gopālas* loudly called "Kṛṣṇa! Kṛṣṇa!" in great anxiety. In order to put out the fire, they all started crying together. They actually thought that their combined tears could extinguish the fire. They did so not out of worry for the safety of their own bodies, but due to their concern over how the fire might harm Kṛṣṇa. Then Kṛṣṇa, the indwelling witness of all, rescued the assembly of cowherd boys by personally putting out the fire. This was His own pastime (*B.r.s.* 3.3.101).

(8) *Pralaya* (devastation)

When the *prāṇa* contacts the element of sky being sheltered in voidness, then the body assumes a condition called devastation. This *pralaya* can be caused either by happiness (*sukha*) or by distress (*dukha*), and is characterized by one becoming completely bereft of activities, of awareness, and even the slightest movement (*B.r.s.* 2.3.58).

Please see and deliberate on these verses describing the four ecstatic symptoms – faltering of the voice, trembling, changing of color, and devastation. When the cowherd boys saw that Lord Hari entered the lake of the serpent Kāliya, they lamented "*Hāy! Hāy!*" as they started loudly weeping and wailing. Being bereft of their Lord (*nātha*) they became helpless (*anātha*) since He went away to grapple with such an unknown fate. Not seeing Kṛṣṇa, all of their lives turned utterly hopeless, and they desperately repeated

"*Hā* Kṛṣṇa! *Hā* Kṛṣṇa!" while burning in the fire of separation. Some trembled violently and became discolored, and others fell unconscious while their faltering voices produced horrible gurgling sounds. Some dropped to the ground and stopped breathing altogether. Thus in Kṛṣṇa's separation the *sakhās* forgot about everything else (*B.r.s.* 3.3.100).

Thus I have briefly described the eight ecstatic symptoms known as *aṣṭa sāttvikā bhāva*. Due to my fear of this book becoming very large, I have not elaborated on these topics. The *siddhas* or perfected souls internally experience all eight of these *sāttvikā bhāvas*, but only one or two symptoms might be revealed externally and thereby seen by other souls. Someone's body may exhibit one symptom, while someone else might show two or three of them. Still others may experience all of these ecstasies for extended periods of time – for hours and hours throughout the entire day and night.

Thus ends the brief description of Sāttvikā.

Vyabhichārī (33 Transitory Assisting Emotions)

The transcendental emotions known as *vyabhichārī* are 33 in number, and they are an inseparable ingredient (*sāmagrī*) that forms the *svarūpa* of *sthāyi-rati*. The five primary mellows of affection: *śānta, dāsya, sakhya, vātsalya* and *madhura*, comprise the fathomless ocean of the mellows of devotion – and the *bhaktas* become madly intoxicated merely by drinking a single drop. In that ocean exists the conglomeration of auxiliary ingredients, which rise momentarily and then sink into the ocean's depths. These are the transcendental emotions known as *vyabhichārī*, or those which circulate about (also called *sanchār*). These *vyabhichārīs* swirl around one's personal ecstatic moods (*bhāva*), and they especially travel towards and congregate about the principal transcendental mellow (*sthāyī*) (*B.r.s.* 2.4.1–2).

Nirveda (indifference); *viṣāda* (lamentation); *dainya* (humility); *glāni* (fatigue); *śrama* (labor); *mada* (intoxication); *garva* (pride); *śankā* (fear); *trāsa* (apprehension); *āvega* (distraction); *unmāda* (madness); *apasmṛti* (forgetfulness); *vyādhi* (disease); *moha* (confusion); *mṛti* (death); *ālasya* (laziness); *jādya* (inertness); *vrīdā* (shyness); *avahitthā* (secretiveness); *smṛti* (remembrance); *vitarka* (argumentativeness); *cintā* (anxiety); *mati* (thoughtfulness); *dhṛti* (patience); *harṣa* (jubilation); *autsukya* (eagerness); *augrya* (ferocity); *amarśa* (anger); *asūyā* (envy); *cāpalya* (fickleness); *nidrā* (drowsiness); *supti* (sleep); and *bodha* (alertness).

Thus I have narrated the 33 *vyabhichārī* emotions. Now please hear the description of how these relate to the *sakhya-rasa*. Except for the three emotions – ferocity, apprehension, and laziness – all the rest remain available for experience in the *sakhya-rasa* (*B.r.s.* 3.3.102).

Yoga (Personal Association) and *Ayoga* (Separation)

There are two ways of experiencing these ecstatic emotions – those felt in *yoga* (being with Kṛṣṇa) and those felt in *ayoga* (being separated from Kṛṣṇa). Since I will describe these later, here I will narrate only the brief codes. When one is removed from the personal association of Kṛṣṇa it is called *ayoga*. In this condition the five emotions of intoxication, jubilation, pride, sleep, and patience cannot be present. In *yoga* (Kṛṣṇa's company) then the five emotions of death, fatigue, disease, forgetfulness and humility are not seen (*B.r.s.* 3.3.103).

Sthāyī (Permanent Relationship)

The symptoms of *sakhya-rati* being the *sthāyī-bhāva* of the *preyo-bhakti-rasa* are described as follows. Both of the cowherd boys [Kṛṣṇa and the devotee] share a mutual exchange of *prema* that is devoid of all feelings of formal reverence. It is an affectionate fondness based on such reciprocal trust that they remain on the level of exact equals. This kind of thickened confidence makes them both think that they are of the exact same disposition; and conversely, when they are separated from each other the passing of a moment seems to be like countless ages (*B.r.s.* 3.3.105–106).

This *sakhya-rati* increases step by step through the levels of *praṇaya* (fondness), *prema* (love), *sneha* (affection) and *rāga* (attachment) – according to the progressive increase of taste found at each level. The ultimate goal (*prayojana*) of the cowherd boys, affection extends up to the stage of *rāga*; please listen to the way in which *rati* expands (*B.r.s.* 3.3.106). Thus the fixed affection (*sthāyī*) which is based on resolute, daring confidence in regard to total equality is known by the name of *sakhya-rati*. Furthermore, this *sakhya-rati* is described as having two main categories–*kevalā* (unalloyed) and *saṅkulā* (mixed). *Kevalā* (unalloyed affection) and *saṇkulā* (mixed affections).

That *rati* which is devoid of any other humor of *rati* is called *kevalā*. And when the *rati* is formed of a mixture of two or three humors it is called *saṅkulā* (*B.r.s.* 2.5.25). In Vraja, the boys headed by Rasāla know of nothing other than pure *dāsya-rati*, the affection of servitude, while the boys headed by Śrīdāma know of nothing other than pure *sakhya-rati*, the affection of friendship. It is seen in Vraja that the superiors headed by Yaśodā perpetually indulge in pure *vātsalya-rati*, the affection of parenthood. Thus I have written of these three personalities in order to illustrate the unalloyed feelings found in *kevalā-rati*. The exhibition of *dāsya*, *sakhya* and *vātsalya* in Vraja are in the *kevalā* category, whereas the humors as exhibited by Uddhava, Bhīma, Mukharā, and those in other cities are in the mixed *saṅkulā* category. This aspect of *saṅkulā-rati* is compared to the desire-fulfilling gem called *cintāmaṇi*, and its realm is mostly the towns of Madhu-purī and Dvārāvati. But the aspect of *kevalā-rati* is compared to the transcendentally superior Kaustubha gem. Indeed, I do not see any mood other than pure eternal friendship.

The *sakhya* affection of Balarāma is mixed with *vātsalya;* the *vātsalya* affection of King Yudhiṣṭhira is mixed with *sakhya* and *dāsya;* the mood of Ugrasena and others is *dāsya* mixed with *vātsalya;* the mood of the older *gopīs* like Mukharā and others is *vātsalya* mixed with *sakhya;* Nārada, and the sons of Mādri (Nakula and Sahadeva) feel *sakhya* mixed with *dasya;* and Rudra, Garuḍa, Uddhava and others feel *dāsya* affection mixed with *sakhya* (*B.r.s.* 3.4.81–83).

Increasing Levels of *Kevalā-Rati*

When *sakhya-rati* further increases in successive stages, the relishable taste correspondingly increases and is known by the name of *praṇaya*. After this form of affection dawns within one's mind, it results in a supreme absorption (*parama āveśa*). Thus it comes to the level of *prema*. When this *kṛṣṇa-prema* melts the heart, the ecstatic liquified consciousness is called *sneha*. Such *sneha* is exhibited at the three places (Vraja, Mathurā and Dvārakā) in two different varieties, namely *ghrita-vat* (like ghee) and *madhu-vat* (like honey). One, like ghee, only melts when it is heated by fire, whereas the other, like honey, is always in a melted state. In Vraja-pur the *sneha* affection is *madhu-vat,* while in Mathurā and Dvārakā-pur it is *ghrita-vat*.

When *sneha* intensifies progressively, one takes certain situations into consideration according to how they will affect Kṛṣṇa's happiness; some things are accepted by the devotee as *anukūla* (favorable) and other things as *pratikūla* (unfavorable). Even one's personal unhappiness is regarded as happiness if it is in relation to

Kṛṣṇa. And without Kṛṣṇa, one's so-called happiness is considered to be unhappiness. When Kṛṣṇa is happy, the devotee is happy. When Kṛṣṇa is unhappy, the devotee is unhappy. When the body of the devotee fully experiences this mood, then the *sneha* proceeds to the next platform called *rāga*. Due to intensified dedication to Śrī Nanda-nandan, one offers unto Him the totality of one's senses, body, mind and resources. Everything about this stage of elevated and resolute attachment (*rāga-niṣṭhā*) is described in the scriptures. According to the geographical location in which it is exhibited, the *rāga* appears in three different varieties of loving affection [or colors, since the word *rāga* also means color]. These are: *nila-rāga* (blue), *kusumbha-rāga* (saffron), and *mañjiṣṭhā-rāga* (bright red). These three modes of affection are sometimes further subdivided into different component aspects. The *mañjiṣṭhā* variety is the most securely fixed *rāga*, for it never diminishes – just as bright red dye never goes away after spilling onto a piece of cloth. The *nīla-rāga* is exhibited at Mathurā, the *kusumbha-rāga* at Dvārakā, and the *mañjiṣṭhā-rāga* at Vraja. Thus I have spoken of their divisions.

Being desirous of attaining the two lotus feet of Śrī Caitanya Mahāprabhu, this Nayanānanda Dāsa speaks about the *preyo-bhakti-rasa*.

Thus ends the third chapter of
Śrī Śrī Preyo-Bhakti-Rasārṇava

CHAPTER FOUR

Symptoms of the Cowherd Boys, Separation and Union

All glories, all glories to Śrī Kṛṣṇa Caitanya and to Lord Nityānanda! All glories to Gopāl Mahanta and to Śrī Sundarānanda!

Features of *Ayoga* (Separation from Kṛṣṇa)

Now please hear the description of the principles of *ayoga* (separation from Kṛṣṇa's personal company) and *yoga* (full experience of His personal company), as they are found in the permanent *sthāyī* mood of friendly *sakhya-rati*. According to the writings of the Gosvāmī, *rati* is always situated within *rasa* in either of the two distinct variations of *ayoga* or *yoga* (*B.r.s.* 3.2.93). The *ayoga* is experienced while apart from Kṛṣṇa; this condition is further subdivided into two aspects, namely *utkaṇṭhā* (anxiety) and *viyoga* (estrangement). First, the *utkaṇṭhā* is felt when the devotee has not yet seen Kṛṣṇa and becomes very eager to see Him. And *viyoga* is felt when the devotee has been beholding Kṛṣṇa and thereafter becomes separated from Him (*B.r.s.* 2.95–96).

(1) *Utkaṇṭhā* (eagerness to see Kṛṣṇa for the first time)

When the young Śrī Arjuna, the son of Kunti, was studying the Dhanur Veda (ancient treatise on archery), he was completely fixed in his training. But upon hearing about the sweet transcendental qualities of Śrī Kṛṣṇa, his mind immediately became very anxious for His *darśana*.

(2) *Viyoga* (separation from Kṛṣṇa's personal company)

It is stated in the scriptures that when one loses Kṛṣṇa's association after having attained it this situation is known by the name of *viyoga* (*B.r.s.* 3.2.114). An illustration of this principle is: When Hari left Vraja and journeyed to Mathurā, from that day onwards all the cowherd boyfriends He left behind became completely bereft of all sense. Very much stricken with the feverish state of separation from Śrī Kṛṣṇa, they babbled amongst themselves in search of Him.

One boy exclaimed, "*Hāi!* O my dear brother! Where have you gone? What offense has been committed to induce you to leave your father, mother and boyfriends? We have all become your humble servants due to your transcendental qualities. Without you, who else could fill your place of esteem among the cowherders? You personally rescued us on the day we entered the mouth of the demon Aghāsura. You protected us from the poisoned waters of the Kāliya lake, and by your own mercy you saved us from a terrible forest fire. O dear Kṛṣṇa, you delivered us from so many calamities in the deep forest, but now being bereft of your company we cannot maintain our own lives! Bestowing the shade of your sheltering protection, you freed us from fear whether in the forest or at home, but now you do not protect us. Why have you done this to us? During those days we were yours, but now we have become strangers to you! Alas, it has become impossible to attain your association! Consumed in the blazing fever of your separation, we have fallen into this greatly disastrous condition, for without your *darśana* our bodies are simply burning up!"

Thus acutely feeling separation from Kṛṣṇa, the *sakhās* became quite pitiful. This condition is proclaimed as *viyoga* (*B.r.s.* 3.3.116).

Daśa-Daśā
The Ten Conditions of Separation

The predicament of feeling Kṛṣṇa's separation in *viyoga* manifests in 10 symptoms, collectively called *daśa-daśā* (the ten conditions). The scriptures describe these states, beginning with *tāpa* (affliction with grief), *kriśatā* (emaciation), and so forth. (*B.r.s.* 3.2.116):

> *aṅgesu tāpaḥ kṛśatā jāgarya 'lambana-śūnyatā*
> *adhṛtir jaḍatā vyādhir unmādo mūrcchitaṁ mṛti*
> *viyoga-saṁbhrama-prīter daśāvasthāḥ prakīrtitaḥ*

> The ten conditions of *viyoga* separation felt by those of loving affection are proclaimed to be: (1) *tāpa* – affliction with fever, (2) *kṛśatā* – emaciation, (3) *jāgarya* – sleeplessness, (4) *alambana-śūnyatā* – helplessness, (5) *adhṛti* – irresolution, (6) *jadatā* – inertness, (7) *vyādhi* – appearing diseased, (8) *unmāda* – madness, (9) *mūrcchita* – unconsciousness, and (10) *mṛti* – death.

Tāpa (Affliction with Fever)

From the day that Lord Hari left for Madhupur, the cowherd boys of Vraja became bereft of their very life-breath. Intensely afflicted with the pain of Śrī Kṛṣṇa's separation they merely remained wherever they were situated, in various places, with completely broken hearts. Some lay down on the ground underneath the Bhāṇḍira banyan tree, blindly hoping that its cooling shade would extinguish the scorching fire of separation; others immersed their bodies in the waters of the Yamunā and still their burning affliction would not go away but only doubled in intensity. Seeing snow during the winter months, they would hurl themselves into it but even that would not mitigate the blazing inferno they suffered without Kṛṣṇa's companionship. Everyone was so tormented in the fire of Kṛṣṇa's separation (*viraha-jvālā*) that they utterly despaired of their own pleasure and well-being (*B.r.s.* 3.3.118).

(2) *Kṛshatā* (Emaciation)

When Kṛṣṇa went to Madhupur in order to liberate King Kaṁsa, all the cowherd boys of Vraja-pur could only speak continuously about Kṛṣṇa. Due to His absence, the sons of the cowherders became so thin that their forms appeared very fragile and slight.

Those bodies made of five elements (*pañcha-bhūta*) became dried-up in Kṛṣṇa's separation. Practically the only element left was air, which became so forceful that it remained flowing through their nostrils in very deep breaths. Being very much stricken with the scorching fever of Śrī Kṛṣṇa's separation, even the bodies of the animals, birds, grasses and creepers of Vraja also became severely emaciated (*B.r.s.* 3.3.119).

(3) *Jāgarya* (Sleeplessness)

From the day that Hari left Vraja and went to Madhupur, all the *sakhās* were unable to keep their composure. They could not tell the difference between day and night nor could they tell the difference between this place and that place; they simply remained wherever they were, scattered here and there. The lotus-like eyes of the cowherd boys continuously welled with tears. And unable to go to sleep they just sat still with closed eyes (*B.r.s.* 3.3.120).

(4) *Alambana-Śūnyatā* (Helplessness)

When one's heart is restless and unsettled, this is called *alambana-śūnyatā* or voidness of support (*B.r.s.* 3.2.117). Without the company of Kṛṣṇa, all the boys of Vraja could not concentrate on any normal activity; indeed, all their actions were fruitless. Śrīdāma, Sudāma, Dāma, Subala, Ujjvala, Labaṇga, Arjjuna, and Sakhā Mahābala all spoke to each other with pathetic statements. These expressions proclaimed the glory of Kṛṣṇa's *viraha-līlā* – His pastime of separation. From the very day Nanda-suta gave up the assembly of His *priya-sakhās* and left Vṛndāvana to enter Madhupur all their life-airs became very hot and feverish. They exclaimed, "Where should I stay? Where should I go? I can't see any way to gain his company!" They repeatedly fell to the ground, repeatedly got up again, and they ran here and there in great confusion. Their very *prāṇa* was never composed, and they continuously lamented and cried "*Hāy! Hāy!*" They could not perform any of their duties, and felt no support whatsoever in life. This was the behavior in Vraja of the cowherd boys while feeling separation from their beloved Śrī Kṛṣṇa.

In that regard is the following Bengali song written by [my brother] Gokula-candra Dās, to be sung in the tune of *Sāraṅga Rāga:*

bhai re! niṭhura boro kān!

chāḍi sakhā-gaṇa, yamunā pulina vana,
kāṅhā oi karalo payān

ḍhoṅḍi ḍhoṅḍi vana, sabahi nirajana,
nāhi bhelo toka raṅga
taba hi viraha-jvara, tāpita antara,
aba sabhai geu saṅga

nāhi dekhi tokara, nayana-sudhākara,
caudiśa dekhi āndhi-ārā
to piyā jīvana, marami jala bhūkhala,
tohasi nayana ki tārā

tila ādha tuyā binu, śūnya hi jīvana,
tri-bhuvana yaichana āgi
kāṅhā se bāchuri dhenu śṛṅga muralī veṇu,
bhulahi so piyā lāgi

bahutahi bhāgima, gopīyā saṅgama,
kabhu jāni hoye tohāri
Gokula-candra dāsa, bolahi tohāra pāśa,
avaso milabo murāri

O my dear brother! O Kṛṣṇa You are so cruel!
Leaving the assembly of cowherd boys
and the gardens on Yamunā's bank.
O where have You gone?

We are searching and searching the forests
and all secluded places,

but we cannot locate Your sportive pastimes.
Therefore burning inside with the fever of separation
we now wander about together.

Since we do not behold You
who bestows nectar unto our eyes,
we now view the fourteen worlds
in complete blindness
for You are truly the pupil of our eyes.
Our very lives so dear to You,
now we grow thin and are dying.

Without you for half a moment,
our lives are totally void,
for the three worlds are now simply empty.
Where are the calves and cows?
And the buffalo horn and flutes?
We have forgotten everything that was dear.

You have unfortunately fled,
and hidden Yourself from our company,
now we do not know anything
about your whereabouts.
This Gokula-candra Dās says
that I am bound by You
and in the end I will again meet with Murāri.

This song confirms the moods found in the statement of *Bhakti-rasāmṛta-sindhu* (3.3.121).

(5) *Adhṛti* (Irresolution)

The following example illustrates how irresolution occurs when sorrow (*duhkha*) becomes prominent. Feeling separation from Śrī Kṛṣṇa, His cowherd boyfriends in Vraja gave up performing all their normal activities, becoming completely bereft of resolve. Abandoning even their duties as *gopālas*, they could not derive the slightest happiness from any endeavor whatsoever. They did not play any games or pranks, nor did they engage in the mellows of laughing and joking, nor participate in fulfilling the joy of their heartfelt desires by mingling together in any way. In Kṛṣṇa's separation they forgot all about their respective activities. Not desiring to keep their own *prāṇa,* they only wished they could die. They stopped adorning their limbs with ornaments, stopped wearing flower garlands, stopped entertaining individual aspirations, and stopped having fun. They stopped tying their hair in topknots, stopped weaving *mālatī* garlands, stopped dancing, singing, and playing musical instruments – they gave up *all* enjoyments. Not wanting to maintain their lives without Kṛṣṇa, they became divested of resolve and thereby deprived of all actions. The *sakhās* thus forgot themselves into oblivion while incessantly recollecting Kṛṣṇa's form within their hearts (*B.r.s.* 3.3.122).

(6) *Jaḍatā* (Inertness)

Inertness is that condition in which one becomes completely void of thinking, due to hearing about or being separated from either a desirable or undesirable object (*B.r.s.* 2.4.107).

An example of how this state of *jaḍatā* occurs in separation is as follows. Burning in the fever of Kṛṣṇa's absence from Vraja, the multitude of *gopas* stopped their activities altogether and became completely inert. Without Kṛṣṇa's company any of their endeavors were useless, and now they lost touch even with the identity of their own bodies. Their limbs shriveled up, their torsos became lean and thin, their clothing just hung loosely. They ceased dressing their hair, maintaining their attire and donning ornaments. No one started mock fights anymore, nor did they crack any jokes, nor enjoy blissful quarrels; they continuously remained hopelessly despondent. The buffalo horn bugle, as well as the *veṇu* flutes and *muralī* flutes were no longer heard anywhere in Vṛndāvana; nor was the mooing of the cows heard, nor did the cuckoo birds sing. Śrīdāma, Sudāma and the rest of the boys no longer danced and sang, for in Kṛṣṇa's separation the assembly of *sakhās* became just like non-moving entities [trees and other plants]. Not even uttering a sound, everyone appeared to be made of dull matter. Their limbs did not twitch; tears trickled from their eyes (*B.r.s.* 3.3.123).

(7) *Vyādhi* (Appearing Diseased)

The condition of *vyādhi* is the appearance of diseases like fever and so forth, caused by separation and other factors that stimulate excesses of the three bodily constituents, namely air, bile and mucous (*B.r.s.* 2.4.90).

When Śrīdāma, Sudāma and the other boys of Vraja were greatly stricken with the blazing fever of Kṛṣṇa's separation their bodies went limp and their limbs were immobilized. In total despondence their forms became paralyzed, devoid of awareness. O Kṛṣṇa, hero of the Yadus! You are the very life of the *sakhās*! The cowherd boys are consumed in the diseased condition of feeling your separation. They are totally bereft of action and consciousness. Thus missing you, the young sons of the cowherders simply lie at the bases of trees (*B.r.s.* 3.3.124).

(8) *Unmāda* (Madness)

The condition called *unmāda* arises when extreme bliss, calamity, or separation causes one's heart to become illusioned to the point of making great mistakes or blunders. The symptoms of such transcendental madness are: laughing loudly like a madman, dancing, singing, pointless actions, babbling, running erratically, outbursts of sobbing, and endeavors that are the opposite of those intended (*B.r.s.* 2.4.79–80).

Without Śrī Kṛṣṇa's *darśana* in Vraja, symptoms of divine madness arose in the bodies of all the Vrajavāsīs. In the delirium of separation the *sakhās* forgot everything; they held not even the slightest remembrance of anything and appeared to be totally deranged. Acting in ways opposed to their normal tasks, their actions were meaningless. In no circle did they perform their proper occupational duties as cowherders. Sometimes calling out "Kṛṣṇa! Kṛṣṇa!" in loud voices, they wailed, "Where has our Prāṇa-sakhā gone leaving us behind?" Mistaking a *tamāl* tree to be Kṛṣṇa they would heartily embrace it; then understanding that they had not attained Kṛṣṇa they would fall unconscious to the ground. Shouting "*Bhāi! Bhāi!* O my dear brother! O my dear brother!" they suddenly dashed off running in any direction. "Where is Kṛṣṇa and Balarāma? I cannot see them anywhere!" They began rolling in the dust until they are completely covered with it. "And where are the *muralī* and *veṇu* flutes?" I cannot see them returning!"

Śrīdāma and Sudāma cry out "*Bhāi re* Kānāi! Why do we not hear the music of the *veṇu* held to your lips? Your dear cows Dhavalī and Śyāmalī run around with their noses held upwards! Why are you not returning, dear brother and playing your *muralī*?" Someone else exclaims, "I used to be your *prāṇa-sakhā*, but now I have become a helpless orphan by not getting a glimpse of you! I used to play games with my brother right here on this very spot. O why have you forsaken me, dear brother, and gone off on some other path?" In this way the cowherd boys rambled on and on with delirious gibberish, sometimes still, sometimes restless, sometimes falling unconscious. They were laughing madly, engaging in useless and unproductive activities, running about without any patience, dancing, babbling senselessly, singing with twisted vocalizations, speaking in utter delusion, shivering in all limbs, nervous and fidgety, crying "KṚṢṆA!" with tears flowing from their eyes.

O! O Mathurā-nātha! O listen. Yadu-vīra! In your separation the *sakhās* have become so agitated! (*B.r.s.* 3.3.125).

(9) *Mūrcchita* (Unconsciousness)

Unconsciousness occurs when one faints for a moment or more. The body is motionless and slack, and foam comes from the mouth. When Hari abandoned Vraja and went to Madhu-pur, all of Gokula went blind. In the town of Mathurā, Bhagavān manifests as Rājeśvar, the king of kings, and He makes the entire universe fortunate by bestowing profuse bliss. Thus all the people of Mathurā Nagar became very happy, but in Gokula as well as Vraja everyone became greatly disturbed. All of Vraja wept in separation from Śrī Kṛṣṇa, and the *sakhās* first went blind and then lost consciousness completely. Their limbs did not move, eyes did not blink, and foam oozed from their mouths as their throats gurgled. Fainting and falling unconscious here and there upon the ground – such has happened to Your dear boyfriends in Gokula-mandala! (*B.r.s.* 3.3.126).

(10) *Mṛti* (Death)

When one gives up their life-air because of lamentation, disease, fright, being beaten, or exhaustion, that is called death. In ecstatic love, its symptoms are inarticulate words, changing of bodily color, slight breathing, hiccups, and so forth (*B.r.s.* 2.4.99).

When the assembly of *sakhās* were experiencing the blazing fire caused by the fever of Śrī Kṛṣṇa's separation they were so afflicted that it was doubtful they would keep living. Some cowherd boys collapsed at the foot of hills in an unconscious condition, while others lay by the banks of rivers with paralyzed limbs and very slight breathing. Plunged into utter desolation, some cried "*Hā* Kṛṣṇa!" and fell unconscious to the ground, lying with faint breathing, slack bodies and closed eyes. Bodies turning pale, now failing to utter a single word. Seeing this, the deer of the forest became astonished. There the deer sprinkled the cowherd boys with their own tears in an effort to revive them. Kṛṣṇa is the breath of those boys. Kṛṣṇa is their life; without the association of Kṛṣṇa life falls into death. Thus was the calamity occurring at Gokulapur. This Nayanānanda becomes agitated just to narrate such things! (*B.r.s.* 3.3.127).

Prakaṭa and Aprakaṭa Līlās

Only the briefest codes have been used to describe the arrangement of *vyabhichārī* emotions that flow within the mellows of the *sakhya-rasa*. Although Kṛṣṇa is said to display His pastimes in two ways: *prakaṭa* (manifest) and *aprakaṭa* (unmanifest). This does not mean that He is two. What I have narrated here were pastimes that occur within the *prakaṭa* version of His *līlā*. While sporting His *prakaṭa-līlā* Kṛṣṇa is seen to come and go, both to and from Vraja, whereas in the *aprakaṭa* mode He is situated perpetually in Vṛndāvana. Nanda-suta never leaves Vraja to go to any other place. In the company of His eternal *sakhās* and *sakhīs* He stays in Vṛndāvana. During the *prakaṭa* pastimes it is Śrī Vāsudeva who travels to Madhu-pur; Nanda-suta uses this circumstance as an opportunity to hide Himself. He still remains in Vṛndāvana but only in an unmanifest manner; thus materialistic persons with mere external vision consider that He is going and coming. Śrī Nanda-suta never goes away or comes back, for He is eternally present in the company of the *gopas* in both *prakaṭa* and *aprakaṭa* modes. The *nitya-siddha* souls who are situated in the *nitya-līlā* keep the *darśana* of Him sporting merrily with His cowherd boy-friends in Vṛndāvana.

Now please listen to an amazing truth about when Hari performs pastimes in Dvārakā. Once Nārada Muni went in his travels from Dvārakā to Vṛndāvana and beheld Rāma and Kṛṣṇa present there just as They were situated before They had apparently left. Stricken with astonishment to see such a scene, the Muni again returned to Dvārakā and saw Kṛṣṇa still there. According to a conversation between Nārada and Yudhiṣṭhira recorded in the *Skānda Purāṇa*, Kṛṣṇa perpetually remains in Vṛndāvana in *prakaṭa* and *aprakaṭa* forms:

vatsair vatsatarībhiś ca sadā krīḍati mādhavaḥ
vṛndāvanāntar gatāh sa-rāmo bālakair vṛtaḥ

> Within the borders of Vṛndāvana, Lord Mādhava continuously enjoys pleasure-pastimes surrounded by the calves, cows, Rāma and the cowherd boys. (*B.r.s.* 3.3.129, quoted from the *Skānda Purāṇa, Mathurā Khanda*)

Kṛṣṇa and Balarāma live eternally in the company of the *gopas* and *gopīs* in both the manifest and unmanifest realms of Vṛndāvana-dhāma. Therefore whatever I have written in this chapter about *viraha* (separation) is only according to the *prakaṭa-līlā* or occasional exhibition of His pastimes within the material sphere. Other than that variation of the *līlā*, the *siddhas* or perfected beings of Vraja-pur never know His separation.

prokteyaṁ virahāvasthā spaṣṭa-līlā 'nusārataḥ
kṛṣṇena viprayogaḥ syān na jātu vraja-vāsinām

This condition of separation from Kṛṣṇa being described is according to the manifest pastimes only. Śrī Kṛṣṇa and the Vrajavāsīs in the eternal unmanifest realm never experience separation at any time. (*B.r.s.* 3.3.128)

For those who are interested, I [Nayanānanda Dās] have written an elaborate description of both the *prakaṭa* and *aprakaṭa-līlā* in my other book named *Kṛṣṇa-bhakti-rasa-kadamba*.

Features of *Yoga* (Association with Kṛṣṇa)

Thus I have spoken of the ten symptoms of *ayoga* (separation) known as *daśa-daśā*. Now I will narrate someting about *yoga*, the personal association of Kṛṣṇa. Please listen.

kṛṣṇena saṅgamo yas tu sa yoga iti kīrtyate
yogo 'pi kathitaḥ siddhis tuṣṭiḥ sthitir iti tridhā

The personal association of Kṛṣṇa is called *yoga* or union. This *yoga* has three subdivisions, namely *siddhi* (perfection), *tuṣṭi* (satisfaction) and *sthiti* (situation). (*B.r.s.* 3.2.129)

(1) *Siddhi* (Perfection)

When one is very eager to obtain the *darśana* of Lord Kṛṣṇa, and thereafter attains that wish, it is called *siddhi yoga* (*B.r.s.* 3.2.130). When Arjuna first met Pundarikākśa (lotus-eyed Kṛṣṇa) in a potter's shop at Drupada Nagar, he was overjoyed to behold the form of Bhagavān, who appeared as beautiful as a painted picture. Thereby Arjuna established friendship with Him and thus he became Kṛṣṇa's *sakhā* (*B.r.s.* 3.3.130).

(2) *Tuṣṭi* (Satisfaction)

When one regains the company of Kṛṣṇa after a period of being apart from Him, it is called *tuṣṭi yoga* (*B.r.s.* 3.2.133). When Kṛṣṇa was playing His pastimes in Dvārakā, He once traveled on pilgrimage (*tīrtha-yātrā*) with full entourage to the holy place of the Kurus (Kurukṣetra). At that time, Śrīdāma, Sudāma and the other pure-hearted residents of Vraja also went there and attained the direct company of Vrajendra-nandana. That Murāri, those *sakhas*, and those wives of the *gopas* thus met together at that holy place. The *sakhās* overflowed with *prema* upon seeing Kṛṣṇa, and it was as if their dead bodies had received the gift of souls again. Attaining the association of Kṛṣṇa their bodies erupted with thrill-bumps and rapturous shivering, and the *sakhās* spread their arms out wide to embrace Him robustly. They soaked His dark-hued body with their tears while He soaked their bodies with His tears. Everyone was immersed in pure *premānanda* at again having obtained the personal company of their Beloved. Thus the entire circle of cowherd boys together experienced *tuṣṭi yoga* or satisfaction upon regaining Kṛṣṇa's association. There is a special description of this condition in the *Śrī Kṛṣṇa Sandarbha* (written by Śrīla Jīva Gosvāmī). Thus I have spoken of satisfaction in union and given its symptoms (*B.r.s.* 3.3.132).

(3) *Sthiti* (Situation)

When one resides always in Kṛṣṇa's personal association and beholds His daily pastimes, the scriptures call that *sthiti yoga* or continuous living situation (*B.r.s.* 3.2.136). What can I say about the limitless good fortune of the cowherd boys in Vraja? They perpetually live with Nanda-suta, the dust of whose lotus feet is sought by ascetics throughout many births of penance – and who still never get a glimpse. That Bhagavān, who cannot be attained by the powerful *yoga* practiced by scores of fully self-controlled *yogīs*, is effortlessly perceived by the *sakhās* of Gokula. How could I possibly describe, even by metaphor, the fortune of the Vrajavāsīs? Those simple cowherd folks have the

Supreme Personality of Godhead – Pūrṇa-brahma Bhagavān – as their personal friend.

Thus I have portrayed the principle of *sthiti yoga*, and how Kṛṣṇa lives together with His *sakhās*. The *Śrīla Bhāgavata* relates this phenomenon in many places.

> *yat-pāda-pāṁsur bahu-janma-kṛcchrato*
> *dhṛtātmabhir yogibhir apy alabhyaḥ*
> *sa eva yad-dṛg-viṣayaḥ svayaṁ sthitaḥ*
> *kiṁ varṇyate diṣṭam ato vrajaukasām*

> *Yogīs* may undergo severe austerities and penances for many births by practicing *yama, niyama, āsana* and *prāṇāyāma*, none of which are easily performed. Yet in due course of time, when these *yogīs* attain perfection in controlling the mind, they will still be unable to taste even a particle of dust from the lotus feet of the Supreme Personality of Godhead. What then can we describe about the great fortune of the inhabitants of Vraja-bhūmi, with whom the Supreme Personality of Godhead personally lived and who saw the Lord face to face? (*Bhāg.* 10.12.12)

The Glory of *Bhakti-rasāmṛta-sindhu*

Thus I have delineated the progression of *vyabhichārī* ecstasies as they are found flowing within the *sakhya-rasa*. These all mix together as ingredients along with the intrinsic form of the *sthāyi-rati*. I bow before the feet of Śrīla Rūpa Gosvāmī, for I have followed certain parts of his book very closely. The *Bhakti-rasāmṛta-sindhu* is a greatly exalted composition, by which the entire universe is nourished with profuse bliss. I have no power to comprehend that work, but by the power of divine grace I have written one or two statements. Within Śrī Rūpa's book the *preyo-bhakti-rasa* is outlined very nicely in verses composed with few words.

The Process of Performing *Bhajan*

The pure unmotivated *sakhya-rasa* is free from any other desires. It is the end of sweetness, and is practiced by many saintly persons. This mellow of fraternity is very, very dear to Śrī Kṛṣṇa-candra, for by its practice He becomes subdued. All the *sakhya-bhaktas* – whether man or woman – ultimately become of male form after fixing their minds continuously. Remaining in the association of their *guru-rūpa-sakhā* (cowherd boy who comes as spiritual master), one becomes the follower of their own cherished *yūtheśvara* (eternal group leader). Rendering *sevā* unto Rāma and Kṛṣṇa according to the proper times of the day, one thus emulates the residents of Vraja while living in two distinct bodies. Without following the residents of Vraja it is impossible to taste that transcendental sweetness found in the personal company of Vrajendra-nandan. By performing *bhajan* of Hari according to the *vidhi-mārga* one goes to Lord Vishnu, whereas by performing *bhajan* according to the *rāga-mārga* one attains Nanda-suta. Some devotees become *sahachara* (male servants) and others become *sahacarī* (female servants), in agreement with the humor of *rati* that they individually cultivate. All of the Lord's devotees *dāsa, dāsī, sakhā, guru* (superior), *preyasī* (girl-friend) each becomes fixed (*niṣṭhā*) in performing the *sādhana* that complements their own *bhāva*. Accepting one of these moods and becoming resolute they attain Śrī Vrajendra-kumār.

Different Goals for Different Flavors of *Bhajan*

Those who emulate the *dāsa* servants by rendering *dāsya-bhakti* ultimately attain residence in Vraja for the purpose of rendering *Kṛṣṇa-seva*. The *bhaktas* of the *vātsalya-rasa* emulate Kṛṣṇa's superiors, and after becoming fixed in that mood they attain Śrī Nanda-nandan. The *sakhya-rasa-bhaktas* emulate the *sakhās* of Vraja, and realizing their *gopa-deha* or body of a cowherd boy they attain the personal *sevā* of Rāma and Kṛṣṇa. The devotees of the *madhura-rasa* attain the *sevā* of Śrī Śrī Rādhā-Kṛṣṇa by emulating the loving affection of the *gopīkās*. Thus by worshiping Hari according to one's own personally resolute emotion (*bhāva-niṣṭhā*), and by systematically following in the footsteps of those of that same mood, one ultimately attains Kṛṣṇa. The devotee who is the best of all is one whose mind is strictly fixed in the *bhāva* that emanates from the spiritual master (*guru-jātīya-bhāva*). In whichever *bhāva* of Vraja one worships Hari, one receives the corresponding bodily form upon attaining Kṛṣṇa in Vraja. It is declared by Kṛṣṇa Himself in the *Nāradīya Purāṇa:*

vrajānusāri-bhāvena yena kena ca sādhakāḥ
bhajitvā mad-gatiṁ prāpya krīḍeyus te mayā saha

In whichever mood the *sādhakas* perform worship,
emulating the residents of Vraja,
they ultimately attain Me accordingly
and enjoy sportive pastimes in My company.

Therefore, my dear mind, please worship Kṛṣṇa and Balarāma along with their dear cowherd boyfriends Śrīdāma and Sudāma. Praising Śrī Caitanya and Śrī Nityānanda with reverence, and praying to Śrīyuta Sundarānanda with humility; glorifying our founding father Parṇī Ṭhākura Gopal whose heart is dedicated to Kṛṣṇa, and who is supremely compassionate; and hoping at the feet of Śrīyuta Gopāl-caraṇ Prabhu, this Nayanānanda Dās narrates *Preyo-Bhakti-Rasārṇava.*

Thus ends the fourth chapter of
Śrī Śrī Preyo-Bhakti-Rasārṇava

CHAPTER FIVE

Sudama Sakha's 64 Associates; The Glories of Kṛṣṇa and Balarāma

navīna-jaladābhaṁ taṁ
kambu-kaṇṭhaṁ manoramam
rāmeṇa ramaṇa-śyāmaṁ
vande kauśeya-vāsanam

He Who has the complexion of a fresh raincloud
Whose conchshell-smooth neck is most charming
Along with Rāma, He's the amorous dark boy
Praises to He Who wears silken garments!

All glories, all glories to the son of Nanda, the Lord of Vraja! All glories to Haladhar who is accompanied by my own cowherd boyfriends! All glories to Dāma, Śrīdāma, and Sudāma! All glories to Mahārāj Nanda! All glories to the *gopas, gopīs* and the moon over Vṛndāvana!

The Glories of Sudāma Sakhā

My dear mind, please become *sakhānuga,* a follower of the cowherd boys, and worship Rāma and Kṛṣṇa. Realizing the *siddha-deha,* visualize the performance of their *sevā.* Becoming a follower of the *priya-sakhās* in Vraja, continuously render service unto Lords Rāma and Kṛṣṇa within your mind. Amongst these dearmost boys, four are outstanding – Śrīdāma, Sudāma, Vasudāma and Kiṅkiṇī. Of these four, one is especially worshipful to me: Sudāma, who is the leader of my group (*yūtheśvar*). He has many servants in his circle. He is beloved to Rāma-Kṛṣṇa and is the abode of happiness and other good qualities. Indeed, the very mellow of their friendship is known as Sudāma. He shares such a level of selfless love (*ahaituka prema*) with Rāma-Kṛṣṇa that it is compared to freshly mined gold cleaned with borax. Sudāma is *parama ānanda-maya* – pervaded with supreme bliss, and he is constantly absorbed in pure *kṛṣṇānanda* – the ecstasy of Kṛṣṇa consciousness. I am merely an ignorant fool; how can I comprehend anything about Sudāma's glories? He knows nothing other than Kṛṣṇa and Balarāma. He considers even a hint of their separation to be like the passing of millions of *yugas*. Please fix your consciousness and incessantly worship Rāma and Kṛṣṇa by counting yourself among Sudāma's followers.

Sudāma's 64 Associates

Now I narrate a description of the eternal associates of Sudāmacandra. Among them all, there are eight principal servants: Sucandra, Śrī Candra-māna, Suranga, Suvinda, Samartha, Karibandhaka, Kumuda and Ananga. I also see the eight foremost friends of Sudāma, and by further listing in turn the eight friends of each of these I will gradually write of 64 boys.

(1) The Friends of Sucandra

Sukantha, Subhanga, Mukunda, Kumuda, Premānanda, Mahānanda, Śrī Jaya-Nandana and Sukhānanda are the eight chief followers of Sucandra. Next I relate the group of Sukanthā.

(2) The Friends of Sukanthā

The *gopas* Sudarpa, Sudambha, Sukanda, Sujaya, Sahanu, Sukhendra, Jayadvrata and Prema-dambha are the chief followers of Sukantha. Next please listen to the eight associates of Sudarpa.

(3) The Friends of Sudarpa

The cowherd boys named Sukhānanda, Premānanda, Sumohana,

Darpānanda, Yaśonanda, Sudhākara, Viśamandha and Kabandha are the eight chief followers of Sudarpa.

(4) The Friends of Sukhānanda

Rasa-candra, Prema-candra, Kāma-chandan, Vasun-dhara, Keli-candra, Lola-candra, Śubhānanda and Sucha-nāgara are Sukhānanda's eight chief associates. Next I will narrate the group of Rasa-candra.

(5) The Friends of Rasa-candra

Sumahendra, Kulānanda, Vimalaka, Ananta, Mahendra, Śrī Ratna-bandha, Vidhānanda and Niḍhi-nanda are the chief followers of Rasa-candra. Now please hear the associates of Sumahendra.

(6) The Friends of Sumahendra

Sumukha, Pura-varddha, Rasāngada,

[NOTE: The original ancient handwritten manuscript has deteriorated at this point. Consequently, the complete listing of the cowherd boyfriends of Sumahendra, plus those of (7) **Sumukha** and three friends of (8) **Rasāngada** are lost.]

. . . Vibhanga, Sānanda, Raktāngada, Sudhānanda and Chandrāngada are the chief followers of Rasāngada. In this way 64 cowherd boyfriends are counted.

Description of Sudāma's Particulars

Now I narrate a description of the dwelling of Sudāma as well as his dress, ornaments and so forth. The town of Vṛṣabhānu-pur is the residence of the *ābhīra* class of cowherd folk, and it extends for two *yojanas* (16 miles). The city is shaped like a hundred-petalled lotus flower. Being the abode of eternal happiness (*nitya-sukha*), it eclipses the celestial kingdom of Lord Indra. Later (in the next chapter) I will comprehensively describe the town of Vṛṣabhānu-pur. The home of Sudāma is inside the western gate. His dwelling has another gateway to the north, which he uses for going outside. His age is *kiśor* (adolescent) and his complexion is fair golden tinged with a reddish luster (*ārakta gaura-varṇa*). He wears variegated ornaments fashioned from precious minerals and gold. His female friend is named Chandrā and his male friend is named Vṛṣabha. His pleasure-forest is Bhadravan a description of which would require limitless writing. Sudāma wears blue silk garments and sports a garland of *kuṇḍa* jasmines around his neck His pet cow is named Śyāmalikā. Now I have mentioned everything.

Meditation on Sudāma

ārakta-gaura śaśi-vaktra vilola-netra
ānanda eva parisundara eva dhīra
krīḍā-gabhīra bhava-bhāra-vimuktaye saḥ
kṛṣṇasya rājati kalā-sakalaḥ sudāmā

His complexion is reddish-golden, face like the moon,
rolling eyes, totally blissful, totally handsome,
very grave, very deep in confidential sports,
he is completely free from the burden
of worldly concerns; he excels in all the arts
designed by Kṛṣṇa – this is Sudāma.

In the *Śrī Govinda-vṛndāvanam* it is stated (1.159–160):

rasiko nāgaro gauraḥ śarad-amburuhekṣaṇaḥ
agranthi-sarala-sthūla unmāda-nṛtya-sundaraḥ
mahā-rāsa-rasāhlāda pulaka-prema-vihvalaḥ
nānā-raṅga-rasopetaḥ sudāmā sa ca kīrtitaḥ

The cowherd boy celebrated as Sudāma is a relisher of confidential mellows (*rasika*), he is very heroic (*nāgara*), his complexion is fair (*gaura*), and his eyes are like lotus flowers blooming in the autumn (*śarat-amburuha-ikśana*). He is detached from all ties (*agranthi*), simple and straightforward (*sarala*), large, plump and strong (*sthūla*), and he is beautified by wild and unrestrained dancing (*unmāda-nṛtya-sundara*). He rejoices in the mellows of the *mahā-rāsa* dance (*mahā-rāsa-rasa-āhlāda*), and is so overwhelmed with ecstatic love that his hairs stand on end (*pulaka-prema-vihvala*). He is endowed with mellows of various types of sport (*nānā-raṅga-rasa-upeta*).

Sudāma's relationship with Kṛṣṇa is that of an intimate boy-friend. In that mood he has not the slightest tinge of awe and reverence (*aiśvarya*). Amongst the different types of *bhāva* (ecstatic emotion), the fraternal *sakhya-bhāva* has a very solid degree of *śraddhā* (faith). The flavor of *sneha* (affection) is like honey (*madhu-vat*), and therefore is called *mañjiṣṭhā rāga* (attachment as charming and durable as the bright red dye made from the "madder" vine). His ceaseless loving intimacy (*prīti*) is such that it is compared to the Kaustubha jewel that is always situated on Kṛṣṇa's chest. His degree of *rati* (attachment) is called *samarthā kevalā* (exclusive competency). In activity his position is that of *pītha-mardana* (confidential friend; literally "back-rubber"), and his service involves collection and preparation of forest flowers. Thus I have mentioned everything about Śrī Sudāma-candra's affairs.

Amongst the four brothers Vṛṣabhānu, Ratna-bhānu, Subhānu and Śrī Bhānu, Sudāma-candra's father is Ratna-bhānu. Śrīmatī Rādhikā is the daughter of Sudāma's elder uncle, and Sudāma is the son of Her uncle (therefore they are cousins). Sudāma's mother is named Śrī Suśilā. His favorite grove is called Sukhotsava (festival of happiness) and is located to the south of lake Syāma-kunda. His personal servants are Madhu-raṇga and Ananta, who stay by his side rendering service both day and night.

The Process of Worship in *Sakhya-Bhāva*

O *sādhaka!* Perpetually realize your *siddha-deha* and worship Rāma and Kṛṣṇa, becoming their follower in Vraja. In the *siddha-deha* you should accompany your spiritual master, whose name is that of one of the *priya-sakhās*, and along with him just render service unto Kṛṣṇa and Balarāma. All the cowherd boys are Rāma and Kṛṣṇa's personal friends. In order for you to become their devoted follower (*anugata*), I write of their various categories such as *suhṛt* (intimate well-wishers) and so forth. The groups of boys headed by Sudāma, Subala, Stoka-Kṛṣṇa and others are all to be counted amongst Rāma and Kṛṣṇa's *sakhās*. It is confirmed in the *Śrīmad-Bhāgavatam* (10.15.20):

śrīdāmā nāma gopālo rāma-keśavayoh sakhā
subala-stoka-kṛṣṇādyā gopah premnedam abruvan

Some of Rāma and Keśava's dear cowherd forest boy-friends – Śrīdāmā, Subala, Stoka-Kṛṣṇa and others – thus lovingly spoke.

As stated in the *Śrī Govinda-vṛndāvanam* (1.149):

ayutāyuta-gopālāḥ sakhāyo rāma-kṛṣṇayoḥ

Rāma and Kṛṣṇa have tens of thousands upon tens of thousands of cowherd boyfriends.

Now please listen as I briefly describe the symptoms of *bhajan*, and the type of meditative visualizations that accompany the process of worship during the time of performing daily *pūjā*. After finishing one's routine duties, the *sādhaka* should focus the attention deep within the heart of hearts and visualize oneself entering Vṛndāvana Purī. This is an extremely secret place, the source of total bliss, and the extraordinarily astonishing realm of Vṛndāvana. It is the topmost level of all your existences (*sarvottama sthāna*), the ultimate difficult-to-reach abode amongst all the difficult-to-reach abodes in creation (*durlabhera durlabha*). It is absolutely enchanting for all souls (*sarva-mohan*) and is the original seat of all potencies (*sarva-śakti-adhiṣṭhāna*). Amongst all the various Vaiṣṇava holy places it is the crest-jewel.

Description of Vṛndāvana from the *Varāha Saṁhitā*

The transcendental earth of Vṛndāvana Bhūmi is far beyond all the clusters of egg-like material universes (*brahmānda-gāna*). This domain revels in fully manifested divinity (*pūrṇa-brahma*), the opulence of pure happiness (*sukhāiśvarya*), and never-ending bliss (*nityānanda-maya*). The spiritual realms headed by Vaikuṇṭha are merely a fractal portion of this sphere. The full potency of Goloka manifests in this area of Gokula, and the borderline region adjoining Vaikuṇṭha manifests as the pastimes of Dvārakā. That sphere of Vṛndāvana is the embodiment of eternal truth (*nitya-satya-rūpī*), and everything there is totally jewellike, being made of desire-fulfilling touchstones. The personified six seasons are always present, blooming their various types of flowers, and the gentle scented breeze gives joy to the universe as it blows.

There are twelve forests in Vṛndāvana beginning with Bhadra – seven to the west of the Kālindī River and five to the east. The five to the east are celebrated as Bhadravan, Śrīvan, Lohavan, Bhāṇḍīravan and Mahāvan. Gokula is within these five forests to the east of the Kālindī. The seven forests to the west of the Yamunā are counted beginning with Tālavan; they are Tālavana, Khadiravan, Bahulāvan, Kāmavan, Kumudavan, Madhuvan and Śrīla Vṛndāvana. Additionally, there are twenty-two *upavan* (sub-forests), beginning with Kadamba-khandi. These are celebrated in the book known as *Varāha Saṁhitā*. In that work these glories of Vṛndāvana are narrated during a conversation between Dharaṇī (the earth goddess) and Lord Varāha (the boar incarnation) as follows:

> *nityam vṛndāvanaṁ nāma brahmāṇḍopari saṁsthitam*
> *pūrna-brahma sukhaiśvaryaṁ nityam ānandam avyayam*
> *vaikuṇṭhādi tadāṁhśāmśaṁ svayam vṛndāvanam bhuvi*
> *yat kiñcid golokaiśvaryaṁ gokule tat pratiṣṭhitam*
> *vaikuṇṭha-vaibhavaṁ yac ca dvārakāyāṁ prakāśayet*

and furthermore:

bhadra-śri-loha-bhāṇḍira-mahā-tāla-khadirakāḥ
bahulā kumudaṁ kāmyaṁ madhu vṛndāvanan tathā
dvādaśaitā vane saṁkhyāḥ kalindyāḥ sapta paścime
pūrve pañca-vanaṁ proktaṁ tatrāsti guhyam uttamam

pūrve tu pañca bhadrādyāḥ tālādyāḥ sapta paścime
anyac copavanaṁ proktaṁ kṛsna-krīḍā-rahaḥ-sthalam
kadamba-khaṇḍakaṁ nandaṁ vanaṁ nandiśvaran tathā

and so forth.

The *Yoga-Pītha* of Kṛṣṇa and the *Sakhās*

The sphere of Gokula-mandala is shaped like a lotus of a thousand petals, and in the whorl and central petals of that lotus is a very secret place. Please meditate on Lord Govinda situated in the center of the lotus stem, as well as His eternal associates headed by Śrīdāma situated as the stamens.

sahasra-patraṁ kamalaṁ gokulūkhyaṁ mahat-padam
karṇikā tan mahad-dhāma govinda-sthānam auyayam

> The exalted region known as Gokula is shaped as a lotus of a thousand petals. In the whorl of that lotus is the grand abode called Govinda-sthāna, which is imperishable. (*Pādma Purāṇa, Pātāla* 38.22)

The ground of that Vṛndāvana Purī is made of desire-fulfilling *cintāmaṇi* gems, and is abounding with hosts of auspicious desire-fulfilling *kalpa-vṛkṣa* trees. In the midst of those forests is one enormous desire tree, with a platform at its base made of solid gold and silver. This is described in the *Gautamīya Tantra* thus (10.153):

kalpa-pādapa-madhyastha-hema-maṇḍapikāgatam

Upon that platform shines a wonderful and splendrous *ratna-siṁhāsana* (jewelled lion-throne); please meditate on the *Yoga-pītha* (central meeting-shrine) situated upon that. This grand altar is formed in eight petals, with four gates on the perimeter and a hexagon in the center within which is carved the *kāma-bīja* (the seed-mantra of desire, namely *klīṁ*). This seed has the characteristic of being *sva-sādhya* – it accomplishes its own purposes. As confirmed in the scriptures:

padmam aṣṭa-dalākāraṁ ṣaṭ-koṇaṁ kāma-garbhitam
catur-asraṁ catur-dvāraṁ yantraṁ sāvaraṇaṁ hareḥ

Please contemplate Govinda in the central whorl of that lotus, surrounded on the filaments by the assembly of cowherd boy-friends. To His right is Śrī Balabhadra, who is the original source of all the Saṇkarṣaṇa expansions. Govinda is surrounded by four *sakhās*: before him is Śrīdāma, to the right is Sudāma, behind is Vasudāma and to the left is Kiṅkiṇī. This is confirmed in the *Krama Dīpikā* (4.128): *diksv atha dāma-sudāma* and so forth. Thus Kṛṣṇa faces west and the *bhaktas* face east, toward Him. It is written that the worshiper engages in *pūjā* facing east. The *Varaha Purāṇa* states:

śrīdāmā paścima-dvāre sudāmā cottare tathā
vasudāmā tathā pūrve kiṅkiṇiś cāpi dakṣiṇe

Śrīdāma is at the gate to the west, Sudāma is at the gate to the north. Vasudāma is at the gate to the east, and Kiṅkiṇī is at the gate to the south.

There are eight personalities situated within the four-gated structure of the whorl of the lotus. One should meditate on the eight petals beginning with the east. Upon the eight petals I see Stoka-Kṛṣṇa, Angśuka, Bhadra-sena, Arjjuna, Subala, Vilāsa, Mahābala and Vṛṣabha. After these I write of further groups of *sakhās* and *upa-sakhās*.

stoka-kṛṣṇāmśukau bhadra-senam arjjunam eva ca
subalañ ca viśālāñ ca tathā gopa-mahābalam
vṛṣabhaṁ pūjayet dikṣu vidikṣu ca yathā-kramam

Along with Kṛṣṇa, one should systematically worship the cowherd boys – Stoka-Kṛṣṇa, Angśuka, Bhadrasena, Arjjuna, Subala, Viśāla, Mahābala and Vṛṣabha – according to their respective positions in different directions around the *Yoga-pitha*.

At the four gates are four heavenly trees: *mandāra, santāna, pārijāta* and *harichandan*. These desire trees stand supporting the rear perimeter of the altar. Beyond these, in all four directions, are innumerable precious cows.

Visualization of Śrī Kṛṣṇa's Beautiful Form in *Pūjā*

Next will be the meditation that is in accordance with famous statements like "*phullendīvara-kānti*" and so on (His complexion is like full-blown blue lotuses). His complexion is that of a fresh raincloud and His age is *kiśor*, His dress, that of a dramatic actor, is embellished with ornaments of jewels and pearls. He wears a yellow *dhotī*, forest flower garlands and *makara*-shaped earrings. His neck is smooth as a conchshell and is endowed with three lines. His cheeks glisten. His crown is topped with a peacock feather and is wound with *guñjā*-berry strands. By His sides radiate a buffalo horn, walking stick, fighting stick, rope, and bamboo flute. One should systematically meditate upon this beautiful form of Govinda beginning from His feet and proceeding up to His face and so forth, all the while steeped in the mood of incessant service unto Him.

Methods for Worshiping Kṛṣṇa in Meditation

One should render continuous loving *sevā*, and in so doing may perform either the *śodaśopachār* (16 offerings), the *pañcopachār* (5 offerings), or the *daśopachār* (10 offerings). Or one may perform the *mahārājopachār* (grand royal offerings) consisting of opulent umbrellas, *cāmara* whisks, mirrors, and so forth; or one may simply worship Him somehow or other with whatever is readily available.

At the time of performing *pūjā*, one should engage in *dhyāna-yoga* meditation and perform *mānasik-sevā* (service visualized within the mind's eye), and be aware of two simultaneous existences – their external form of a *sādhaka* and their internal form as a *siddha*. Uncovering the form of Madana Mohan from within the heart, one first offers *pādya* (water for washing) unto His lotus feet. Next one offers *arghya* (presentations) by installing within a conchshell various items like barley grains, cut *dūrvā* grass, and *chandan*. After that one smears His limbs with bathing oil, and sprinkles His divine body with water scented with camphor. Then one offers fresh garments, paints auspicious *tilak* upon His forehead, fixes ornaments and so forth, again performing *pādya* (footwash). Next comes *madhuparka* (an oblation of mixed honey, ghee, yogurt, milk and sugar), then *ācamanīya* (mouthwash), then the scents of sandalwood, nice flowers and flower garlands. Performing *maṇgal āratī* by waving incense and lamps, one afterwards offers *naivedya* (eatables) consisting of sweets, ripened fruits and water. Again offering *ācamanīya* (mouthwash) and *pādya* (footwash), next comes *asana* (seating), *tāmbūla* (betel), *pālañka* (bedding) and *śayana* (putting to sleep). All these things are considered favorable service (*anukūla sevā*). One certainly earns the merciful glance of Lord Kṛṣṇa by offering *cāmara* whisks, fans, mirrors, clothing, and service unto His lotus feet.

The Glories of Balarāma and Kṛṣṇa

Balarāma-candra is radiant like the full moon; his bodily complexion is so white that it looks like the mixed luster of conchshell and crystal. His eyes are rolling due to the intoxication of drinking honey. Long jewelled earrings dangle from his ears. Sometimes he holds a plow, club, or buffalo horn in his left hand, and sometimes he holds a small *venu* flute, walking stick, long *muralī* flute or horn. Wearing a bright blue *dhotī*, appearing like the moon rising above a raincloud, he mesmerizes the entire universe. As stated in the *Varāha Purāṇa:*

śuddha-sphaṭika-saṅkāśam raktāmbuja-dalekṣaṇam
rohiṇī-tanayaṁ rāmaṁ kāma-pālaṁ bhajāmy aham

Similar in complexion to pure crystal
with eyes like the petals of red lotuses
He's the son of Mother Rohinī named Rāma –
I worship the guardian of transcendental desire.

Seeing the *darśana* of Rāma and Kṛṣṇa's beautiful forms situated together, their youthful splendor as Yugala Kiśor steals the minds of the cowherd boys. To put it in another Bengali meter:

śyāmala dhavala duhuṅ raja virāj
jala-dham śaśa-dhara aichana sāj
jala-dhara śyāma rāma-kāṅti
indra-nila saha phaṭikera bhāti

The pair of dark and light auras are resplendent
like a raincloud and the moon
together ornamenting the sky
The complexions of raincloud Śyāma along with Rāma
appear dazzling like a sapphire
along with a crystal.

rāma-bāme hari-mohana śobhā
jalada pita-vasana capalābhā
lāṅgala-muṣala veṇu vīṇā
tri-bhaṅga-bhaṅgima duṅhu surata-pravīṇa

Hari by the left side of Rāma is enchantingly lustrous
like a raincloud adorned
with a flowing brilliant yellow cloth
They carry a plow, club, flute and vīṇā.
Posing in three-fold bending postures
Both of them are fully proficient
in the techniques of intimate love.

śyāma-gale kunda-karavī rārna-mālā
śveta śyāmala aṅge korota ujolā
kiśora vayesa veśa-rūpa anupāma
caudike vraja-śiśu dāma sudāma

Around the neck of Śyāma is a *kuṇḍa* (jasmine) garland
Around the neck of Rāma is a *karavī* (oleander) garland
which makes their dark and light limbs
appear splendrously radiant
Their age of *kiśor* and their dress and beauty
are absolutely matchless
They are surrounded by the boys of Vraja
like Śrīdāma and Sudāma.

hāsi hāsāyata sahacara meli
gopa-go-dhana-saha korota hi keli
bhaja mana yugala-kiśora dono bhāi
śiva śuka nārada yāko dheyāi

Meeting with their friends they laugh
and make each other laugh
With the *gopas* and the cows
they perform very playful sports.
My dear mind, please worship
these two Yugala Kiśor brothers
upon whom Śiva, Śuka and Nārada meditate.

There is also a nice Sanskrit verse that runs thus:

jaladhara-śaśi-varṇau gopa-veśau kiśorau
sahacara-gaṇa-vṛndaiḥ krīḍamānau vrajeśau
naṭa-vara-jita-veśau nila-pītāmbarāḍhyau
jagata-janana-hetū rāma-kṛṣṇau nato 'smi

The pair of complexions like a raincloud and the moon
The pair dressed as cowherds, the pair of youths
The pair engaged in sporting with the assembly
of their friends; The pair who are Lords of Vraja
The pair whose dress eclipses that of
the best of dancers

The pair fond of wearing blue and yellow garments
The pair who are the source of all living entities
in the universe –
I bow to the pair known as Rāma and Kṛṣṇa.

The Non-different Kṛṣṇa and Balarāma

He who is Kṛṣṇa is He who is Rāma – they are one substance. This is the statement of the *Āgama* scriptures, the *Purāṇas* and the *Bhāgavata*. Any person who thinks that these two are different will never be delivered from the material world at any time.

As stated in the *Ādi Saṁhitā:*

yaḥ kṛṣṇaḥ so 'pi rāmaḥ syād yo rāmaḥ kṛṣṇa eva saḥ
anayor antarādarśi saṁsārān na nivarttate

He Who is Kṛṣṇa is He Who is Rāma, and He Who is Rāma is He Who is Kṛṣṇa. Anyone who sees Them as being different will never leave the world of birth and death.

From the *Pādma Purāṇa, Uttarā Khanda:*

yo vai kṛṣṇaḥ sa vai rāmo yo rāmaḥ kṛṣṇa eva saḥ
yuvayor nāntaraṁ me 'stī prasida tvaṁ jagan-maya

He Who is Kṛṣṇa is certainly He Who is Rāma, and He Who is Rāma is certainly He Who is Kṛṣṇa. These two youths are nondifferent. O pervaders of the universe! May you be pleased with me!

From the *Hari Vaṁśa,* spoken by the sage named Vaishampāyana (Vi. 7.4):

eka-kāryāntarāgatāv eka-dehau dvidhā-kṛtau
eka-caryau mahā-vīryāv ekasya śiśutāṅgatau

This pair acts for one purpose
although appearing different;
This pair is one body; This pair has split into two;

This pair moves and walks as one;
This pair is greatly chivalrous;
This pair, of one substance,
appears in the bodies of two young boys.

The sages say that in Vraja, Kṛṣṇa and Balarāma are one substance that takes two names for the purpose of performing playful *līlās*. Any person who merely speaks of Them as being different goes to hell, even if he is very pious.

rāme kṛṣṇe ca yo jivo vibhinnātmaṁ karoti ca
vāso 'pi niraye tasya vadantīti maharṣayaḥ

That *jīva* who makes a distinction between the souls of Rāma and Kṛṣṇa verily lives in hell. This is spoken by the great sages.

In this regard, just see what is written in the *Hari Vaṁśa* in India. It is a statement that Kṛṣṇa-candra Himself had spoken to Balabhadra. Kṛṣṇa said, "Dear brother Balarāma, please listen! Whatever I am, that is you. We are one body having become two. Furthermore, for the purpose of *līlā* we will again become two bodies and manifest our pastimes in the material world by assuming the forms of human beings."

Also from the *Hari Vaṁśa* (Vi. 14.48):

ahaṁ yah sa bhāvena yaḥ saḥ so 'ham sanātanaḥ
dvāv eva vihitau hy āvām eka-dehau mahābalau

"That which I am, you are also He. That which is He is eternally Me. We have only become two; We are certainly one in two bodies, a pair endowed with great power."

Śrī Kṛṣṇa had spoken as follows to Balabhadra, in reference to the pastime of killing the demon Pralamba:

yathāham api lokānāṁ tathā tvaṁ tac ca me matam
ubhāv eka-śarīrau svo jagadarthe dvidhā-kṛtau

aham vā śāśvataḥ kṛṣṇas tvam vā śeṣah purātanaḥ
sa balena bhavān pūrṇas trailokyāntara-darśanaḥ

"Just as I am among the people, just so are You, as this is My intention. Both of Us are one body appearing as two for the welfare of the world. I am the eternal Kṛṣṇa, and You are the primordial Śeṣa. By dint of Your power, You are the total witness of everything within the three worlds."

The partial expansion of that same Balabhadra is Ananta Himself, who bears all the worlds upon His thousands of heads. Furthermore it is stated: *yasyāmśāmś ena vidhṛtā jagati jagatah prabho:* The Lord is He whose portion of a plenary portion sustains all the planets in the universe. Rāma is the original cause of everything; He is the *mūla-saṇkarāṇa*. The creation and maintenance of the material world is performed by His mere partial expansion. This Baladeva remains pervading the entire universe just as the threads of a cloth are woven lengthwise and crosswise. That is confirmed in *Śrī Daśama* (the Tenth Canto) of *Śrī Bhāgavata* thus (10.15.35): *naitac citraṁ bhagavati:* "This act [the killing of Dhenukāsura by Balarāma] is not an amazing accomplishment for the Supreme Personality of Godhead."

These two foremost personalities are the original Soul of all souls. Because they are the cause of the entire creation, therefore they are worshipable for all living entities in the creation. They are the Mother and Father of the universe in the guise of Rāma and Kṛṣṇa. They are all-adorable, the root of all existences, and they exhibit their own plenary portions in all spheres. When these two incarnate, they are a fully complete manifestation. They sport at Vraja for the welfare of the world. This is confirmed in *Śrīmad-Bhāgavatam* (10.28.32) by the statement of Akrura: *pradhāna-puruṣāv ādyau:* "These two persons are the foremost beings, the original Supreme Personalities." Rāma and Kṛṣṇa perform their eternal pastimes (*nitya-līlā*) in Vṛndāvana, and they never leave Vraja at any time to go anywhere else. At Dvārakā, Śrī Rāma and Kṛṣṇa manifest their expansions known as *vilāsa-rūpa* with the four names Vāsudeva, Rāma, Śrī Pradyumna and Aniruddha. But the most complete (*pūrṇatama*) forms of Kṛṣṇa and Rāma remain perpetually in Vraja.

vatsair vatsatarībhiś ca sadā krīḍati mādhavaḥ
vṛndāvanāntar gataḥ sarāmo bālakair vṛtaḥ

Within the borders of Vṛndāvana, Lord Mādhava continuously enjoys pleasure pastimes surrounded by the calves, cows, Rāma and the cowherd boys. (*B.r.s.* 3.3.129, quoted from the *Skānda Purāṇa, Mathurā Khanda*)

Kṛṣṇa performs eternal pastimes along with His cowherd boyfriends while situated at Vṛndāvana in both *prakaṭa* manifestations and *aprakaṭa* manifestations. The realm of Goloka Vṛndāvana is included within the perimeter of Vṛndāvana. He perpetually sports His *nitya-līlā* in both places.

Rāma and Kṛṣṇa Served by the Assembly of *Gopīs*

In the company of cowherd girls who are eternal (*nitya*), genuine (*satya*), and beyond the material modes (*guṇātītā*), Kṛṣṇa performs eternal pastimes in the mood of great fun. The earth of Goloka is totally full of all universal opulences (*aiśvarya*), and that is where Rāma and Kṛṣṇa expand their amusements.

Within the inner chambers of Kṛṣṇa's palace, the cowherd girls tend to various aspects of clothing and ornamentation in rendering service unto Him, while some of them wave *cāmara* whisks in their hands. Balarāma sits facing Kṛṣṇa on the same *āsana*, with his matchless complexion eclipsing millions of moons. This pastime of Kṛṣṇa and Rāma dallying in the midst of many women is clearly narrated in the *Bhāgavata Purāṇa*. It is also stated in the *Govinda-vṛndāvanam* (1.117–119):

antaḥpura-nivāsinyo gopyaś cāyuta-saṁkhyakāḥ
padma-hastāś ca tāḥ sarvāḥ koṭi-vaiśvānara-prabhāḥ
tābhiḥ parivṛtaḥ kṛṣṇaḥ śuśubhe paramaḥ pumān
tasyāgre bhagavān rāma āsīnaḥ sama āsane

> There are ten thousand *gopīs* residing in Lord Kṛṣṇa's palace. All of them have lotus-like hands and are radiant in complexion like ten million blazing fires. Surrounded by them, Kṛṣṇa the Supreme Personality shines in great splendor. Facing Kṛṣṇa is Bhagavān Rāma, seated upon the same cushion.

Please behold the sportive pastimes performed during the *prakaṭa-līlā* (manifest in the visible material sphere). Rāma and Kṛṣṇa share limitless delights in the company of the assembly of *gopīs*. These extremely astonishing pastimes are the reservoir of *premānanda* (loving bliss), and are imperceptible for people conditioned by the modes of material nature (*prākṛta manuṣya*).

The Pastimes of Rāma and Kṛṣṇa with the *Gopīs*

One night Rāma and Kṛṣṇa were exhibiting great prowess as they went together to a secret place in Vṛndāvana. Both the brothers then filled the holes of their flutes with musical sounds that enchant the entire universe. These melodies attracted the minds of the young girls of Vraja. Listening to the sound of the flutes, the *gopīs* became very excited. Two kinds of *gopīkās* blissfully began to adorn themselves those who are *Rāma-priyā* (beloveds of Balarāma) and those who are *Kṛṣṇa-priyā* (beloveds of Kṛṣṇa). Both of these groups then proceeded through the forest to see Rāma and Kṛṣṇa, and they were so jubilant that they became deeply immersed in the mood of grand mischievous delight. When they finally beheld the *darśana* of Rāma and Kṛṣṇa in the bower house, all the girls exclaimed auspicious vibrations of "*Jai! Jai!*" Everyone then enjoyed with blissful hearts as Rāma and Kṛṣṇa sported lavish diversions along with the assembly of *gopīs*. Hand-in-hand, the girls formed a circle while in the center Rāma and Kṛṣṇa sported in great playfulness. Making a myriad of jokes, playing a myriad of pranks, they clapped their hands and sang sweet songs. Decorated with various kinds of ornaments, and forest garlands about their necks, the boys wearing blue and yellow garments were thus surrounded by a host of cowherd girls.

This scene is described in the *Śrīmad-Bhāgavatam* (10.34.20–21) thus:

> *kadācid atha govindo rāmaś cādbhuta-vikramaḥ*
> *vijahratur vane rātryāṁ madhya-gau vraja-yoṣitām*
> *upagīyamānau lalitaṁ strī-janair baddha-sauhṛdaiḥ*
> *sv-alaṅkṛtānuliptāṅgau sragvinau virajo-'mbarau*

> Once Lord Govinda and His brother Rāma, the exhibitors of amazing prowess, were playing amongst the young girls of Vraja in the forest at night. They were praised by the charming songs of the *gopīs*, who were bound to them with ties of intimate affection. The brothers were nicely adorned, their limbs were anointed with sandalwood paste, and they wore flower garlands and spotless clothing.

Killing the Demon Named Śaṇkhachūḍa

At that time, a servant of the demigod Kuvera named Śaṇkhachūḍa arrived and watched the pastimes of Rāma and Kṛṣṇa. The demon became overwhelmed with lust by seeing the *gopīkās*, and in his mind he contemplated abducting them. Thinking like this he came before them, causing Kṛṣṇa to reflect to Himself. "Who is this?" Then Balarāma secretly spoke to Bhagavān. "Behold the servant of Kuvera standing before us." The two brothers ran to console the *gopīs*, and then they uprooted large *śāla* trees with which to destroy the *guhyaka* (demigod attendant of Kuvera). Seeing this, Śaṇkhachūdā understood their insurmountable strength and began to run away, but after a short distance Kṛṣṇa caught hold of him and angrily slew him. Completely pulverizing the demon's body by the repeated striking of His fists, Kṛṣṇa took the jewel from his crown and presented it to His older brother. *Śaṇkha chūḍa iti khyāto:* His name was Śaṇkhachūḍa (*Bhāgavatam* 10.34.25). The *gopīs* were astonished to see the might of Rāma and Kṛṣṇa exhibited before them in the violent killing of Śaṇkha-chūḍa. Balarāma stood in front of them giving protection and reassurance. Who could understand their shocked reaction to Kṛṣṇa's prowess? While Śaṇkhachūḍa was having this terrible fight with Kṛṣṇa, Haladhar calmed the *gopīs* by assuring them, "Please don't be afraid!" As Śrī Rādhikā watched the fight, She trembled intensely in great fear, thinking, "I don't know what's happening to Kṛṣṇa! Alas, how will this end!" She loudly called to Him, "*He* Vrajendra-nandan!" while all the other *gopīs* loudly exclaimed with cries of lamentation "*Hā! Ha!*"

In this way, Rāma and Kṛṣṇa continuously sport along with the *gopīs* throughout the entire day and night in Vṛndāvana.

śaṅkha-cūḍam adhirūḍha-vikramaṁ
prekṣya vistṛta-bhujaṁ jighṛkṣayā
hā vrajendra-tanayeti vādinī
kampa-sampadam adhatta rādhikā

Seeing the greatly powerful demon Śaṇkhachūḍa spreading his arms in an attempt to abduct Her, Rādhikā called out, "O son of the King of Vraja!" and started to tremble in fear (*B.r.s.* 2.3.44).

ghorā khaṇḍita śaṅkha-cūḍam ajiraṁ rudhe śivā tāmasī
brahmiṣṭhaśvasanaḥ śama-stuti-kathā-prāleyam āsiñcati
agre rāmaḥ sudhā-rucir vijayate kṛṣṇa-pramodocitaṁ
rādhāyās tad api praphullam abhajan mlāniṁ na bhāvāmbujam

On one side of the courtyard the dead body of Śaṇkhachūḍa was lying, surrounded by many jackals steeped in the dense darkness of the mode of ignorance. On another side were many learned *brāhmaṇas* offering nice prayers, which were soothing as the sprinkling mist of a cool breeze. In front of Kṛṣṇa, Rāma was standing, his nectar-luster causing a calming effect. But even amid all these different circumstances of soothing and disturbing effects, the fully-blossomed lotus flower of ecstatic conjugal love that Kṛṣṇa felt for Śrī Rādhā could not wither in the least (*B.r.s.* 3.5.23).

The demon Śaṇkhachūḍa was killed at night, and then the next morning at daybreak the *gopīs* returned to their own homes.

[NOTE: According to the *Brahma Vaivarta Purāṇa*, Śrī Rādhikā once became irritated with the cowherd boy Sudāma during a pastime in Goloka and cursed him to be born as a demon. Thus he became Śaṇkhachūḍa during a *prakaṭa-līlā* in the material sphere, and was subsequently killed by Kṛṣṇa, thereby being freed from the curse.]

Kṛṣṇa's Words in Praise of His Elder Brother

After that pastime, one day Kṛṣṇa spoke some loving words unto Balarāma in the mood of fraternal affection (*sakhya-bhāva*). Just see this statement in the *Daśama* (Tenth Canto of *Śrīmad-Bhāgavatam* 10.15.4-8). Kṛṣṇa said, "*Śuno bhāi!* Listen, dear brother! *Ohe* Balarāma! These daughters of the cowherd folk in Vraja are very fortunate! The *gopīs* that receive the embrace of your arms thereby become the most glorious cowherd girls in Vraja. The goddess of fortune Lakṣmī had desired the embrace of your arms, but she could only wish for them since she never attained them. But these young girls have received the embrace of those arms, and therefore the *gopīs* are most fortunate. Your lotus feet have delighted this forest, and so the earth has become blessed, as is Giri Govardhana. The grass, trees, streams and so forth, as well as all the animals and birds feel that their births have become fulfilled by the touch of your lotus feet."

Thus spoke Bhagavān unto Balarāma; please hear further evidence of this statement as recorded in the *Daśama* (10.15.8):

dhanyeyam adya dharaṇī tṛṇa-vīrudhas tvat-
pāda-spṛśo druma-latāḥ karajābhimṛṣṭāḥ
nadyo 'drayaḥ khaga-mṛgāḥ sadayāvalokair
gopyo 'ntareṇa bhujayor api yat-spṛhā śrīḥ

This earth is now fortunate because her grasses and bushes are touched by your feet, and because her trees and vines are plucked by your fingernails. You bless her rivers, hills, birds, and animals with your merciful

> glances. You embrace the *gopīs* between your arms, a favor cherished by the goddess of fortune herself.

In his commentary on this verse, Gosvāmī Śrī Sanātana has explained this glory of the *gopīs* as follows: *śrīr api yatspṛhā yasmai spṛhayati kevalam ity arthah. ataḥ sarvebhyo gopīṣv evādhika-dhanyatā paryavasyati:* That was the only desire cherished even by Lakṣmī. This is the meaning. Therefore it is concluded that the fortune of the *gopīs* is much greater than that of everyone else (*Śrī Bṛhad Bhāgavatāmṛtaṁ* 2.7.107).

Kṛṣṇa's Body is Never Material

In this way they indulge in their pleasure pastimes of both the *prakaṭa* and *aprakaṭa* realms, which can never be understood by materialistic persons. Taking on the form of a human being, Kṛṣṇa engages in human-like enjoyments in the company of family and friends, although such actions could never be imitated by ordinary persons. Sporting eternal amusements along with eternal *sakhās* and *sakhīs*, Kṛṣṇa and His transcendental family do not have material bodies. Enacting human deeds in the figure of a human being, He enjoys exactly according to His own desires from moment-to-moment. That person who says Kṛṣṇa has a material body becomes a great sinner (*mahā-pāpī*), a punishable offender (*daṇḍya*) and the lowest among men (*narādhama*). Similarly, the associates of Kṛṣṇa have bodies according to their own desire and sport for the pleasure of Kṛṣṇa in such transcendental forms. As stated (by Lord Brahmā) in the *Bhāgavatam* (10.14.2):

> *asyāpi deva vapuso mad-anugrahasya*
> *svecchā-mayasya na tu bhūta-mayasya ko 'pi*

> O Lord, this bodily form of Yours, in which You have shown favor to me, is manifest of Your own desire; it is certainly not a product of matter.

Thus Rāma and Kṛṣṇa perpetually enjoy life along with the *gopas* and *gopīs*, without any separation at all, in both the *prakaṭa* and *aprakaṭa* realms of Vraja. It is mentioned in the *Kṛṣṇa Yāmala:*

yatraiva bhagavān kṛṣṇas tatra vṛndāvanaṁ vanam
tatraiva rādhikā nityā bhadrā candrāvalīti ca
tatraiva balarāmas tu gopa-gopyo varāṅganaḥ

Where Kṛṣṇa, the Supreme Personality of Godhead, is certainly existing, that is the forest of Vṛndāvana. There Rādhikā certainly is existing eternally, as are Bhadrā and Chandrāvali also. There Balarāma certainly is existing, as are the cowherd boys and the cowherd girls of beautiful form.

Anyone who does not meditate internally on such pastimes of Rāma and Kṛṣṇa becomes the receptacle of all miseries and remains suffering within the material sphere. As stated in the *Ādi Saṁhitā:*

kīrtanīyau rāma-kṛṣṇau śāstra-samvādam icchatā
anyathā hy aprapattiḥ syād bahūnāṁ janmanāṁ vibho

O radiant one, the pair Rāma and Kṛṣṇa should be glorified according to the statements of the scriptures. Those who desire to glorify something else will fall down into many repeated births and deaths.

Totally renouncing all desires for unrestricted material happiness, mundane enjoyment, or even liberation, and eradicating all hopes and endeavors for women and wealth incessantly contemplate within the Vraja of your heart Kṛṣṇa and Balarāma along with the cowherd boys of Vṛndāvana-dhāma.

sukha-śuddhaṁ tathā mokṣaṁ hitvā tu bhaja re manaḥ
hṛn-madhye gokule kṛṣṇaṁ rāmañ ca bālakaiḥ saha

O mind! Having given up pure happiness and liberation, please worship Kṛṣṇa and Rāma along with the cowherd boys in the Gokula of the heart.

Thus, my dear mind, I have instructed you with this evidence. Now just worship Rāma and Kṛṣṇa and deliver me! I am praying at the feet of Śrī Caitanya and Nityānanda, and offering my mind unto

Abhirām and Sundarānanda. May I remember birth after birth the feet of Śrī Gopāl (Parṇī Gopāl) and Śrī Gopāl Caraṇ (my father). There is bliss in hearing the book *Preyo-Bhakti-Rasārṇava*. Thus the fifth chapter is narrated by this Nayanānanda.

Thus ends the fifth chapter of
Śrī Śrī Preyo-Bhakti-Rasārṇava

CHAPTER SIX

The Residences of Sudāma and His Associates

śrī-rāma-keśavau vande
vrajādhīśau jagat-patī
paramānanda-dātārau
śrīdāmādibhir āvṛtau

I bow to the splendrous brothers, Rāma and Keśava
the Masters of Vraja, the Lords of the universe
Who are the Bestowers of supreme bliss
Who are surrounded by Their boyfriends
headed by Śrīdāma.

All glories, all glories to Rāma-Kṛṣṇa, and Their dear cowherd boyfriends! In the perfect spiritual body as well as in the body of a practitioner (*siddha-sādhaka-deha*), please remember the realm of Vṛndāvana. Becoming a follower of the residents of Vraja within your heart, just remain fixed in emulating your most cherished eternal *rāgātmikā* personality. In the company of your *guru-rūpa-sakhā*, or spiritual master in the form of a cowherd boy, wear the dress of a *gopa* and always worship Hari in your *mānasik-siddha-deha* (spiritual body visualized in the mind). The dear cowherd boy named Sudāma is the abode of bliss. Along with him, worship Kṛṣṇa and Balarāma in Vraja. Sakhā Sudāma's group consists of 64 cowherd boys. Consider yourself to be one of the boys in their circle. To facilitate such awareness, I now speak of the residence of that Sudāma-candra, as well as the arrangements for adorning him with nice clothing, ornaments and so forth. He lives along with his own associates in the town of Vṛṣabhānu-pur. Now I will narrate descriptions of the splendor of this town. Just contemplate him deeply and directly behold this place within your heart.

Description of the Town of King Vṛṣabhānu

Vṛṣabhānu Purī is shaped like a lotus flower of a thousand petals. It is extremely astonishing, just like a place of eternal deathlessness. The town extends for a circumference of two *yojanas* (16 miles). Even the celestial abode of King Indra called Amarāvati could never be compared to this domain. Here are the residences of countless, countless cowherd folk, all of which are nicely beautified by various clusters of trees and gardens. Numerous species of flowers are in full bloom at the same time, and there are rows upon rows of *champaka* flowers, plus *mālatī* and *kuṇḍa* jasmines. Hovering amongst the flowers are many bees that are maddened in craving for honey. The nicely scented breeze blows very gently in these gardens. Here and there are lakes and ponds, resplendent with many species of lotus flowers such as the *kumuda* and *kanvasāra*. Many birds are present upon the waters of the lakes such as swans, ducks and herons, and cuckoos are singing while the peacocks dance. The bases of some of the trees scattered about are encircled with jewelled platforms. The trees most conducive for these arrangements are the banyan, fig, white lily and mango. There are various types of birds moving and sitting amongst these trees such as female and male parrots, plus there are storks in the tall grasses where noisy crickets and cicada bugs are busily chirping.

In this place there are uncountable residences of the cowherd folk, the *gopas,* and these homes are made of bricks. Each of the paths and platforms are studded with gemstones, and they are kept very clean by having very fragrant sandalwood paste mixed with musk sprinkled all around. The meeting hall of the townspeople is surrounded by a large brick wall with ramparts; it is an ornate building made of gold, silver, and emeralds. In the center of that is the residence of King Vṛṣabhānu. His palace, surrounded by a moat, is made of solid gold and silver. Being the principal residence of total universal opulence there is perpetual bliss in this realm. All the people living here are continually very happy in transcendental euphoria. All the houses are beautified by flags fluttering in the breeze, arranged in sequences according to the colors white, yellow, blue and red. Here and there sit full waterpots decorated with freshly sprouted twigs. The four directions remain pleasantly auspicious due to forest flower garlands hanging from the walls.

The sounds of various musical instruments such as the *dundubhi* kettledrums, *ānaha,* large *ḍhāka* bass drum; bow-shaped stringed *pinaka,* droning *tamburā, mṛdaṇga* drum, *dampha* tambourine; dish-shaped *jhānjha* gong, and *mahurā* reeds can be heard playing. The dwelling of the Rāj is surrounded by a moat and is bordered on all four sides by jewelled walls with parapets. To the west is the royal gate, which is fitted with a smaller entrance door. Adjoining this to the north is another gate. There are thousands upon thousands of jewelled pillars fixed in row after row, which are all made of solid crystal, solid coral and so forth, and are studded with various gemstones. The main gate is decorated with hanging clusters of pearls, plus banners and ribbons and *cāmara* whisks swaying in the breeze. What can I possibly say about the splendor of this royal gate? Fashioned by the celestial architect Viśvakarma, this gate completely captivates the mind.

In front of the outside gateway is a raised platform completely studded with jewels. Royal swans, storks and other birds are attracted to come and sport here. Near this platform are flowering trees fixed in orderly rows of *kadamba, champaka, nāgeśvara* and other trees. To the left side of the royal gate shines a divine lake, the surface of which is made quite splendrous by being scattered with different kinds of lotus flowers. In front of this lake are many nice and especially radiant fruit trees such as betel, jackfruit, mango, banana, wood-apple, coconut and rose-apple. This lake has two opposing landings that are inlaid with tile mosaics. To the south of the royal gate are uncountable *gośālās* (cowsheds). To the west of these are the homes of many other cowherd folk. In front of the northern gate is a very magnificent mansion, within which many female dancers are dancing. In front of this building is a lake abound all around in jewels, where various birds sing and bees buzz. So far I have described the grandeur of the outer areas of Vṛṣabhānu-pur. The devotees will view this within their own heart of hearts.

The Inner Chambers

After this I now narrate a description of the inner chambers of the palace. I have never seen a place anywhere in all these three worlds that could be compared to this realm. Within the royal gate there is a second royal courtyard area that is lined all around with variegated gardens. Structural columns studded with various jewels stand in row after row, holding up a resplendent jewelled canopy. The inner columns, composed of solid crystal embedded with silver, and being decorated with sprays of pearl strands, altogether make this pavilion especially shimmer like the rays of the moon. In this place the cowherd boys Śrīdāma and Sudāma sport various pastimes along with their boyfriends according to different times and circumstances. Beyond this spot are five more celestial courtyards where different kinds of animals and birds choose to live. To the east of this are four different open square compounds enclosed by buildings which shimmer radiantly with an effulgence like the moonlight. The compound to the east is the abode of the cowherd man Ratna-bhānu (King Vṛṣabhānu's younger brother, the father of Sudāma). Please listen as I describe that residence.

Ratna-bhānu's Palace

On the northern side of Ratna-bhānu's home is a gateway surrounded by rows and rows of pillars made of various minerals and studded with jewels. In that house the cowherd boy Sudāma-candra along with his friends eat the sweets and other foodstuffs given by his mother. Through a portal to the west is his own private residence made of jewels and pearls. Female and male parrots sing there and utter very sweet statements, while multi-colored banners, ribbons and *cāmara* whisks sway in the breeze. In this place is the jewelled bedstead where Sudāma-candra takes rest and lounges about. To the north of his bedroom is another door which he uses to go outside. In this outer area is a large *pārijāta* tree, bound at its base by a raised golden platform. Sudāma takes his own associates and congregates with them there. In the company of Sucandra and the others, Sudāma gets dressed and decorated at that spot. During those particular times, you should be attentive and meditate on being there also, performing your specific service.

To the east of Sudāma-candra's residence is an enchantingly ornate villa. It has four nicely-designed gateways all around, and the breeze blows very gently there. At that place, Sudāma-candra's sister Śrī Rūpa Mañjarī plays along with her girlfriends. In front of these four gates shine four magnificent trees of different species, namely *santāna, pārijāta, champaka,* and *kimśuka.* Thus I have described the compound to the east. Now please hear about the building to the south.

Subhanu and Bhānu's Joined Palaces

The building to the south is the residence of the cowherd man Subhānu (King Vṛṣabhānu's younger brother). It is an extremely brilliant structure, being constructed of various jewels and minerals. The building to the west of this is the residence of the cowherd man Bhānu (another of King Vṛṣabhānu's brothers). Both of these buildings, situated in one place facing south and west respectively are so splendrous that I cannot even see or describe all of their glory.

The Treasury Building

The structure to the north comprises the inner chambers of King Vṛṣabhānu. Therein is the immense treasury building, which is so opulent that it is the ultimate seat of Rāj-Lakṣmī (the treasure of the king, or the goddess of royal fortune). The main treasury house is filled with vast quantities of riches, foodstuffs, and diverse kinds of precious stones, and it is accessed by a gate to the east.

This building is fashioned with a thousand gem-studded pillars and is so nicely constructed that it puts to shame Sura-pur, the celestial abode of the demigods.

Mother Kīrtidā's Quarters

To the south of here is another gateway that leads to the residence of the cowherd boy Sudāma. He lives there inside a jewelled temple. To the west of this I see yet another portal. There is no comparison to this, for it is filled with the aura of limitless effulgent gemstones. I understand that through this western gate is the quarters of mother Kīrtidā. This complex is graced with various pillars, jewelled mosaics and so forth. To the north of there is another smaller gate. Thus I have described the situation of her residence.

The Ratna-śālā

To the east of mother Kīrtidā's dwelling is a building called *Ratna-śālā*, the jewel-house. It is constructed with jewels, coral, minerals, and pearl-strands. The four gates of this building are adorned with wonderful *cāmara* whisks tied with bunches of ribbons, and it is exquisitely fashioned with beautiful pillars, jewel-studded walls and so forth. At this place Śrīmatī Rādhikā plays numerous games in the company of Her girlfriends, and they sport merrily amidst much laughter and joking. There her sister Ananga Mañjarī and other maidservants tend to clothing and ornaments along with their own girlfriends. In the eastern section of this building shines a raised and bejewelled altar that is so wonderfully constructed that it is like the abode of all artistic crafts. Five classes of *sakhīs* assemble here and tend to clothing, ornaments, and creating different kinds of bodily ornaments by weaving garlands of various flowers. Thus I have described something about the inner chambers. From time to time (when services are to be rendered here), the devotees will catch a glimpse of this place.

The Homes of Sudāma's 8 Chief Boyfriends

Now please listen as I describe the residences and so forth of the eight chief cowherd boyfriends who are attached to the service of Sudāma-candra.

(1) Sucandra

In the western wing of Vṛṣabhānu's palace is the home of the cowherd man Sura Gopāl. First, please listen as I describe this place. His house has gateways facing east and north. It is a very splendrous home featuring wonderfully variegated shapes. From the eastern gate through and beyond the third inner compound is a very charming mansion, constructed around a large square enclosure. A door to the north of this leads to the residence of the cowherd boy Sucandra. That place is totally jewellike due to being adorned with a myriad of precious gems. Sucandra lives there and sports various pastimes in the company of Suranga, Suvinda, Jayasmṛta, and many others. The name of Sucandra's father is Sura Gopa, and his mother is known as Padmā. Sucandra's complexion is fair-golden (*gaura*) and he wears blue garments. His caste is *vaiśya* and he likes to dress as a dramatic actor.

(2) Sukantha

To the north of Sucandra's residence is the place of the cowherd man Jaya Gopa. His residence is a spacious mansion built around a courtyard and completely covered with jewels. Through a gate to the south adorned with jewels and other opulences is the residence of the cowherd boy Sukantha. There he plays along with his friends named Subhanga, Sudarpa and others. The name of Sukantha's father is Jaya Gopa, and his mother is Sumedhā. His complexion is variegated shades of dark (*nana-varṇa śyāma*), he wears garments of red color, and his caste is *vaiśya*.

(3) Sudarpa

On the southern side of King Vṛṣabhānu's palace is the residence of the cowherd man Śubhānanda, which is decorated with many jewels and other precious substances. Through the northern gate and beyond one courtyard, in between four mansions and through the south gate, is another house. This ornate structure of pinkish hue has rows and rows of pillars all around. This is the abode of the cowherd boy Sudarpa Gopāl. Here he plays with many boyfriends such as Sudambha, Sukanda, Sujaya and others. Sudarpa's father is named Śrī Śubhānanda, and his mother is known as Śrī Kāmadā. His complexion is red-tinted fair-golden (*rakta-gaura*), he wears blue garments, and he is of the cowherd caste known as *ābhīra*.

(4) Sukhānanda

The mansion to the east of here is the residence of the cowherd man Udambara Gopa. His home within the eastern gate is very lovely, being painted with many wonderful murals. There sports the cowherd boy named Sukhānanda. In that remarkably colorful home, he likes to play various sports in the company of his own boyfriends named Premānanda, Sumohana, Darpānanda, Yaśonanda, and many other boys. Sukhānanda's father is named Udambara, his mother is Mānava Devī, and his residence caste is *gurjara*. His complexion is dark (*śyāma*), he wears yellow garments and his age is *kiśor*, fresh adolescence. Thus I have described the particulars of Sukhānanda Gopa.

(5) Rasa-candra

Near the eastern corner of this residence is the home of the cowherd man Candra Gopa. This building is surrounded by brick walls that are studded with gemstones. The complex has two gateways, one to the south and one to the west; the southern gate leads to the outer area. Through this gate and beyond two other courtyards is the home of the boy Rasa-candra. He plays there along with his friends Premānanda, Keli-candra, Kāma-chandana, Vasundhara, and others. Rasa-candra's father is named

Candra Gopa and his mother is known as Sudhā. Rasa-candra's complexion is combined dark and fair (*śyāma-gaura*), and he wears garments that are red. He is celebrated throughout the world as belonging to the *gurjara* caste.

(6) Sumahendra

To the east of the royal palace is the home of the great soul named Kulānanda. His incomparable residence shines in great colorful variety. It is surrounded on all four sides by magnificent brick walls that have two gates, to the east and to the west. Through the eastern gate and beyond the second courtyard is a charming compound surrounding a square plaza, a dwelling which is just full of jewelled decorations. By the eastern gate there is an extremely splendrous blue residence. That is where the cowherd boy Sumahendra Gopa sports. Within this four-walled compound, the house appears spotlessly pure due to being totally inlaid with blue *mahendraka* stones. Sumahendra's father is known as Kulānanda, and his mother is known throughout the scriptures as Chandrā. Sumahendra is blackish in complexion (*śyāma*), he wears white garments, and his caste is *paśupāl*, keeper of animals. Thus I have spoken the particulars about Sumahendra.

(7) Sumukha

On the southern side of Nandīśvar (and north of Vṛṣabhānu-pur) is the residence of the cowherd man Kānta Gopa. His palatial mansion is very enchanting, indeed its novel construction is ingenious. There are two gateways to this house, to the north and to the west. Through the western gate and beyond the first courtyard shines a radiant compound surrounding a square plaza that is the residence of the cowherd boy named Sumukha Gopāl. Within this mansion he plays and has mock fights along with Sunānanda, Pura-baddha, Pramarddhaka and other loving friends that are inhabitants of this part of town. The father of Sumukha Gopa is named Kānta, and his mother is known as Kāḍambinī. His complexion is fair-golden (*gaura*), he wears blue garments, and his caste is *paśupāl*, keeper of animals. Thus I have spoken something about the *gopāl* named Sumukha.

(8) Rasāngada

To the east of Kānta Gopa's residence is the very enchanting abode of the cowherd man Purandara Gopāl. Through the northern gate of this compound is a dwelling which is rendered exceptionally fascinating due to being made entirely of solid gold. This is the quarters of the cowherd boy Rasāngada. His father is named Śrī Pura, and his mother is Padmāvatī. His complexion is reddish-gold (*rakta-gaura*), he wears blue garments and performs the duties of a protector of cows. Of the *puśupāl* caste, Rasangada plays there along with his friends Candrangada, Vibhanga, and others.

Thus I have spoken a little about of the splendor of Vṛṣabhānupur. All I know is: who could possibly describe everything about this place? The devotees who are *sudāma-bhāvānkita* – marked with the mood of following the cowherd boy Sudāma, realize a *siddha-deha* (perfect spiritual body) and always live in this place performing *mānasik-sevā*, devotional service visualized within the mind.

Thus ends the description of Vṛṣabhānu-pur

Description of the Splendor of Nandīśvar

All glories, all glories to the *priya-sakhās*, the very dear cowherd boyfriends of Balarāma and Kṛṣṇa! O my dear mind! Please fix your consciousness on them continuously and worship them in Vṛndāvana!

The realm of Gokula-maṇḍala is formed just like a lotus flower of a thousand petals, and all the deepest mysteries of the universe are flourishing within the whorl of that lotus. In this central area is the extremely matchless town of Nandīśvar. The ground of that sphere, composed entirely of desire-fulfilling touchstones (*cintāmaṇi*), has no comparison anywhere else in the universe.

Nothing that Lord Brahma has ever created in the material world can be compared to this place. Indeed, all the vast and magnificent spiritual realms headed by Vaikuṇtha are situated merely as minute portions of this place. Nandiśvar is a supremely mysterious domain and is far beyond the perception gained by following mere rules and regulations (*vidhi*). This realm is understood only by the best of the very dear devotees of the Lord (*bhakta priya-vara*).

Kṛṣṇa's Eternal Pastimes

Śrī Kṛṣṇa's eternal pastimes (*nitya-līlā*) take place in Vṛndāvana and Kṛṣṇa always remains at this place in His manifest (*prakaṭa*) and unmanifest (*aprakaṭa*) forms. To the devotees His pastimes remain *prakaṭa* and thus they always behold such sports. For others these same pastimes are invisible and thus remain *aprakaṭa*. Just as Kṛṣṇa is eternal, similarly His pastimes are eternal, and this is why I have spoken of the process of worship (*sādhana*) performed by the devotees in order to attain the *nitya-deha* or eternal spiritual body. Thereby the *sādhakas* may realize an eternal spiritual body and live in Vraja performing service throughout the day and night. In the company of your *guru-rūpa-sakhā*, spiritual master in the form of a cowherd boy just worship Balarāma and Kṛṣṇa in Vraja with a blissful heart along with your own group of cowherd boyfriends.

Description of the Town

Now I will narrate a brief description of the town of Nandīśvar Pur. Please meditate on this place within your *siddha-sādhaka-deha* (both internal and external bodies). Nandīśvar Puri extends for a distance of two *yojanas* (16 miles), and many secrets are embraced within this perimeter. There are uncountable *gośālās* (cowsheds) made of jewels and other splendrous treasures. There are various beautifully-constructed buildings that make the area look like Sura-pur the abode of the gods. There are forests and gardens full of many *kalpa-tarus* (desire-fulfilling trees), as well as other celestial plants. Everywhere there are hundreds and hundreds of trees, creepers, animals and birds. Here and there are jewelled altars, very pleasantly fashioned, and the bases of trees are bound all around with solid gold platforms studded with rubies. The ground of Vraja-bhūmi is composed of *cintāmaṇi* jewels, and is so opulent that all the majesties of all the goddesses of fortune in the entire creation are present there. The flowers everywhere are all blooming at the same time, for this realm is the headquarters of the personified six seasons. The atmosphere is just like a cosmic bubble within which resides *nityānanda-sukha,* the pure happiness of eternal bliss.

The Palace of King Nanda

In the center of this region is the royal palace of the king, Śrī Nanda Rāj. Even the abode of Lord Indra could never be offered as a comparison to such a structure. Within the complex there are thousands of temples and residences composed of jewels and other wonderful things, all enclosed by an enormous wall. There are two main gates to the royal palace, one to the north and one to the west. The northern gate is used for royal business affairs. The doors of this gateway are studded with many varieties of costly jewels, and are bordered by thousands and thousands of very nicely constructed pillars. These grand pillars are made from pure crystal, coral, pearls, various kinds of minerals, rubies, lapis lazuli, and pure silver. Soothing white *cāmara* whisks and colorful ribbons hang from the walls, and on top of the walls is a wonderful thatched roofing composed of jewelled rods, above which many flags flutter. In front of the gate shines a splendrous raised platform totally inlaid with jewels. It is constructed so fantastically that it is like the reservoir of all artistic crafts.

Surrounding this platform are five special trees called *deva-taru,* trees of the gods. Whatever desires one may have are perfectly fulfilled by these trees. On the eastern side is a celestial *santāna* tree, and on the southern side is a *pārijāta* tree. To the west is a *kalpa-vṛkṣa* tree, and to the north is a *hari-candana* tree. In the very center of the platform is a *mandāra* tree. Please note attentively that this *mandāra* tree in the center of the platform represents the residence of the personified six seasons.

Just inside the royal gate is a *haritāla* tree, which always resounds with the chirping of numberless kinds of birds. In front of this tree is an effulgent lake in which dwell diverse kinds of water fowl. Assorted species of lotus flowers like *kumuda* and *kamala* are in full bloom, and each and every flower resounds with the buzzing of groups of bees. Different types of birds such as swans, ducks, *sarālīs,* storks and herons are present, and many other kinds are incessantly chirping and cooing. All four sides of this lake are banked with divine *ghāts* (landings) having celestial steps. Surrounding each of these *ghāts* are incomparably gorgeous divine trees. Here are many trees such as jackfruit, banana, orange, white-lily, screwpine, mango, flamboyant, evergreen, rose-apple, betel, coconut, *nāgeśvar, campaka, bakula, kadamba,* and wood-apple. There are also many flowers blooming such as jasmine, nutmeg vine, *tagara,* rose, *gunāchi, yuthi, sevatī, rangina,* oleander, and white water lily. What can I say about the magnificence of all these different types of flowers? Amongst the *pārijāta, gaja-kunda, sugandhi* and *pārali* flowers resounds the very nice vibration of bees that are hovering here and there.

The Royal Assembly Hall

In the city of Nandiśvar live the five brothers: Nanda, Upananda, Abhinanda, Sananda, and Nandana. The palace complex of Nanda Mahārāja is situated in the center and is surrounded on all four sides by the palace complexes of the other brothers headed by Upananda.

These five palaces are surrounded by tall walls which have golden towers topped with flags waving in the breeze. In the central area amongst the fifteen courtyards of this compound is a very enchanting structure. Upon viewing it one's heart cannot remain calm. Thousands upon thousands of pillars shine in row upon row. Supported on top of them are vast awnings decorated with suspended strands of pearls. The courtyard here is splendrously adorned by a raised platform trimmed with silk draperies and designed as if by magic. Upon this stage dancing girls perform their art very nicely.

On the southem side of the main stage is an incomparably splendrous archway. That is where Śrī Hari sits in the evening and watches dancers and singers. Talented artists perform singing, dancing and playing of musical instruments for Śrī Hari and the assembly of His cowherd boyfriends, while all of their hearts become excited with great jubilation. After first mentioning those confidential pastimes that take place here during the evening time, now I describe details of the tenth courtyard. This most confidential place is constructed in a matchless circular formation where Bhagavān, the Supreme Personality of Godhead, conducts playful games in the company of His cowherd boyfriends. This place is known as *Raṅga-sthala* (Arena of Sports), and beyond that there are twenty buildings in the inner chamber. Beyond the twentieth courtyard is another very charming mansion complex which illuminates the ten directions with its effulgence. All four sides of this golden abode are totally inlaid with countless rubies, pearls, and coral.

Lord Balarāma's Quarters

Through a gate to the south of here is the kitchen, which has two doors with windows in there. This is where Rohiṇi Devī cooks while maidservants prepare the various ingredients. To the west of this main kitchen is a large door made of silver, which leads to a very nicely constructed residence rendered quite brilliant with the effulgence of moonstones. It is surrounded by untold thousands of jewelled pillars that are decorated with *cāmara* whisks, strands of pearls, coral and rubies. Within this building is a wonderful golden bedstead surrounded with blue draperies, and trimmed with the colors of various substances like vermillion. There sits Rohiṇī-kumār, Lord Balarāma the son of mother Rohiṇī while so many servants and maidservants render *sevā* unto Him. Through the eastern gate from here is the main storehouse, which is filled with vast reservoirs of gems, pearls, and various kinds of valuable minerals. There resides Nanda Gopa and Mātā Yaśomatī, who are also attended by many servants and maidservants.

Lord Kṛṣṇa's Quarters

Through the northern gate from there is a most enchanting dwelling decorated by many flags fluttering in the breeze. This palace is fashioned in various colors, such as that of vermillion and so forth, and the jewelled pillars are marvelous, being inlaid with artful designs of rubies. All four sides of the building are adorned with white and blue clay pots, *cāmara* whisks with bejewelled handles, and bunches of colorful ribbons that glitter their jewellike auras all around. Golden towers made of precious stones and pearls display waving banners of various colors like white and yellow. This dwelling is furnished on all four sides with windows and doors, and the gem-studded doorframes are fitted with solid gold doors. In the center of this dwelling is a very brilliant jewelled bedstead covered with different kinds of shimmering cloths. Upon this bedstead Vrajendra-suta, Śrī Kṛṣṇa, the son of the King of Vraja takes rest. Now and then at the appropriate time, the *sādhaka-bhakta* beholds the *darśana* of this scene.

To the east of here shines a very enchanting building where gentle scented breezes always blow. This building is made of gems and is endowed with four gates. There is nothing like it to be seen anywhere in the three worlds. In front of the eastern gate is a *tamāl* tree and a raised platform studded with uncountable precious stones. Upon this platform live so many different types of birds. The *śārīs* and *śukas* (female and male parrots) make various sounds that are very pleasing to the ear. To hear the utterances of these birds is just like hearing the recitation of the Vedas, and these birds sing of the pastimes of Kṛṣṇa with very sweet voices. Underneath this *tamāl* tree, Śrī Nanda-nandana sits to perform his morning duties such as washing his face and brushing his teeth.

In front of the western gate is a *pārijāta* tree whose flowers are nicely scented just like *aguru* perfume. The jewel-studded town of Nandīśvar is rendered fragrant by the scent of these flowers, and at the base of this tree Lord Hari occasionally takes a brief rest. In front of the southern gate there is a jewelled palace which is graced by many pillars and a platform close by. Near the northern gate is a very nicely-constructed altar formed of various minerals that glow like the moon. In the courtyard of this place shines a wonderful awning adorned with numerous opulences like gemstones and strands of pearls. At this place male dancers sing and perform their art before Kṛṣṇa, who is seated in the center of a ruby-studded altar. He sports numerous pastimes here along with His *sakhās* (close boyfriends) and *upa-sakhās* (distant boyfriends). They make jokes, decorate each other with clothing and ornaments, and thus manifest limitless graceful charm. At that place, and at those times, the devotees who are followers of the cowherd boys (*sakhānugā*) render services in the company of their *sakhā-rūpa-guru* (their spiritual master in the form of a cowherd boy). Thus I have spoken somewhat of the splendor of Nandīśvar-pur. Hearing about this increases the enticement of the minds of the devotees.

I offer prayers at the feet of Śrī Caitanya, and bow at the lotus feet of Lord Nityānanda. My Prabhu, Śrīyuta Sundarānanda Thākur Gopāl is supremely merciful to the fallen and bereft souls. Desiring only the feet of *guru*, Kṛṣṇa and the Vaiṣṇavas. I have written this book named *Preyo-Bhakti-Rasārṇava*. Dās Nayanānanda thus offers prayers at the end of this sixth chapter.

Thus ends the sixth chapter of
Śrī Śrī Preyo-Bhakti-Rasārṇava

CHAPTER SEVEN

Prātaḥ-Kaliya-Sevā: Services During Morning Pastimes (6:00–8:24 A.M.)

tam vande gokulānandaṁ
nayanānanda-sundaram
rāmena parāmanandaṁ
govindaṁ nanda-nandanam

I pray to Him, the giver of bliss to Gokula
  The most beautiful one who gives bliss to the eyes
In supreme bliss along with His brother Rāma
  The delighter of the cows, the delighter of Nanda.

All glories to the Son of Nanda, Lord Hari, the Moon over Gokula! All glories to Śrī Rāma and Mukunda along with all of Their associates!

The Process of Spontaneous Worship

Listen, listen, dear friends! I make this request of you: Incessantly worship Lord Hari on the *rāga-marga,* the path of spontaneous devotion. All the Vrajavāsīs, the residents of Vraja, are fixed up in spontaneous devotion to Kṛṣṇa (*rāgātmikā niṣṭā*). This includes those in the category of *dāsa* (servant), *sakhā* (cowherd boyfriends), *guru-varga* (superiors), and *preyasī* (beloved cowherd girifriends). Nicely fix up your own mood (*bhāva*) amongst them (as if you were one of them), and become their follower according to your own spontaneously desired disposition (*rāgātmikā*). In your two distinct bodies (*siddha-sādhaka-deha*), namely the internal spiritual body and the external body of a practitioner, just render service day and night unto Śrī Nanda-nandana according to the different times of day. In your external physical body (*sādhaka-deha*) render services by collecting flowers and so forth, and also by offering sweets, grains, fruits and water at different times. Engage in *śravana* (hearing), *kīrtana* (chanting), *smarana* (remembering), *pāda-sevānam* (massaging the Deity's lotus feet), *dāsya* (remaining as the servant), and *sakhya* (becoming His close friend), and according to the process of this friendship offer the totality of your soul unto Him (*ātma-samarpaṇa*).

Always living in Vraja by visualizing your spiritual *siddha-deha* within your mind, you enter into your own eternal group (*yūtha*) and directly engage in *sākśāt-govinda-sevā* (personal service to Lord Govinda). Beginning from *prātaḥ-kāla* (the morning time) all the way up to *mahā-nisha* (nighttime), just render unalloyed service that is appropriate for the particular period. Many of the unique *līlās* of Lord Kṛṣṇa are described in the *Purāṇas*, such as His pastimes of *bālya* (childhood), *pauganda* (boyhood), and *kiśor* (youth), which are all eternal *līlās* performed in the company of His *sakhās* and *sakhīs*. The devotees will behold a vision of each of these pastimes.

The *līlās* are divided into two types: *prakaṭa* (manifest) and *aprakaṭa* (unmanifest). Those daily pastimes that remain invisible to souls within the material creation are called *aprakaṭa*. The devotees continually engage in remembrance of the *prakaṭa līlās*, and by realizing a *siddha-deha* they reside within Vraja. Just as Kṛṣṇa is eternal, similarly His pastimes are also eternal, and His associates such as boyfriends, girlfriends, fathers and mothers have been described in the *Purāṇas*. All these pastimes of Kṛṣṇa are witnessed by those who become the followers of the cowherd boys, cowherd girls and Kṛṣṇa's superiors.

Oh my dear mind! Just worship Rāma and Kṛṣṇa along with the cowherd boys, and render *aṣṭa-kālīya-sevā* according to the different times of day. Lord Kṛṣṇa's activities within Vraja are enacted only out of pure divine sweetness (*mādhurya*), so please accept the service of such pastimes throughout the day and night. His pastimes of killing demons and so forth are enacted only to display His majestic opulence (*aiśvarya*). Overlooking these things, please render *prema-sevā* (selfless loving service) and you will taste His *mādhurya*.

Now, I will briefly describe the process of *bhajan* performed by those who are inclined toward *rāgānugā* (spontaneous loving devotion), particularly of those who are *priya-sakhā-anugata* – the followers of Kṛṣṇa's dearmost, closest cowherd boyfriends.

Dawn: Lord Kṛṣṇa is Awakened

At dawn, Vṛṣabhānu-pur is very beautiful. In that peaceful atmosphere, all the *priya-sakhās* headed by Śrīdāma are awakened by the sound of Balarāma's buffalo horn. Then the *upa-sakhās* (the greater assembly of cowherd boys) come together and congregate with Śrīdama and Sudāma. After performing their morning duties they all go to the town of Nandiśvar to get the *darśana* of Kṛṣṇa. Śrīdāma, Sudāma, Dāma, Subala, Bhadra-sena, Stoka-Kṛṣṇa, Mahābala, Kiṅkiṇī, Ujjvala, Gobhata, Arjjuna and the other cowherd boys thus travel to the headquarters of Nanda Mahārāja while completely maddened with ecstatic *prema*. Arriving at the palace, they stand out in the courtyard and very jubilantly call, "*Utho! Utho! Kotah Kṛṣṇa?*" ("Get up! Get up! Where is Kṛṣṇa?") This is related in *Śrī-Govinda-līlāmṛtam* (2.8):

> *tāvad gobhaṭa-bhadrasena-subala-śrī-stoka-kṛṣṇarjjunāḥ*
> *śrīdāmojjvala-dāma-kiṅkiṇī-sudāmādyāḥ sakhāyoḥ gṛhāt*
> *āgatya tvaritā mudābhimilitāḥ śrī-sīrinā prāṅgane*
> *kṛṣṇotiṣṭha nijeṣṭha-goṣṭha-maya bho ity āhvayantaḥ sthitāḥ*

At that time Kṛṣṇa's boyfriends Gobhata, Bhadra-sena, Subala, Stoka-Kṛṣṇa, Arjjuna, Śrīdāma, Ujjvala, Dāma, Kiṅkiṇī, Sudāma and the rest hastily arrive from their homes and joyfully meet with Śrī Balarāma out in the courtyard. They stand together and call, "Kṛṣṇa! Get up! Let's go to Your beloved cowshed! *Bho*!"

Then these boys go along with Mother Yaśodā to Kṛṣṇa's sleeping chamber, where He is presently reclining.

navīna ghana-sārābhaṁ
śyāmam pīta-paṭāvṛtam
ratna-pālaṅka-madhyasthaṁ
suṣuptaṁ tatra cintayed

The essential complexion of a fresh raincloud
the dark boy is covered with yellow sheets
Situated upon a fine jewelled bedstead
sleeping – one should meditate on Him there.

In an ornately jewelled temple, lying upon a pleasant bedstead, Nanda-suta is fast asleep amongst the various colorful pillows. At that particular time, everyone first watches Him for a while, then His servants step forward and try to stir Him from His rest. Nanda Rāṇī personally performs the *maṅgal-ārati*, after which she gives Him benedictions while offering freshly cut barley and *durvā* grass. Yaśodā calls Him to give up His rest, and with a damp cloth she cleans the face of the Lord.

In this regard, there is a song by Gokula-candra Dās as follows:

uṭho uṭho mora, nandera nandan,
prabhāta hoilo rāti
aṅgane dāṅḍāyā, royeche sakala,
bālaka tomāra sāthī
mukhera upari, mu 'khāni diyā,
ḍākaye yaśodā rāṇī
koto sukha pāyā, ghumāicho śuyā,
āmi kichu nāhi jāni
nayana meliyā, dekhaho cahiyā,
udoya hoilo bhānu
śrīdāma sudāma, ḍākaye saghana,
utho bhāyyā ohe kānu

aṅga moḍā diyā, uṭhilo satvare,
sundara yādava rāy
mukha prakṣāli, gokula candrahi,
jala jhāri loyā jāy

Get up! Get up, my Nanda-nandana!
The night is over, and morning is here!
Out in the courtyard all of your young boyfriends
are standing and waiting for you!

Thus Yaśodā Rāṇī exclaims to Him while applying a wash-cloth to His face.

How much happiness you get by thus sleeping
and lying about. I cannot understand a bit!
Open up Your eyes and see – the sun has arisen!

Śrīdama and Sudama are also calling very loudly, "*Utho bhāyyā! Ohe Kānu!*" ("Get up, dear brother! O Kānu!") Finally stretching His limbs, the beautiful Yādava Rāi promptly gets up. To go and wash His face, Gokula-candra narrates, He picks up a waterpot and leaves.

Going to Milk the Cows

Having gotten up from bed, Hari sits down on an *āsana* and eats some sweet things given by His mother. Seeing His boyfriends present makes Kṛṣṇa very blissful, and He satisfies all of them according to His inclination of *prema*. Afterwards He ascends a jewelled platform and performs morning duties such as washing His face and brushing His teeth. Then He goes to milk the cows in the company of His boyfriends and servants, sporting in great happiness all the while. Calling each of the cows by name, Kṛṣṇa and Balarāma enter the cowshed in the company of their cowherd boyfriends. Kṛṣṇa calls, "Gangā! Sarali! Kālī! Piśaṅgī! Piyalī! Haṁsi! Sumukhi! Tungī! Vanamāli!" Balarāma also calls His own cows. "Hansinī! Kānāri! Dhavali!" And then they all get busy at once milking the cows. This is described in the *Govinda-līlāmṛtam* 2.37–38:

gopālo 'pi sva-gośālāṁ sa-rāma-madhu-maṅgalaḥ
sakāvya-gīspati sāyaṁ śaśī-vāmbaramāviśaṁ
dadhāra dyusadaṁ rāmo dhavalāvali-veṣṭitah
kailāsa-gaṇḍa-śailālī-madhyasthairāvata-bhramam

As Gopāla entered His own barn along with Rāma and Madhu-maṅgala, He appeared like the moon rising in the twilight sky along with Venus and Jupiter by its side. The demigods mistook Rāma surrounded by the multitudes of cows to be Airāvata, the white elephant-carrier of Lord Indra, surrounded by the vast snow-capped mountain range of Kailāsa.

Kṛṣṇa milks some cows Himself, and He has His servants milk other cows. Finally they complete the sportive pastime of milking the cows.

Dancing in the Morning

Next, various pastimes take place in the company of the cowherd boys. Seeing those sports, Nanda Rāṇī experiences limitless bliss. With Śyāma to the left and Rāma to the right gathering with Śrīdāma and the other boys, they play different types of games while joking, dancing, and singing. Nanda Rāṇī comes out with trays of condensed milk and sweet creamy butter in both of her hands in order to feed Rāma and Kṛṣṇa and their boyfriends. All the boys sit down to eat the *kśīra* and fresh butter. By eating again and again according to the wishes of Mā, they achieve the full relishable taste. Nanda Rāṇī says, "Oh listen Gopāl! Let me see You dance, and then I will give You some sweet tasty butter!"

In this regard there is another song by Gokula-candra Dās, to be sung in any melody thus:

dhoriyā māyera kara, nāce bhālo naṭa-bara,
dadhi dugdha sara nanī lobhe
śyāma-sundara tanu, lāgiyāche tāhe reṇu,
jala-bindhu meghe jeno śobhe
hari mukha cāhi rāṇī, ānande kohoye vāṇī,
nāce bhālo mora yadu-maṇi
hero āiso nanda-rāy, ānanda bahiyā jāy,
dekho nija sutera nācani
śaśi jiti o mukha, dekhiyā sabāra sukha,
āra nāco bole bāra-bāra
heno-kāle nanda āsi, cumba khāya rāśi rāśi,
sukha pāiyā parama āsāra
gopa-gopī cāribhite, ānanda pāiyā cite,
dekhe nṛtya sabe jādu jāra
gokula-candrera vānī, śuno ogo nanda-rāṇī,
nāce bhānu prāṇa sabakāra

Holding onto His mother's hand, the Best of Dancers nicely dances, being desirous of yogurt, milk, condensed milk and cream. Particles of kicked-up dust adhere to the body of Śyāmasundara, appearing splendrous just like drops of water upon a cloud.

Yaśodā Rāṇī looks upon the face of Hari and in great bliss exclaims the words, "You dance very nicely, my Jewel of the Yadus! O Nanda, come and see how much bliss is flowing here! Behold the dancing of your own son!

Everyone is so happy to see that face which conquers the beauty of the full moon, and they say again and again – "Dance more, dance more!" At that time Nanda comes and administers heaps and heaps of kisses, obtaining a torrential downpour of happiness.

The hearts of all the elderly *gopas* and *gopīs* who are presently surrounding this scene attain great bliss to behold the absorbing enchantment of this dancing.

Then Gokula-candra says "Listen, O Nanda Rāṇī! This dancing is only expressing the grace and beauty found in everyone's hearts!"

Grasping Hari by the hand, Nanda Rāṇī pulls Him into her lap and showers His lotus face with seemingly thousands upon thousands of kisses. Filling His hands with *kśīra* and fresh butter, she makes Hari eat again and again while rocking Him in her lap. After washing His mouth He chews betel nuts.

The Cowherd Boys Return to their Homes

Gradually all the cowherd boys personally bid farewell to Kṛṣṇa one by one. Śrīdāma, Sudāma, Dāma, Subala, Ujjvala, Angśu, Bhadra-sena and Mahābala return to their respective homes, and while traveling on the footpath they sing songs of the pastimes of Rāma and Kṛṣṇa.

When Śrīdāma, Sudāma and the other cowherd boy leaders arrive at home, they go and milk their own cows in the company of their boyfriends. After that, their feet are washed by their respective servants, and their limbs massaged with scented oil. They are bathed in warm water, dried off, offered fresh garments, fed sweets and sweet rice and other palatable items, and are given cool water to drink. Then they chew on betel nuts while reclining on pleasant jewelled couches, and take rest for a little while. These pastimes progress up to the fourth *daṇḍa* (7:12–7:36 A.M.) At the appropriate times, in the appropriate ways, these pastimes are visualized by the devotees while services are performed in meditation.

Kṛṣṇa and Balarāma in the Inner Chambers

After the cowherd boys bid farewell from the presence of Kṛṣṇa, then Rāma and Kṛṣṇa go along with their male servants to the inner chambers. Balarāma and Kṛṣṇa sit on divine jewelled seats while the servants massage their limbs with scented oil. Now and then, different cowherd boys gradually arrive from their respective homes. After meeting with them individually, the Brothers come out to congregate with all the assembled Vrajavāsīs. Kṛṣṇa bows at the feet of His father and mother, then goes into the house along with His cowherd boyfriends. Fresh butter, sweet rice, various sweets and *laḍḍus* are shared by Kṛṣṇa, Balarāma and their friends. Afterwards reclining on their *āsanas* and chewing betel nuts, they greet their friends Śrīdāma and Sudāma and others when they return. There is much outrageous fun in joking along with Śrīdāma and the boys. Thus in the company of the *priya-sakhās* they relish the enjoyment of great and robust bliss.

Then there is some whispering and secret discussions with Subala and others. At that time Madhu-maṅgala and his friends arrive and meet with them. It is a mind-enchanting scene of Rāma and Kṛṣṇa sitting in the center while the assembly of their cowherd boyfriends surround them on all sides. To Kṛṣṇa's right sits Śrī Balarāma, whose eyes madly roll about. He is dressed in the costume of a wrestler. He is the best of dancers, and He is the enchanter of Cupid. According to the time and situation, the devotees who are following the cowherd boys (*sakhānuga*) render service that is in accordance with their own most cherished ambition.

To the Sporting Arena

Then all the boys get up and proceed to the *Raṅga-sthala,* their Sporting Arena. There they engage in mock fighting with Śrīdāma and the others. Subala watches these boyish antics from the sidelines, and his limbs appear greatly thrilled by exchanging joking words and wise-cracking comments with some cowherd boy associate. Afterwards wandering to this place and that place, all the boys admire the different kinds of animals and birds. They listen to the recitations of the *śārī* and *śuka* parrots, and watch the dancing of the peacocks.

To the Morning Meal

Meanwhile, in the kitchen Śrīmatī Rohiṇī is busy cooking various kinds of rice, vegetables, sweet rice, and so forth. After the cooking is finished and the kitchen is nicely cleaned, all the foodstuffs are sent out and placed on a wonderful jewelled platform.

When Yaśodā calls, Kṛṣṇa and all the other boys proceed toward the kitchen. Groups of servants wash the boys feet, and the entire assembly comes into the dining hall. Rāma and Kṛṣṇa sit down upon a golden platform. To their left, facing north, sits the group of cowherd boys headed by Subala. To Kṛṣṇa's right sits Balarāma, Nanda, Upananda, and the cowherd boys headed by Śrīdāma, Sudāma and others. Śrīmatī Rohiṇī serves the nice foodstuffs consisting of various types of rice and vegetables that are dripping with ghee. After the meal is finished, the boys wash their mouths and then go to recline on *āsanas* and chew betel nuts. All the cowherd boys bid farewell and return to their respective homes, where they mitigate their fatigue by reclining upon wonderful and colorful couches. Their servants render *sevā* by massaging their feet. At this time, those in their *siddha-deha* behold that vision, which is depicted as follows:

> *itthaṁ bhuktvā tu govindo bhrātṛbhiḥ sakhībhir mudā*
> *ācamya bhakṣayet pūrṇaṁ tataḥ śayyāṁ samāviśet*
>
> After Govinda thus happily eats along with His brother and friends, He washes up, chews betel, and then reclines upon a couch.

Preparations for Herding the Cows

After one *daṇḍa* passes (24 minutes), they arise and rinse out their mouths with scented water. Again they chew betel nuts that are scented with camphor, and they go outside to sit on divine *āsanas*. Gradually Śrīdāma, Sudāma, Subala, Stoka-Kṛṣṇa, Angśu, Bhadra-sena, Mahābala and all the other boys individually come and meet with Kṛṣṇa, who becomes very blissful upon seeing His friends. Śrīdāma steps forward and exclaims, "O Son of Nanda! Today I will herd the cows in the playful fun of Your company!" But Mother Yaśomatī hears this talk of going to the forest, and she becomes very disturbed at heart and cannot calm her mind. She exclaims, "Śrīdāma! Sudāma! *Ore!* What are you saying? Why are you telling tales suggesting that such young children will go to the forest? All of you are the wealth of my soul and indeed the pupils of my eyes! Not seeing Hari for even a second, I become blind! If Hari were to step outside this house to play, then for even that brief moment of not seeing Him I shall be unable to maintain my life!" Balarāma smiles and smiles and comes before Mother Yaśodā, announcing, "I personally accept full responsibility for Kānāi in the forest. I will take Him along in the midst of the assembly of boys, and will keep Him right in front of me at all times. I will not even let Him go alone to the bank of the Yamunā River. We feel great happiness by playing in the company of Kānu. For this reason, all of these cowherd boys are now gazing at His moonlike face!"

Then Śrīdāma stands up and says, "Listen Yaśomatī! Hari is the very life-force of all these boys. He is their best friend!" Hearing this statement, Nanda Rāṇī replies, "O listen, Śrīdāma! Hari is the wealth of my life and Balarāma is my eyes. Without my eyes or life, how will I remain alive? Without Rāma and Kṛṣṇa, a single *daṇḍa* seems like the passing of hundreds of *yugas*!" Then Balarāma becomes solicitous and says, "Mātā, please don't worry about Gopāl! For those born of the *vaiśya* caste, life is centered around cows; indeed, protecting cows is their *dharma*. Without practically learning these things, how can we properly perform the occupational duties of cowherders?" Hearing this statement by Rāma, Nanda Rāṇī replies with faltering words, and upon hearing her statement the cowherd boys begin to smile. She says, "Listen dear son Balarāma! I make this request of you: I ask that you do not take Hari to any forest that is very far away. Please remain close by the Yamunā River and you can graze the cows there. But no matter what anyone says, you are not to go to any forests that are very far away. Only under these conditions, Haladhar, can you take my Kṛṣṇa along!"

Dressing Kṛṣṇa and Balarama

After saying this, Mother Yaśodā commences decorating Kṛṣṇa with clothing and ornaments, feeling very blissful inside. She ties His turban, fixes His crown, puts a peacock feather upon it, and weaves strands of *guñjā* berries and fresh twigs upon it. She arranges the tresses of His hair and paints *tilak* on His forehead with musk-paste. She fixes long earrings that dangle upon His two round cheeks, and places a pearl on the forward part of His nose. She puts jewelled necklaces around His conchshell-smooth neck, and places a forest-flower garland upon His chest that is marked with *śrīvatsa*. She puts bangles on His wrists and armlets on His arms. She ties the strings to secure His waistbell ornament, and fixes it upon His waist that looks like that of a lion. His costume as the best of dramatic dancers (*naṭa-bara*) is further adorned by many decorations being added to it. Kṛṣṇa's thighs conquer the beauty of banana tree trunks, and his eyebrows look like curved bows shooting the arrows of Cupid. His feet are adorned with ankle-bells, and in His hand is an enchanting flute.

Thus decorating Rāma and Kṛṣṇa, Mother Yaśodā looks upon both their faces. She thinks to herself, "How could I possibly let them go?" but the words do not even come out of her mouth. She showers the faces of Rāma and Kṛṣṇa with seemingly thousands upon thousands of kisses while her body becomes overwhelmed with ecstatic bliss. Chanting a *mantra-kavaca* as a shield, she bathes both of their bodies with the nectar-tears falling from her eyes.

The Cowherding Party Assembles

Thereafter, Balarāma blows his buffalo horn to signal all the cowherd boys headed by Śrīdāma and Sudāma to assemble there. The four directions resound with the auspicious vibrations of "*Jai! Jai!* All glories! All glories!" while the *brāhmaṇas* recite Vedic hymns of glorification. All the cowherd boys come forward and bow down to Rāṇī, and then Kṛṣṇa and Balarāma offer prayers at the feet of their Mā. The cowherd men headed by Nanda and his brothers Upananda, Sananda, and the others ceremoniously offer

Kṛṣṇa into the hands of His boyfriends. All the elderly *gopas* and *gopīs*, who are full of tearful eyes and wet faces, gaze upon the countenances of Rāma and Kṛṣṇa. The two boys first offer respects to their mother and father, and then offer respects to their other superiors as the *brāhmaṇas* chant, "*Ciraṁ jiva! Ciraṁ jīva!* May you live long! May you live long!"

Then Nanda Lāl, the dear son of Mahārāja Nanda, comes out of the house, keeping in front of Him uncountable cows and limitless cowherd boyfriends. Thus I have spoken of the pastimes commencing from *prātaḥ-kāla*, morning time. For the period of one *prahar*, Kṛṣṇa is situated within the assembly of His father's royal palace. The *darśana* of this *līlā* will be seen by the *bhaktas*. Afterwards, at the tenth *daṇḍa* (9:36–10:00 A.M.) they all leave for the pasturelands. All glories, all glories to Rāma-Kṛṣṇa, and the assembly of their boyfriends! There will certainly be bliss for one who hears the narration of this book.

Thus ends the seventh chapter of

Śrī Śrī Preyo-Bhakti-Rasārṇava

CHAPTER EIGHT

Pūrvahna-Kalīya-Sevā:
Services During Forenoon Pastimes
(8:24–10:48 A.M.)

go-gopālaḥ ganāvītaṁ
govindaṁ goṣṭha-gaṁ mudā
rāmena ramaṇa-śyāmaṁ
vande 'ham vana-mālinam

Surrounded by the cows and cowherd boys,
Govinda happily proceeds
toward the pastureland.
That beloved dark boy who is accompanied by Rāma
I bow to the one adorned
with a garland of forest flowers.

All glories to Rāma-Kṛṣṇa, Śrīdāma, and Sudāma! All glories, all glories to the Vrajavāsīs and to Vṛndāvana dhām!

The Cowherding Procession Leaves Town

Keeping countless thousands upon thousands of cows and calves before them, thousands and thousands of cowherd boys run behind and surround them. The boys sound their buffalo horn bugles "*Dhaan! Dhaan!*" and they make the cows move along by shouting "*Hai! Hai!*" and "*Aha! Aha!*" There are pleasant musical sounds that proclaim divine auspiciousness being played on small *veṇu* flutes, stringed *vīṇās*, and long *murlī* flutes that accompany their joyful singing. The entire sphere of Gokula-mandala becomes completely pervaded by these sounds, and the air vibrates with the echoes of limitless *dumpha* tambourines, *mṛdaṅga* drums, and *madala* tom-toms. The young girls of Vraja come outside, and they all turn their faces in the same direction to watch Rāma and Kṛṣṇa. Many of the beautiful girls chant the auspicious sound "*Jai! Jai!*" while others standing here and there by the side of the road recite *mangalācaraṇa* prayers of invocation.

The main gate through which the cows and boys will pass is nicely decorated with full water pots, mango branches, banana leaves, flower garlands, mounds of white rice, and flags. All the boys run along carrying mesh lunch bags brought from their own homes, within which are four kinds of foodstuffs. They shout the cowherding sounds "*Aba! Aba!*" clap their hands and call "*Hai! Hai! Aha! Aha!*" which makes the cows jump, collide into each other, and then begin moving forward.

Mother Yaśomatī has been following them up to the halfway point out of town, and there she offers Hari into the hands of His most beloved friends. She says, "Take away my very life-force and go to the forest! Please pay careful attention that He will be protected at all times. Now this body of mine, completely bereft of life, will simply remain motionless at home!" Then Nanda Rāṇī just stands there, gazing with fixed attention as tears cascade from her lotus eyes, soaking her own clothes. Nanda, Upananda, and other superiors instruct the boys in the proper techniques for tending the cows. Everyone follows the boys and cows to the outskirts of the town, being unable to give them up, and keeps watching until they approach the edge of the forest. Nanda Mahārāja cannot keep his composure, nor can he turn his eyes away. Again, again and yet again, he looks upon the moonlike face of Hari. The two brothers finally bow to their father, take their boyfriends and drive the cows forward. All the men and women of Vraja just stand there with their faces lifted, up to the very last moment that Hari remains within their vision. Afterwards, all the cowherd girls along with Nanda and the other townspeople sadly return to their respective homes with tearful eyes.

Blissful Boys in the Pasture

The two brothers Rāma and Kṛṣṇa then decorate the pastureland with their presence along with countless boys and countless cows. What can I say about the splendor of all these boys together? The scene looks just like the glowing full moon surrounded by the host of stars. Some boys, of the same age as Kṛṣṇa and Balarāma, consider themselves on an exactly equal level. They have the same way of arranging their dress and ornaments, and their beauty is the same. Some boys are younger, some boys are older, and others only think of themselves as being younger or older; among these groups, their dress and ornaments are all similar. The boys also have many different complexions. Some are darkish (*śyāma*), some are white, some are yellow, some are lotus-colored, some are like sapphires, some are variegated (of many colors), some are red, some are fair-golden (*gaura*), some are pale yellow, and some are tawny brown. They are decorated with various ornaments made of jewels, pearls, and gold. Wearing colorful turbans of blue, yellow, white and red, they hold flutes, *vīṇās,* sticks for driving the cows, walking sticks and fighting sticks. They wear artistic loincloths, and their garments are arranged just like dramatic actors. Lavishly decorated from the tops of their heads to the tips of their toes, they sport *vaijayantī* garlands woven from colorfully variegated forest flowers.

Thus the young boys of Vraja proceed along, driving the cows with shouts of "*Hai! Hai!*" while in the midst of them Rāma and Kṛṣṇa are merrily dancing and dancing. The cowherd boys then enter into the forest of Vṛndāvana, the place of supreme secrets that are limitless and particularly transcendental. There they begin performing various excellent pastimes such as dancing, singing, rolling on the ground, laughing, and exhibiting great boyish pride. The pastimes they enjoyed on the previous day are then recounted aloud and all of them gather together to perform various confidential sports. Some boys blow their buffalo horn bugles, some fill the air with flute sounds, some make sounds with their throats, some call the calves with their flutes, and some make loud shouts. Thus they all exhibit various talents.

Pastimes in Bhāṇḍiṛavan

Someone calls for Kānāi and says, "*Bhāi re!* O brother! Let's all go and play at the base of the Bhāṇḍīra tree!" Thus the boys all proceed to the forest called Bhāṇḍiṛavan. This place is nicely colored and scented by a myriad of blossoming flowers. There are limitless kinds of diverse birds there. The sweetly-scented breeze flows very gently, while male and female bees buzz and peacocks joyfully dance. All the leaves, twigs and flowers are extremely soft and pleasant. It is very cool in the shade underneath the very charming banyan tree called Bhāṇḍiṛa. The trunk of the tree is surrounded with solid gold, and in front of it is a raised platform. On that platform, Guṇa-nidhī (Kṛṣṇa, the abode of all divine qualities) briefly rests for one *daṇḍa* (24 minutes) with His cowherd boyfriends. During that period of rest there is an opportunity for those who are followers of the cowherd boys to render services. The different episodes of Kṛṣṇa's playful pastimes at Bhāṇḍiṛavan are causes of pure astonishment. Devotees should contemplate performing services in their *siddha-deha* during each of those pastimes.

Kṛṣṇa's complexion is just like clusters of melted black eye-ointment buffed to a lustrous shine. He wears yellow cloth and adornments that conquer the best of dramatic actors. A pair of earrings dangle from His ears, and they swing upon His two cheeks. He has nice *tilak* painted on His forehead with dark musk, and around His neck is a flower garland. His face is soft and soothing like the full moon in the autumn month of Śarat. The dot of bright *candan* on His forehead appears like the moon arisen from behind a dark cloud. His eyes are spread wide just like *indīvara* lotus petals, and His eyebrows look like bows of Cupid. Such a *rūpa-mādhurī* (pure sweetness of transcendental beauty) cannot be found anywhere else! Upon His head is a nice turban crowned with a peacock feather and is tied with strands of flowers, which attract bumblebees to hover about as they float from flower to flower.

To the right of Śyāma stays Haladhar Rāma, and on either side stays Śrīdāma and Sudāma. At that lovely place the assembly of boys begin to dance. In the center is Śrīdāma, Sudāma and

Kṛṣṇa-candra, dancing with Balarāma. Kṛṣṇa's sports at Bhāṇḍīravan are so extremely enchanting that we have composed some nice verses to describe it. Please listen.

Song to be sung in the melody of *Tudi rāga:*

sakhā saṅge raṅge hari kori nṛtya gāna
kṣaṇeka basiyā tāhā korilā viśrāma
tārapara nānā miṣṭha sāmagrī bhakṣaṇa
suśītala jala-pāna pūṛna ācamana

sakarpūra tāmbula tahā korilā bhakṣaṇa
sucandra pabhṛti kore aṅga samvāhana
madhura ukti narma-kathā subalādi sane
hāsya-parihāsa kore loiyā priya-gaṇe

bāhu-yuddha daṇḍādaṇḍi hastāhasti kriyā
laguḍālaguḍi yuddha priya sakhā loiyā
vāhya vāhaka-krīḍā koroye kakhana
skandhe vahi loiyā jāy hāraye ye jana

eka-bāra rāmera gana krīḍā jinilo
śrīdāmake kori skandhe kānāi rohilo
kabhu śrīdāmera skandhe cāpe bhagavān
jāre sambhavaye sei-bhāve nayana

In the company of the cowherd boys Hari plays, and they dance and sing. Then they sit down and rest for a few moments. Afterwards they eat various kinds of sweet preparations, drink very cool water, and when they're done they wash their mouths.

Next they chew on betel scented with camphor, as the boys headed by Sucandra massage the limbs of Kṛṣṇa and Balarāma. They share sweet statements and jokes with Subala and the other dear ones amidst much smiling, joking and laughter.

> Then Kṛṣṇa and Balarāma take their dearmost friends and begin mock fighting sports. They play arm-wrestling, stick-fighting, hand-boxing, and club-fighting amongst the *priya-sakhās*. Next they play a game in which the losers of a contest must carry the winners upon their shoulders.
>
> Once while playing this game, Balarāma's group was victorious, so Kānāi was obliged to take Śrīdāma upon His own shoulders. Sometimes on other occasions, Bhagavān sits upon the shoulders of Śrīdāma. Whoever believes that these things are possible will accordingly behold them with their own eyes.

Thus along with Śrīdāma and the other cowherd boys, they play the game of riding upon each other's shoulders. At anytime anyone can conquer anyone, for they all play as equals. Sometimes they dance and dance and play musical instruments with great joy in their hearts. With delightful abandon they imitate the warbling sounds and the walking style of the swans. Some of them imitate the sounds of the cuckoos and peacocks, while others race around in imitation of the monkeys. Some assume very fearsome stances by imitating the walking of lions and tigers. Thus the cowherd boys make different kinds of jokes while feeling great bliss in their hearts. After this, the two brothers Kṛṣṇa and Balarāma are rendered various services, and after that the assembly proceeds toward Gokula. In this way, they spend up to the twelfth *daṇḍa* (10:24–10:48 A.M.) playing in the forest of Bhāṇḍīra. Consequently the *līlā-sukha* (happiness of the pastimes) of Rāma and Kṛṣṇa is very wonderful.

Pastimes in Kāmyavan

Then taking along the *sakhās* and *upa-sakhās* they arrive at the forest of Kāmyakavan while driving and driving the cows and calves ahead of them. The forest of Śrī Kāmya is very dear to Śrī Kṛṣṇa, and He performs many secret pastimes here along with

His boyfriends. All the cows become very excited and proceed quickly while Kṛṣṇa is immersed in bliss enjoying the pastimes of the cowherd boys. Thus they dance, sing, and make jokes. From a distance, a cowherd boy runs as he exclaims to the others, "I will go ahead of you and touch Kānāi first!" Another boy takes flowers in his hand and speaks to Śrī Kṛṣṇa, "I am unable to run!" while grasping and tugging on Kṛṣṇa's garment. Some boys climb up in the trees and pick freshly ripened fruits, while someone narrates into Śrī Kṛṣṇa's ears the beauty of the borderings around the flower gardens. The very sight of the forest locations here and there is a most auspicious and mysterious vision. The splendor of these forests is limitless and cannot possibly be described.

Upon the lakes are blossoming lotus flowers of the variety *kamala* and *kahlār*, and from each flower is heard the resounding buzzing of limitless bees. There are diverse species of flowers scattered about, including land-growing lotuses as well as water-growing lotuses, lily-of-the-valley and also *nāgeśvar, campaka, kunda, tagara*, and *mālatī*. Here and there are secret forest places shining with the splendor of the mysterious *kalpa-vṛkṣa* trees. Thus wandering this way and that, all the cowherd boys and the cows arrive on the bank of the Yamunā River. The boys drink the water of the Yamunā by filling their palms, and then they jump in to have a big water fight. After finishing their water sports, they come up on the bank of the river and put on dry clothes.

Pastimes in Bahulāvan

Next the multitudes of cowherd boys signal the cows with their flutes, thereby gathering them together, and they all move along toward the forest of Bahulāvan. Having gone to that forest they converge at the base of a celestial *santāna* tree, and from there they become very ecstatic by viewing the area around that place. The boys pick forest flowers and weave different kinds of garlands. Collecting forest minerals of various colors, they decorate their bodily limbs.

Śrīdāma comes forward and says, O Nanda-nandana! Our bodies are agitated by hunger and our mouths are all dried up! From home we brought four kinds of foods: there are many different varieties of curries, fried foods, sweet rice, and spicy minced vegetables. Sitting down in this place, please enjoy a forest feast! After that then we will again be able to run around along with the cowherd boys!" Hearing this speech, Hari replies, "*Bhālo! Bhālo!* Very good, very nice idea! Due to being so engrossed in playing games today, it has gotten very late. Bring forward the plates and set them up in rows. Spread out the cloth and place the containers of foodstuffs upon it." Thus all the cowherd boys sit around in a circle, keeping Kṛṣṇa in the center, and they enjoy great fun and mischief while partaking of this forest feast. Eating and eating the nice foodstuffs, they relish a myriad of wonderful tastes, and they also accept the remnants that touch the lips of Kṛṣṇa.

Thus Bhagavān, the Supreme Personality of Godhead, enjoys a grand picnic in the company of His cowherd boyfriends, after which they go to a charming pond to drink its water. Then Lord Hari washes His mouth, sits upon a raised platform and accepts betel nuts to chew.

The cowherd boy servants wave fans and *cāmara* whisks while some servant massages His lotus feet. Then He takes a very brief rest. I behold these pastimes of the assembly of cowherd boys occuring at the thirteenth and fourteenth *daṇḍas* (10:48–11:12, 11:12–11:36 A.M.) and therefore I write of such *līlās*. During these same periods being described, the *sādhaka* performs *sevā* in great fun, sporting in his *siddha-deha* along with his *guru-rūpa-sakhā,* his spiritual master in the form of a cowherd boy.

Pastimes in Madhuvan

After wandering around throughout the forest of Bahulāvan the groups of *sakhas, upa-sakhās,* and all the cows and calves then proceed to the forest of Madhuvan. Stopping by the pond called Madhu-kund, Balarāma commences the sport of drinking honey. Dressed like a wrestler, Lord Haladhar then takes a little rest.

Govinda sits at the base of the wrestling-tree, surrounded in all four directions by the assembly of His friends. What can I say of the glory of the jewelled altar radiating the aura of pure gold? On the right side of Kṛṣṇa is Rāma who shines with the effulgence of a silver mountain. Rāma's eyes are rolling and his lips are trembling, and due to drinking excessive amounts of intoxicating honey his body and limbs are shivering. Seeing the bewildered and ridiculous actions of Balarāma, the assembly of boys are overjoyed, and they play with him by making different kinds of jokes and laughter. Śrī Baladeva, who is known as Rohiṇī-kumār (the darling boy of mother Rohiṇī), sits to Kṛṣṇa's right, and they are encircled by the cowherd boys headed by Śrīdāma, Subala, Ujjvala, Madhu-maṅgala, and others who are all exuberantly drinking honey by the bank of Madhu-kund.

Then Bhagavān initiates the sport of playing with a ball in the company of the cowherd boys. But there is no one among them who could possibly equal Balarāma in his skill at playing ball. A boy catches the ball and runs chasing the others while everyone shouts, "Get them! Hit them with the ball!" Some boys run far away and hide behind trees. One brother shouts, "Śāntalī! Śāntalī! Over here!" If anyone gets hit with the ball then they become prisoners of Balarāma. In this way numerous fun games are performed at Madhuvan as the *sādhaka* devotees follow these pastimes according to the time of day and render appropriate services within the mind.

Pastimes by the Bank of the Yamunā River

After playing games in the forest of Madhuvan, Kṛṣṇa and Balarāma take their cowherd boyfriends to a forest on the bank of the Yamunā River and sit down. The cows come to the bank of the Yamunā and drink the water, and then lie down to rest at the base of *kadamba* trees. After drinking the refreshing water the cows become very happy to be in the shade, and in great bliss some feed their calves milk. At that place Balarāma and Kṛṣṇa take rest in the company of *sakhās* and *upa-sakhās* like Śrīdāma and Sudāma.

Various fruits are picked and set around in a festive array including the stems of lotuses, jackfruit, bananas, marmelos, mangoes and *piyāla* nuts. Thus various fruits from the water and from the land are collected and prepared, and then Rāma and Kṛṣṇa along with their cowherd boyfriends commence eating. After that they wash their mouths and chew on betel nuts while gazing at the splendor of the forest with blissful minds.

There in the shelter of very cooling shade, all the cowherd boys collect soft leaves and flowers one by one.

Using various species of fresh twigs and flowers they construct a divine throne on top of the jewelled platform. This platform is surrounded on all four sides by auspicious trees and vines adorned with flowers, from which the buzzing of bees can be heard. Many types of birds make soft sweet sounds. The bees madly wander from tree to tree in search of honey. This entire forest is perfumed with a myriad of pleasant fragrances. A single divine mystery that is pervaded with perpetual bliss thus wanders all about the forest.

Kṛṣṇa's Bathing Ceremony and Coronation

Śrīdāma and Sudāma then exclaim, "What can we say about this splendrous display? The aura at the trunks of these trees conquers the magnificence of King Indra's heavenly abode! We have made a lion-throne out of flowers and twigs, and upon that throne we will install Śrī Nanda-nandana as the king. Here in this forest on the bank of the Yamunā River, Kṛṣṇa will become the monarch and all of us will become his subjects! We will mitigate the fear of evil King Kaṁsa and will put an end to all wicked activities, thus enveloping cowherd boys everywhere in pure bliss!" Hearing this, all the *sakhās* become very jubilant and start arranging the magnificent royal coronation ceremony of Balarāma and Kṛṣṇa. They seat Hari upon the lion-throne made of flowers and, bringing water from the Yamunā River, they perform His *abhiṣek* (bathing ceremony). Thus the auspicious sounds of "*Jai! Jai!*" resound throughout that forest as each and every boy present shouts "*Jai Kṛṣṇa! Kṛṣṇa!*"

The two brothers are surrounded on all sides by cowherd boy-friends; some are standing far away, while others are standing nearby. Balarāma is to the right side of Kṛṣṇa, and on Kṛṣṇa's left is Śrīdāma. Closest are Sudāma and Vasudāma and others. In front of Kṛṣṇa and Balarāma are Subala, Ujjvala and Madhu-maṅgala, being members of the *narma* class of *sakhās,* and they converse about numerous confidential topics. Bhadra-sena stands behind Kṛṣṇa and Balarāma holding up the umbrella, while Śāraṅga Gopāl stands holding a water pot. Bhagavān leans upon the shoulder of Śrīdāma while Suviśāla and Viśālākśa prepare and offer betel. Rasāla arranges their garments while Kusumollāsa applies *chandan.* Puṣpa-hāsa and others render service to their various bodily limbs. The servants headed by Raktaka and Patraka hold their buffalo horn bugles and walking sticks. Madhu-vrata and others wave *cāmara* whisks while Sura-bandha, Karpura, Kusuma and others massage Kṛṣṇa's lotus feet. At this very time the *sādhaka* realizes the *siddha-deha* and renders services while remaining under the shelter of the *guru-rūpa-sakhā,* spiritual master as cowherd boy.

A Meditation on Kṛṣṇa's Lovely Form

Now, in that regard here is a *dhyāna:*

nava-jala-dhara-varṇa cikkana ujjvala
sūrya-koṭi sama-prabhā candra-koṭi śītala
cāru pītāmbara śobhā vidyutera jyoti
mukutā grathita mālā jeno baka-pāṅti

Colored like a fresh raincloud
  but smooth, lustrous and brilliant . . .
Radiant like millions of suns
  yet cooling like millions of moons.
Charming yellow cloth splendrous
  like the effulgence of lightning.
Pearl necklace like a row of white herons.

nitya nava yauvana sundara kalevara
koṭi kandarpa nindi varaṇa sundara
nitya-līlā sukhānanda-magna sakhā-gaṇa
vṛndāvana pura-pati rāja vilasana

Whose lovely form is eternally
in the bloom of fresh youth.
Beautiful complexion conquering millions of Cupids.
Whose cowherd boyfriends are deeply engrossed
in the blissful happiness of eternal pastimes.
The Monarch of the town of Vṛndāvana.
The King who likes to enjoy sportive delights.

kandarpa dhanuka jini bhru-yugala śobhā
kapāle candana-bindu śaśadhara ābhā
alakā kuntala tāhe śire śikhi-pakhā
kasturi tilaka bhāle candanera rekhā

Whose two eyebrows vanquish
the splendor of Cupid's bow.
The dots of *chandan* upon His cheeks
are radiant like full moons.
Whose curling locks and tresses
are topped by a peacock's tailfeather.
Dark musk-paste *tilak* upon His forehead
is bordered by lines of bright *chandan*.

kaṭi-taṭe pīta-dhatī kāñcīra sahite
kari śuṇḍa bhuja-yuga valayā tahāte
nakha-gaṇa koṭi candra kore jhalamala
rakta kiśalaya dyuti ati kara-tala

Upon His hips is a yellow *dhotī*
along with a belt of tinkling bells.
His two arms look like the trunks of elephants
and are adorned with bracelets.
His fingernails shimmer like millions of moons.

The palms of His hands have the glowing
  reddish luster of fresh young leaf-shoots.

caraṇe rañjita baṅka nūpura śobhita
jāhā dekhi mane hoy madana lobhita
dakṣiṇe śrī-balarāma candramā baraṇa
nīla-paṭṭa paridhāna ghūrnita locana

His feet resound with the splendor
  of anklebells placed at a slant.
Seeing which brings to mind
  these are enticing even for Cupid.
To Kṛṣṇa's right is Śrī Balarāma
  whose complexion is like the full moon.
He is wearing blue cloth
  and his eyes are rolling in intoxication.

śrīdāmera gaura-kānti aṅga jhalamala
sudāma prabhṛti kṛṣṇa veṣṭhita sakala
rāja-lakṣaṇa-yukta rāja ābharana
rāja patra mitra saba saṅge sakhā-gaṇa

Next to him is Śrīdāṃa whose fair-golden
  bodily complexion is sparkling.
Thus Kṛṣṇa is completely surrounded
  by all the boys headed by Sudāma.
They tend to Him with royal ornaments
  and paraphernalia engraved opulently
    with royal symbols.
In the company of the cowherd boys
  they act out dramatic roles
    as if they were royal ministers,
      counsellors, friends and so forth.

At this time those devotees who are taking shelter of the mood of Sudāma (*sudāma-bhāvāśritā*) should perform services by following humbly in the footsteps of Śrī Sudāma-candra. Please serve Balarāma and Kṛṣṇa in accordance with your own most cherished goal, while in contemplation of their *svarūpa-veśa* (ontological guise).

Thus the *pūrvahna-sevā* or services rendered during the forenoon period extend up to the fifteenth *daṇḍa* (11:36–12:00 noon). Now I will speak of the *madhyāhna-sevā* or services rendered during the midday period. Please listen with undivided attention. By the mercy of Śrī Caitanya, Nityānanda and Sundarānanda Ṭhākura, this Nayanānanda sings the book *Preyo-Bhakti-Rasārṇava*.

Thus ends the eighth chapter of
Śrī Śrī Preyo-Bhakti-Rasārṇava

CHAPTER NINE

Madhyāhna-Kālīya-Seva and *Aparāhna-Kālīya-Seva*

Services During Midday and Afternoon Pastimes

(10:48 A.M.–3:36 P.M. and 3:36–6:00 P.M.)

namaḥ kamala-netrāya
srag-viṇe pīta-vāsase
cāru-citra śikhanḍāya
namas tasmai ghana-tviṣe

Obeisances to He of lotus-petal eyes
to He who wears flower garlands and yellow cloth
to He who wears a lovely peacock feather
Obeisances to He whose complexion
is raincloud-dark!

Glory to Hari, the Son of Nanda, to Giridhārī, the lifter of Govardhana Hill! Glory to Haladhar, the holder of the plow, and to Yamunā-tīra Bihārī, who sports on the bank of the Yamunā River! Glory glory to Śrīdāma, Sudāma and all the assembled cowherd boys! Glory, glory to Śrī Gokula, the moon over Gokula, along with all His associates!

Games by the Bank of the Yamunā

After that, during *madhyahna-kāla* (the midday period), Balarāma and Kṛṣṇa play numerous games along with their boyfriends at the base of a *kadamba* tree by the bank of the Yamunā. They make jokes and laugh and engage in various kinds of mischievous pranks. Wandering around as a single group they pick forest flowers. In eagerness to find fresh green grasses the cows have wandered off a little, and now all the cowherd boys follow behind and tend to them. They protect the cows very carefully out of fear of King Kaṁsa and therefore always keep the cows right by their sides at all times. In this way I have described how Hari engages all the boys in herding the cows. Kṛṣṇa personally plays games with Subala, Arjjuna, Haladhar, Śrīdāma, Sudāma, Subhadra, Maṇḍalī-bhadra, and Vasudāma. Thus Gopa-Kānta, the beloved of the cowherd boys, frolics on the bank of the Yamunā River. It should be known that these sportive pastimes continue up to the sixteenth *daṇḍa* (12:00 noon–12:24 P.M.)

Pastimes in Śrīvan

After that Śrī Nanda-suta, along with Subala and several other confidential friends, leaves the general assembly of boys and goes to a solitary place on the pretext of searching for some stray cows. At that time, Haladhar takes charge of all the cowherd boys headed by Śrīdāma, and they go to the forest of Śrīvan to search for other cows. While tending the cows, Balarāma and the other boys perform numerous sports while enjoying the pastimes of boyhood. They pick flowers, climb trees and enjoy tasting fresh fruits. They dance and sing and clap their hands, and play their armpits in a musical way. They jump here and there and exclaim "*Aba! Aba!*" while herding the cows, and they play on flutes and buffalo horn bugles. They behold the splendor of the visions of the forest, decorate their bodies with red clay pigments, and with the gait of maddened elephants they flail their limbs as they run. Thus the cowherd boys play in the company of Rāma and wander throughout this forest of Śrīvan up until the eighteenth *daṇḍa* (12:48–1:12 P.M.)

Pastimes in Kumudavan

After this, Balabhadra accompanied by Śrīdāma, Sudāma and the others proceed to the forest of Kumudavan. In this forest the various blossoming flowers sweeten the breeze, the bees sing and the peacocks dance. The *śārī* and *śuka* parrots chant and the cuckoos make the sound "*kuhu, kuhu*." The forest birds all chirp as the cranes and herons warble. Haladhar then begins arm-wrestling and stick-fighting along with Subhadra, Maṇḍālī-bhadra and other boyfriends. Many birds sit in the trees making diverse kinds of chirping sounds, and some of the boys imitate those same sounds. Some boys dance just like the peacocks do, and some of them walk just like the swans do. Someone imitates a maddened elephant and someone acts just like a lion. Others move like frogs, others move like snakes, others move like baby elephants. Thus the boys play childish games, swimming in the *rasa*-laden mellow-sports of Rāma's company. In this regard there is the following song:

nāce haladhara saṅge, sahacara ānande,
bālaka meliyā
jeno ghanāgame, nāce śikhi-gaṇe,
kāme unamatta hoiyā
valayā kaṅkane, nūpura caraṇe,
rana-ghana bājai
kare kara dhori, koriyā kuṇḍalī,
haladhara nācai
śrīdāma sudāma, subhadra arjjuna,
kare dhore bani tāla
viśāla vṛṣabha, bhadra mahābala,
kohe nāce bhāyyā bhālo
tā dekhi vipine, mṛga pakṣi-gaṇe,
ānande avaśa hoiyā
gāyata kokila, śikhi-kula nāce,
haladhara mukha cāyā
bhramara bhramarī, uḍata parikara,
pika-rava beḍiyā
e dāsa nayana, ānande magana,
vipina bihāra dekhiyā

Dancing in the company of Haladhar, the boys mingle with their friends in great bliss just as the peacocks become maddened with desire and dance when the rainclouds arrive.

By their bracelets, bangles, and bells upon their ankles, they resound with profuse dance vibrations. Holding hands and forming a circle, Haladhar dances.

Śrīdāma is there plus Sudāma, Subhadra, and Arjjuna, holding hands and dancing to the beat.

Also Viśāla, Vṛṣabha, Bhadra, Mahābala. While they are dancing they exclaim, "*Bhāyyā bhālo!* Oh, brother! Very nice dancing!"

Beholding this sight within the forest, the animals and the birds become stunned in bliss. The cuckoos sing as the peacocks dance, all gazing at the face of Haladhar.

The male and female bees fly around in groups and the sound of the cuckoos is all-pervading. This servant named Nayana is immersed in bliss beholding these sports in the forest.

Thus Śrī Rāma becomes flushed with color while performing these fun pastimes within the forest of Kumudavan. Sitting down at that place they eat some sweet preparations. Thus the cow-herd boys are situated in Kumudavan until the twentieth *daṇḍa* (1:36–2:00 PM).

Pastimes in Bhadravan

After that everyone leaves to go to the forest of Bhadravan. Śrīdāma, Sudāma, and all the other boys in their company enjoy various mellows with Balabhadra as they wander from forest to forest. Arriving in front of Śyāma-kunda, everyone becomes ecstatic to behold the splendrous beauty of that divine lake. Śyāma-kunda is embellished with various trees and creepers embracing each other. Numerous types of flowers are blooming as bees fly from blossom to blossom. At that place they rest briefly at the base of a *tamāl* tree while the songs of the cuckoos and the bees steal their minds and ears.

To the south of Śyama-kunda is the grove of Śrīdama known as *Śata-varga* (hundreds of divisions). In that grove there is one bower that is extremely astonishing. It is known as the dancing-grove (*nātyakunja*) of Gopāl Śrīdāma. It is completely studded with jewels and constructed in variegated ways. This dancing grove glows with a color that is pinkish. To the eastern side is a very excellent banyan tree which has hundreds and hundreds of thousands of branches and sub-branches. Under the pleasantly cooling shade of that tree is a platform made of solid gold. It is a place of supreme bliss where no discord could possibly exist.

Thus Balarāma comes to that place in the company of his boy-friends, and he rests upon the platform for a brief nap. The followers of Śrīdāma, who are always in great bliss, prepare various sweet edibles and fruits. One by one they bring the preparations and offer them to Rāma and in the company of his friends Haladhar enjoys eating these palatable items. After drinking cool water he tastes betel nuts. At that place and at that time, please render service unto him. All these pastimes of the cowherd boys playing merrily in the company of Balabhadra continue up to the twenty-second *daṇḍa* (2:24–2:48 PM).

To the east of this place, at a little distance away is a very enchanting sporting-grove (*raṅga-kunja*) which is a festival of happiness. It is the exceptionally fascinating grove of Sudāma-candra. Full of blossoming flowers, its coloring is pinkish. This grove is surrounded by creepers and bushes and is decorated with various types of birds. Bees fly to each and every flower in search of honey. In front of the southern gate is a tree known by the name of *Hari-tālikā*. At its base is an altar formed of various jewels inlaid into solid crystal. Upon this platform is a lion-throne of a hundred levels that has no comparison anywhere. To the south of here is a grove by the name *Rasālaya* (abode of mellows), which belongs to the group of boys headed by Sucandra. This is the headquarters for Sucandra and the other *sakhās* and *upa-sakhās* that are followers of Sudāma-candra. Now Haladhar takes Śrīdāma and the others to that place and they all become very blissful to behold the splendor of that sporting grove.

A Picnic of Sweets

At that time Bhagavān Śrī Kṛṣṇa suddenly returns, accompanied by Subala, Ujjvala, and Madhu-maṅgala. All the cowherd boys become so ecstatic that they are plunged into the ocean of loving bliss (*premānanda*). Kṛṣṇa satisfies his dearmost friends with the nectar speeches of His very sweet words. Then Śrī Rāma and Kṛṣṇa take all the boys headed by Śrīdāma and Sudāma, and sitting in that grove they enjoy a festival of happiness. In the center is Naṭabara Hari, the best of dancers, and to His right is Rāma. To His left sits Śrīdāma and Sudāma, and in front is Subala and Ujjvala. All the other boys sit in their appropriate positions. At that place the followers of Sudāma engage in serving out different kinds of sweet preparations. They distribute fruits, flowers, assorted sweets, curries and sweet rice. They serve *capātis* with sugar on them, and cow's milk mixed with ghee. Balarāma and Kṛṣṇa enjoy eating along with Śrīdāma, Sudāma, Dāma, Vasudāma, Kiṅkiṇī, Subhadra, Maṇḍalī-bhadra, Subala and the others. Sudāma offers a forest fruit to Kṛṣṇa, and Kṛṣṇa and Haladhar enjoy sharing it in great happiness. All their boyfriends are relishing supreme bliss. After they finish, they wash their mouths and sit down on *āsanas* upon raised platforms where they chew betel nuts.

At that place the followers of Sudama render services by which Balarāma and Kṛṣṇa become supremely satisfied. Sucandra weaves a flower garland and places it around Kṛṣṇa's neck. This forest garland swings and displays the pearls and coral that are woven into it. Sukantha takes *kunkum* from the Malaya hills, rubs dark *aguru* wood into it, mixes in some camphor and rubs it on the bodies and limbs of Kṛṣṇa and Balarāma. Then Sudarpa Gopāl waves a white *cāmara* whisk while Sukhānanda very blissfully offers them fresh betel nuts. Rasa-candra brings the water pitcher before them, and Sumahendra holds an umbrella made of fresh twigs and leaves. Sumukha and others massage their limbs as Rasangada massages

Kṛṣṇa's feet. Kṛṣṇa leans on the shoulder of Śrīdāma, and Subala stands before him while a myriad of graceful activities are performed in the joy of supreme bliss. What can I say about the magnificence of Balarāma sitting on the same seat with Kṛṣṇa? The effulgence of their two beautiful forms appears as if the sun and moon have arisen simultaneously. These youthful *Yugala-kiśor* brothers agitate the mind with their sheer beauty of fresh adolescence. One realizes the *siddha-deha* in the company of *guru-rūpa-sakhā,* cowherd boy in the form of one's spiritual master, and thereby participates in this scene. Thus outlines the service to Balarāma and Kṛṣṇa at the end of *madhyahna-kāla,* the midday period. At this point I have narrated up to the twenty-fourth *daṇḍa* (3:12–3:36 P.M.)

Aparāhna Sevā: Services During Afternoon Pastimes

Ball Playing and other Robust Sports

In the afternoon period Lord Hari plays different kinds of games with His friends, being so requested by the boys. Wandering throughout the forest, they go here and there in great bliss while beholding the splendor of the forest together. Along with His *priya-sakhās* Śrīdāma, Sudāma and Dāma, they happily play ball and other sports. While playing ball, Kṛṣṇa and Śrīdāma engage in mutual pushing and shoving. Sometimes these two have fierce fights while deeply absorbed in *premānanda,* and at other times they become friends and embrace each other warmly. Different boys each receive Bhagavān in their own respective places, and thus they accept Him into their own groups and treat Him equally, just as if He were one of themselves. Sometimes they all go from Vṛndāvana to another forest, and sometimes they go to Govardhana Hill. Rāma takes a few of his friends and goes elsewhere in search of straying cows. They look in different forests, caves, riverbanks and follow streams all throughout the countryside.

On the bank of the river by the base of Govardhana Hill, Kṛṣṇa begins playing a very fast-paced sport called *Hādu-gudu.* This is when someone has to touch the opponent by extending their foot, and by running quickly someone else has to grab hold of the opponent's feet. Thus playing different kinds of sportive games with their friends, they all enjoy romping in the gardens of Govardhana. These games continue up to the twenty-sixth *daṇḍa* (4:00–4:24), and the devotees who are meditating on them should perform their services at the appropriate moments.

Collecting the Wandering Cows

Now Haladhar sounds his buffalo horn bugle to inform everyone that it is time to go. All the boys hear it and freeze in place while exclaiming to each other, "*Are bhāi! Bhāi!* O brother brother!" At the sound of Balarāma's bugle all the boys become mesmerized, and they each cease relishing the mellows of the sports that they were tasting. Then Hari takes all His friends to gather the cows and they wander throughout the different groves of the forest. Some look in caves, in woods on the hillsides, or in bower-houses. Others run to distant places to search by the bank of the river and amongst the banyan trees. Becoming quite alarmed due to not finding all the cows, the boys incessantly call out their names. Seeing this Kānāi says, "*Bhāi re!* O my dear brother Śrīdāma! I will bring the cows back with the sound of My flute. Please watch carefully!"

Then Kṛṣṇa vibrates His flute with the sounds of the cows names, and all the cows immediately come running in search of the source of this music. Galloping along with their tails and their heads lifted high in the air, the cows promptly come and stand before Kṛṣṇa. Mooing and mooing, they gaze at Him with fixed eyes, and they touch the body of Śyāma by swishing the ends of their tails upon His back. Śrīdāma and Sudāma exclaim, "Subala, *are bhāi!* O dear brother Subala! There is no one else among our brothers as glorious as this Kṛṣṇa! He brought the cows in by playing upon His flute! We never heard of anyone else who could do that! *Are bhāi!* Just see the feats performed by Kānāi!"

Driving the Cows Back Home

Next, all the boys pasture the cows while they pick flowers and fruits from the forest. They have a snack of these fruits and also some sweets and drinking water, and then chew betel. After this, the cowherd boys assemble together and drive the cows toward the path back home. The boys call and call the names of all the cows and calves: "Dhavalī! Śyāmali! Kālī! Piyalī! Haṁsī! Piśāṅgī! Śavalī! Śrīngī! Kurangī! Raṅgī! Vamśī!" Thus the assembly of cowherd boys drive the cows forward by shouting, "*Hai! Hai!*" and "*Aha! Aha!*" The atmosphere is pervaded by the profuse sounds of their buffalo horns "*Dhaan! Dhaan!*" as well as by the sounds of their flutes. The auspicious echoes of the buffalo horns bugling in the forest are mixed with the sounds of kettle drums and many other instruments like small *dumpha* drums, *muraja* tom-toms, and assorted melodious musical instruments. The cowherd boys clap their hands, make funny sounds with their hands in their armpits, and drive the cows forward with calls of, "*Aba! Aba!*" while they bugle, play flutes and sing. The incessant mooing of the cows is like a song of praise for their calves, as if they were chanting "*Jai! Jai!*" The thunderous reverberations of this grand procession completely saturate the area of Gokula-maṇḍala, and all the people living throughout the land glorify them by exclaiming, "*Jai Rāma-Kṛṣṇa Jai!*" The boys Śrīdāma, Sudāma, Dāma, Subala, Ujjvala, Subhadra, Maṇḍalī-bhadra, and Mahābala come forward to gather with Rāma and Kṛṣṇa, and they settle all the cows to graze on the edge of the town.

The Exciting Return to Nandiśvar

At this point Balarāma and Kṛṣṇa along with their boyfriends enjoy the sport of watching animals playfully fighting with each other. Amongst the herds of cows there are bulls fighting with bulls, and calves fighting with calves. One maddened bull is chasing a cow that is in season. Rāma and Kṛṣṇa along with their boyfriends delightedly watch this scene. These pastimes with Kṛṣṇa continue to the twenty-eighth *daṇḍa* (4:48–5:12).

Finally, they arise quickly in order to return home. Thus Hari performs His eternal pastimes by taking His cowherd boyfriends along and walking on the ground of Vṛndāvana which He renders pleasing by the touch of His own feet. The cows move forward as the boys of Vraja run behind them. In the center of the assembly of boys, Rāma and Kṛṣṇa are situated just as the moon is surrounded by a halo. Their bodies are smeared with the dust raised by the hooves of the cows. Thus the two brothers Rāma and Kṛṣṇa appear very dusty. The cloud of dust from the hooves of the cows rises high into the orb of the sky as the cows *moo* and *moo* and progress toward home. The sounds of the bugles, flutes, "*Hai! Hai!*" and the lowing sounds of the cows are heard by all the *gopas* and *gopīs* who are residing at home, and thus they become very jubilant. Leaving aside their household activities, they rush toward the path that comes from the pastureland at the edge of town. Nanda, Upananda and others also go along with Yaśodā. All the Vrajapur-vāsīs give up everything they were doing and run for the *darśana* of Rāma and Kṛṣṇa. All the beautiful young girls, and the women of the town as well as the housewives come outside their homes and stand looking down the path, waiting for the vision of Rāma and Kṛṣṇa.

Rāma and Kānu proceed along while sporting merrily in the company of their friends. They shout, "*Aba! Aba!*" and clap their hands and play enchanting *veṇu* flutes. The sounds of the bugles "*Dhaan! Dhaan!*" mixes with the vibrations of flutes and other horns. Some boys walk in the forefront carrying flags and banners. The boys in this assembly are dressed in similar costumes, they appear to have similar forms, and in their midst are Rāma and Kṛṣṇa who walk along majestically like a pair of elephants. They playfully pose and swing their limbs and assume other enchanting postures. These two young *Yugala Kiśor* boys advance, along with their two closest friends. Dressed just like dramatic actors, they excite and entice the minds of the entire universe.

The Beauty of *Yugala Kiśor*

Do their splendors have the complexion of a pair of mountains, one made of silver and the other made of dark eye ointment? One holds a buffalo horn, the other holds a *murlī* flute. One has blue garments, the other has yellow. Both of them destroy all fear of material misery, suffering and calamity. Their beauty defeats that of Cupid, and they illuminate the total creation. Thus my *Yugala Kiśor* returns from the forest. Upon their lovely and variegated colorful turbans are peacock feathers. They have long curly locks, and streaks of sandalwood paste are on their foreheads. The arms of both of them are incomparable. They have beautiful lotuslike eyes, and their noses put to shame that of Garuḍa, king of birds. Earrings swing from their ears and tap their cheeks. Upon their conchshell-smooth necks sway garlands of jasmine flowers. Their hands look like pairs of lotus flowers and their arms look like the trunks of elephants. Their wrists are decorated with bangles, and by their pleasing sides are their walking sticks. Both of their hips are adorned with blue and yellow cloths, and their ornamental waistbells tinkle, thereby eclipsing the songs of the bumblebees. The walking motions of their graceful forms defeat the movements of the wagtail bird. Upon the dust of the earth they leave their footprints marked with the lines of a flag, thunderbolt, elephant goad and so forth. In front of them and behind them cowherd boys move along in the form of a circle, and in the center these two brothers are dancing and dancing.

The Assembly Enters Nandiśvar Town

Suddenly the *gopas* and *gopīs* who are standing and waiting catch sight of them from afar, beholding the dress of *Yugala Kiśor* and their lotus-like faces. This *darśana* immediately causes the auspicious sounds of, "*Jai! Jai!*" and "*Ulu! Ulu!*" to arise, and in all directions there is an ecstatic and tumultuous uproar of these jubilant exclamations.

After this, each of the cowherd boys gradually withdraws from the group and continues along their own path. Taking their personal associates with them, they depart for their respective homes. Śrīdāma and Sudāma lovingly embrace the saddened Kṛṣṇa, and with a faltering voice He satisfies them. Holding Subala's hands, Kṛṣṇa bids farewell with sweet words and then proceeds in the direction of His own home while His eyes are dripping and dripping with tears. He shares appropriate parting words with Maṇdālī-bhadra and other boys, while yet other boys bow down at Kṛṣṇa's feet. Thus individually speaking with Kṛṣṇa and bidding farewell, they each take their own group of cows and drive them home. Rāma and Kṛṣṇa continue onward to Nandiśvar, approaching their home in the company of their own friends.

Returning to Vṛṣabhānu-pur

Afterwards Śrīdāma, Sudāma, and others continue from Nandiśvar and travel toward their home in Vṛṣabhānu-pur. Arriving there, each of the members of this group of cowherd boys drive their own cows to their respective homes. All the ladies living in the town exclaim, "*Jai! Jai!*" and in all four directions this auspicious sound of, "*Jai! Jai!*" can be heard arising. Entering the town, Śrīdāma and Sudāma play enchanting *veṇu* flutes. Hearing this music, Ratna-bhānu comes forward. Seeing his father; Sudāma bows at his feet. Then Ratna-bhānu takes Sudāma onto his lap and kisses his face. Finally Śrīdāma also is greeted and enters his own home.

Services Rendered to Sudāma

Next I will narrate some particulars about Sudāma-candra's *sevā*, services rendered by the practicing devotees. Mother Suśilā calls out upon seeing Sudāma, "*Aya re! Aya re!* Oh, he has come. He has come!" Taking her son onto her lap, she mitigates all his fatigue. His limbs are covered with the dust of the cows and he is sprinkled with drops of perspiration. His moonlike face has become drawn due to the heat of the sun's rays. Then his servants take him and seat him upon a jewelled lion-throne while they wave soothing *cāmara* whisks. The servants wash his feet with very cool water and massage his limbs with scented oil. After the massage and bath they dress him in clothing and then smear his limbs with sandalwood paste. Suśilā brings an offering of numerous sweets, and Sudāma eats them in the company of his own associates. Then, going to sit on an *āsana* he chews betel nuts, and he calls for the cowherd boys who are his own followers. Sucandra, Śrī Candra-mana, and other followers come for the afternoon audience of Sudāma. Seeing Sucandra and the others, Sudāma feels great bliss, while Ratna-bhānu and Subhadra enjoy hearing him tell pleasurable stories of Kṛṣṇa's blissful pastimes. Taking his own friends along, Sudāma next goes to the *gośālā* where they move from spot to spot while milking the cows. This pastime should be remembered in the *siddha-deha,* and one should thereby become marked by the *bhāva* (the ecstatic mood) of Sudāma. One should meditate on the *svarūpa* (the original form) of Kṛṣṇa and become one of His followers in the company *of guru-rūpa-sakhā,* the spiritual master in the form of a cowherd boy.

O Śrī Caitanya! O Avadhūta (the divine madman Nityānanda)! O Śrī Sundarānanda! Please show mercy to this fallen soul! O *Gaurānga-bhakta-vṛnda* (assembled devotees of Lord Gaurānga)! This book *Preyo-Bhakti-Rasārṇava* is the giver of supreme jubilation. Now the ninth chapter has been narrated by Nayanānanda Dās. I have extensively described *aparāhna-sevā,* service during the afternoon pastimes. Next I will give an indication of *sāyahna-sevā,* service during the twilight time.

Thus ends the ninth chapter of

Śrī Śrī Preyo-Bhakti-Rasārṇava

CHAPTER TEN

Sāyāhna-Kālīya-Sevā and *Rātri-Kālīya-Sevā*

Services During Dusk and Evening Pastimes

(6:00–8:24 P.M. and 8:24–10:48 P.M.)

navina jalada-śyāmaṁ
rāmena vana-mālinam
tri-bhaṅga-bhaṅgimākāraṁ
vande 'ham nanda-nandanam

Who is dark like a fresh raindoud
Who along with Rāma
is adorned with flower garlands
Whose form is bent in a three-fold pose
I praise the darling boy of Nanda!

All glories, all glories to Rāma-Kṛṣṇa, and to Śrīdāma and Sudāma! All glories to the Vrajavāsīs! All glories to Vṛndāvana dhām!

Kṛṣṇa and Balarāma Return Home

Rāma and Kṛṣṇa move toward the palace of Nanda Mahārāja while all directions resound with auspicious vibrations of welcome and good will. Coming out of the house, Nanda-Rāṇī runs to take Hari onto her own lap to her heart's content. Tears fall from Rāṇī's eyes as she holds His left hand, and gazing upon Rāma and Kṛṣṇa's faces she begins to kiss them. Pouring cool water for them to drink, she performs various auspicious rituals, and finally takes Rāma and Kṛṣṇa into her own house. Seating them upon a jewelled lion-throne, she puts divine clothing on them, then she settles both the brothers next to each other on a single *āsana*. Exclaiming with concern, "Oh, you did not know how many hardships you would have to face in the forest!" She takes her own garment and wipes their moonlike faces. Seeing that their faces are drawn from the heat of the sun and that their lips are dry, she declares, "*Ore* Haladhar! I will never again let you go to the forest!"

Kṛṣṇa's Evening *Ārati* Ceremony

Male servants come forward and wash the feet of Kṛṣṇa and Balarāma, while others take *cāmara* whisks and fan soothing breezes. Their limbs are massaged with nicely scented oil, and their bodies are rinsed by pouring refreshing water. Towelling off their bodies, they are given yellow and blue clothes, then one servant brings forward the *pādya-patra* bowl and washes their feet. After this they are seated upon a jewelled lion-throne with Śrī Balarāma to the right and Śyāma to the left, Rāṇī Yaśodā lights up a series of ghee-lamps upon a golden tray. Nicely scenting the wicks with camphor, she then performs the *āratrika* of Kṛṣṇa while the assembled *gopīs* cheer with the auspicious vibrations of "*Jai! Jai!*" Then Yaśomatī also offers the lamps to Balabhadra. Thus performing the *ārati* while Kṛṣṇa is in the company of His friends, she then wipes His limbs and face with a cloth. She brings forward pitchers and offers them scented water as well as sweets, *capātis* with sugar, plus various fruits, curds, and milk mixed with cream. Rāma and Kṛṣṇa eat all these things along with their friends, then drink some water and chew on betel nuts.

Finally Haladhar and Rāya take a brief rest; afterwards they get up and proceed to the *gośālā* for milking the cows. Hari milks the cows along with His servants; He personally milks some cows and has other boys milk the other cows. After finishing they go and sit in the *Mohan Mandir* (enchanting temple). The progression of these pastimes continues for two *daṇḍas* into the night (6:00–6:24, 6:24–6:48 P.M.). Both Kṛṣṇa and Balarāma then rest upon jewelled bedsteads.

Arising one *daṇḍa* later (6:48–7:12), they meet with Viśāla, Vṛṣabha and others. Then Śrī Nanda-nandana proceeds along with Rāma and the other *sakhās* to the quarters through the east gate and is seated. At that time the boys headed by Śrīdāma and Sudāma arrive and congregate with Kṛṣṇa and Balarāma. Kṛṣṇa becomes very satisfied to see Śrīdāma and the rest, and He offers them His own seat within that assembly. Gradually all the boys come one by one like Subala, Ujjvala, Madhu-maṅgala and other friends of the confidential *narma* class. These pastimes occur at the fourth *daṇḍa* of the nighttime (7:12–7:36 P.M.). After this, I will describe the *rāja-sabhā* (Royal Assembly Hall). During all of these respective periods, the *sādhaka* should realize the *siddha-deha* and worship Rāma and Kṛṣṇa by following the *guru*.

Artistic Performances in the Royal Assembly Hall

After this, Śrī Rāma and Kṛṣṇa don the elegant costumes of royalty including divine cloth and various ornaments. Taking His boyfriends along, Kṛṣṇa goes outside into the courtyard and sits upon an opulent throne within a garden-temple. The cowherd boys all sit upon fancy carpets in their respective positions, lined up this way and that in row after row. In the center sits Śrī Kṛṣṇa in His royal garb, with Balarāma to His right and Śrīdāma and Sudāma to His left. The followers of Śrīdāma and Sudāma sit nearby and the groups headed by Subala and Arjjuna sit in front. Thus Hari presides majestically amongst many friends like Subhadra, Maṇḍālī-bhadra and six kinds of *sakhās*. The servants stand close holding lamps aloft on stands while the assembly of *brāhmaṇas* recites auspicious hymns of benediction. That arena becomes completely packed with the gathering of townspeople, and the awning overhead sparkles radiantly. Even the congregation of *brāhmaṇas* at Lord Indra's celestial assembly hall in Amarāvatī fades into insignificance before this majestic audience at Nandīśvar in Goloka. Everyone present is absorbed in the bliss of continual spiritual joy as they behold the performances of various kinds of singing, musical concerts and ecstatic dancing. Talented singers vocalize choruses and dancing girls cavort while scores of drummers sit in rows and beat *mṛdaṅgas, mādala* and *dampha* drums. Actors and actresses sing and display their immortal arts. Everyone laughs at the different types of comedy performances including hilarious portrayals of prostitutes taking the role of so-called heroines. Bells ring, eyebrows are knitted into frowns, and musical notes flutter along with the beats of *mādala* and *mṛdaṅga* drums that are lined up and reverberating in the courtyard. The dramatic performers blissfully sing of the transcendental qualities of Balarāma and Kṛṣṇa, and while singing to the beat they cast sidelong glances to behold Their moonlike faces. Thus Śrī Nanda-nandana is gloriously present beneath the ornate royal parasol radiant in majestic royal attire, seated upon the fabulous royal throne. His charming bodily limbs are smeared with sandalwood paste, and servants wave peacock-feather fans and *cāmara* whisks. His golden clothing glitters with the effulgence of lightning and appears to be like rows of clouds (the sequins, sparkling auras) sporting along with a fresh raincloud (His dark bodily complexion). Upon His chest is a forest-flower garland, and upon His head is a strand of tiny woven flowers. Thus seated to the left of Rāma – oh what majesty is displayed by Śrī Nanda-dulāl!

Finally rewarding the talented artists for their outstanding performance, He generously lavishes each of them with gifts of opulent cloth, precious gemstones, and so forth. After this the presentations of dancing and singing are concluded with a grand finale, and the artists bid farewell and depart.

The Outrageous Madhu-maṅgal Performs

After this, Kṛṣṇa's boyfriend Śrī Madhu-maṅgal takes center stage and devises a myriad of quarrelsome jokes and thereby instigates bouts of ecstatic wrangling. Sometimes he appears in the disguise of the backward *kāhāro* race and remains at a distance like an outcaste; sometimes he appears in the disguise of a woman and seductively casts sidelong glances; sometimes he appears in the disguise of a dacoit and makes fearsome and menacing gestures; and sometimes he contorts his bodily limbs in various caricatures and makes everyone laugh uproariously. In this way Kṛṣṇa and His friends enjoy numerous excellent amusements including dancing, singing and so forth.

Kṛṣṇa and Balarāma Retire to the Inner Chambers

Finally Yaśomatī calls, "Please finish your pastimes for the day!" Then Kṛṣṇa embraces the boys headed by Śrīdāma, and He satisfies the boys headed by Subala with sweet words. Thus bidding appropriate farewells and having last-minute discussions, all the *sakhās* leave for their own homes. After Mā calls Him again Kṛṣṇa leaves and enters the inner chambers along with His mother and Rohiṇī-nandana. Washing His face with sweetly-scented water, Śrī Nanda-nandana goes to sit with His father.

Rohiṇī personally cooks and then calls Rāma and Kṛṣṇa to come and eat. Thus everyone including Nanda, Upananda, Sananda, Nandana and the rest goes to the dining hall. After finishing the evening meal they chew betel and then depart for their own quarters. Kṛṣṇa and Balarāma again go to the Mohan Mandir (enchanting temple) where wonderful flower-couches have been fashioned, and each reclines to rest upon their own. There the *dāsa* and *dāsī* servants attend to their feet; tell me who in the universe is as fortunate as such servants. These pastimes continue up to the eighth *daṇḍa* of the night (8:48–9:12 P.M.). At this point you should meditate on their resting pastime. Thus ends the description of the *sāyāhna-līlā* (pastimes at dusk).

Rātri Sevā:
Services During Evening Pastimes Returning to Vṛṣabhanu-pur

After this, I narrate how all the cowherd boys return to their own homes. Śrīdāma and Sudāma take their own associates and light lamps to start the trek back to Vṛṣabhānu-pur. They engage in various jokes with their friends along the way and thereby relish the sportive mellows of laughter. Next going to the *gośālā* they visit with their cows, and then they congregate with their friends. Continuing to the gardens, Śrīdāma and Sudāma are seated in the center while the assembly of boys sit surrounding them. There they busy themselves with confidential amusements like dancing, singing, playing musical instruments, making jokes, playing dice, and generally becoming boisterous and unruly in ecstatic bliss. On some days they hear the songs of talented singers, and on other days dancers exhibit their art. Thus Vṛṣabhānu Purī becomes pervaded with music and song that causes every man and woman of the town to remain totally jubilant at all times.

Sudāma Retires to the Inner Chambers

Finally Śrīdāma and Sudāma embrace each other and depart for their respective resting quarters. When Śrī Sudāma arrives at his own home he bids farewell to his *sakhās* and *upa-sakhās*. Mother Suśīlā affectionately wipes his face and feeds him an assortment of sweets and four kinds of foodstuffs. Washing his mouth, he is seated upon a divine *āsana* as servants prepare betel packets and offer them to him. The boys Madhu-raṅga and Anantaka are Sudāma's very dear personal servants; being in full knowledge of all his secrets they remain perpetually by his side. Then entering the western gateway to his jewelled bedroom, Sudāma finally lies down to take rest upon a flower *āsana* atop a jewelled bedstead. His two servants then massage his feet by applying lustrous oil; in hot weather they make cooling breezes by waving *cāmara* whisks.

Realizing one's own *siddha-deha* during all of these different times, just take *darśana* of Kṛṣṇa in full knowledge of His *svarūpa*. These services are completed at the tenth *daṇḍa* of the night (9:36–10:00 P.M). Please listen attentively to my concluding words about how the day finally ends.

While sleeping at night Sudāma sees Rāma and Kṛṣṇa in his dreams, for he cannot live a moment even in his own home without the constant company of those two. All the pastimes that he performed that day in the company of Rāma and Kṛṣṇa – either at home, in the pasture, while tending the cows, or going to Vṛndāvana – all of these pastimes he beholds in his dreams. Thus he confirms to himself that he never gives up Kṛṣṇa.

Even while dreaming, Sudāma talks in his sleep and exclaims the cowherding sounds, "*Hai! Hai!*" and says aloud, "*Are!* Rāma and Kṛṣṇa! O brothers! Where have the cows gone?"

Now the devotees should internally realize the *nitya-siddha-deha* and serve all these pastimes that occurred during the day even in their own dreams. Living in Vraja in the company of one's *guru-rūpa-sakhā*, just worship Rāma and Kṛṣṇa always by accepting the *sakhya-bhāva*, the mood of a cowherd boy. Giving up all other aspirations, worship *Yugala Kiśor* the youthful pair Kṛṣṇa and Balarāma renouncing all desires as well for *dharma, artha, kāma,* and *mokṣa*.

Conclusion

Hoping at the feet of Śrī Caitanya, Nityānanda and Sundarānanda Ṭhākura, thus Nayanānanda Dās narrates the tenth chapter. This book *Preyo-Bhakti-Rasārṇava* is just like nectar, and the devotees who are fond of *sakhya-rasa* should always drink it. That person who recites or hears it with proper faith finally attains the feet of Rāma and Kṛṣṇa. Even if one is infested with all sins and afflictions, such a person becomes purified at heart and very quickly realizes the personal service of Rāma and Kṛṣṇa. One whose mind is fixed (*niṣṭhā*) on tasting the *prema- rasa* of the *sakhya-bhāva* would certainly taste this book.

After reading the writings of Śrī Rūpa Gosvāmī I have very humbly written this book, in simple poetry. I am extremely insignificant and my mentality is that of a sense-gratifier and a doer of wicked deeds. How could I possibly have the *śakti* to render this composition? Only the favor of Śrī Guru and the compassion of the Vaiṣṇavas has enabled me with the potency to describe these things in poetic meter. My most worshipable objects are the feet of Prabhu Gopāl (my father); I hold his lotus feet upon my head. By the strength of his order I can see, although I am a great fool. That Prabhu became very merciful and showed me his favor. His most worshipable object is Śrī Prabhu Kānu Rāma and his most worshipable object is Śrī Hari Caraṇa. He is the dear one of Pānu Gopāl. This Pānuyā Gopāl is one of the personal associates of Lord Gopāl; everyone is aware of his glories. Within the forest he bestowed *hari-nāma-mantra* upon a tiger by reciting the holy names into its ear. He turned the foodstuffs of Konakār into flowers, and by his touch the thieves on the footpath were blinded. What more can I say about the glories of that Gopāl? He is the favorite object of mercy for Sundara.

Śrīyuta Sundarānanda [in Gaurāṅga-*līlā*] is the same as Sudāma [the cowherd boy of Kṛṣṇa-*līlā*] and he is one of the foremost personal associates (*pārśada*) of Śrī Nityānanda and Caitanya. He is Balarāma and Kṛṣṇa's *priya-sakhā* (dear cowherd boyfriend), and the son of Ratna-bhānu (Vṛṣabhānu Mahārāja's brother). In Kali-yuga he takes birth as Śrīyuta Sundara. O my dear mind! Incessantly worship this Śrīyuta Sundarānanda along with the feet of Lords Nityānanda and Caitanya! My crest-jewels are the devotees of Śrī Caitanya Mahāprabhu. I fold my hands and bow my head millions and millions of times unto them. All glories to the great souls known as *dvādaśa-gopāl,* the twelve chief cowherd boys! I offer my obeisances at all of their feet, one by one. I offer thousands of obeisances unto the lotus feet of the Vaiṣṇavas. My humble prayer is that they will forgive the offenses committed by this person. I am exclusively meditating on the lotus feet of the great souls Abhirām, Śundarānanda and Gopāl. Trusting in the feet of Prabhu Gopāl this book manifested as *Preyo-Bhakti-Rasārṇava.*

This servant Nayanānanda is the humble attendant of Gopāl. My elder brother is Śrīyuta Gokula-candra. I have seen a few *sūtras*, some concise notes that were written by him in various places. In accordance with those, and in remembrance of his intention I have composed this book and spread it afar.

Thus ends *Śrī Śrī Preyo-Bhakti-Rasārṇava* *"The Nectar Ocean of Fraternal Devotion"* by Nayanānanda Dās Ṭhākura

Scriptures quoted by Ṭhākura Nayanānanda in the text of *Śrī Śrī Preyo-Bhakti-Rasārṇava*

Śrīmad-Bhāgavatam

Pādma Purāṇa

Skānda Purāṇa

Nāradīya Purāṇa

Varāha Purāṇa

Varāha Saṁhitā

Ādi Saṁhitā

Hari Vaṁśa

Pañca-Rātra

Gautamiya Tantra

Govinda Vṛndāvanam

Kṛṣṇa Yāmala

Krama Dīpikā

Bhakti-Rasāmṛta-Sindhu

Ujjvala Nīlamaṇi

Rādhā-Kṛṣṇa-Gaṇoddeśa-Dīpikā

Bṛhad Bhāgavatāmṛtam

Laghu Toṣaṇī

Govinda Līlāmṛtam

Bengali *kīrtana padas* written by Gokula-candra Dās (Gokulānanda), Nayanānanda's elder brother

Notes on parallel *Bhakti-rasāmṛta-sindhu* and *Nectar of Devotion* quotations

In Chapters One through Four of *Śrī Śrī Preyo-Bhakti-Rasārṇava*, Ṭhākura Nayanānanda has scrutinizingly analyzed particular sections of Śrīla Rūpa Goswāmī's glorious *Bhakti-rasāmṛta-sindhu*.

For the reader who wishes to study these sections alongside the equally glorious *Nectar of Devotion* by His Divine Grace A. C. Bhaktivedānta Swāmī Prabhupāda, we offer the following list of parallel references.

Column 1 represents *Bhakti-rasāmṛta-sindhu* quotes, according to Wave, Chapter and verse; column 2 gives the corresponding chapters of *Nectar of Devotion*. Thus whenever you see a particular *B.r.s.* verse, you can refer to the chart and then look in the N.O.D. to see further elucidations on these topics by His Divine Grace.

B.r.s.	N.O.D.
1.2.74–92	(6) How to Discharge Devotional Service
1.2.270–287	(15) Spontaneous Devotional Service
1.2.288–309	(16) Spontaneous Devotion Further Described
2.1.301–330	(26) Stimulation for Ecstatic Love
2.3.1–58	(28) Existential Ecstatic Love
2.4.1–90	(29) Expressions of Love for Kṛṣṇa
The most important sections regarding the cowherd boys:	
3.3.1–42	(41) Fraternal Devotion
3.3.57–136	(42) Fraternal Loving Affairs

Disciplic Succession of Cowherd Boys in the Village of Maṅgala-dihi, West Bengal

Śrī Nityānanda Prabhu

Sundarānanda Gopāl

Parṇī Gopāl

Kāśināth

Kānu-Rāma

Gopāl-Caraṇ

Gokulānanda & Nayanānanda

Jagadānanda

Dvārakānāth

Lord Nityānanda Balarāma's eternal associate is Śrī Sundarānanda Gopāl; Sundarānanda's chief disciple was Parṇī Gopāl (Pānuyā Gopāl); Parṇī Gopāl's disciple Kāśināth had a son named Kānu-Rāma and Gopāl accepted him as an adopted son and gave him initiation; Kānu-Rāma's son Gopāl-Caraṇ had two sons named Gokulānanda and Nayanānanda; Gokulānanda's son was Jagadānanda, whose grandson was Dvārakānāth.

The Twelve Cowherd Boys of Vraja

Intimate boyfriends of Lord Balarāma who also take birth as the principal associates of Śrī Nityānanda Prabhu as listed in *Śrī Caitanya-caritāmṛta, Ādi-līlā,* Chapter 22, texts 13–48.

1 – Śrīdāma: Abhirām Ṭhākura

2 – Sudāma: Sundarānanda Gopāl

3 – Mahābala: Kamalākara Pippalāi

4 – Subala: Gauridās Paṇḍit

5 – Arjjuna: Parameśvara Dās

6 – Vasudāma: Paṇḍit Dhanānjaya

7 – Mahābāhu: Maheśa Paṇḍit

8 – Stoka-Kṛṣṇa: Puruṣottama Paṇḍit

9 – Labaṇga: Kālā Kṛṣṇadās

10 – Dāma: Nāgara Puruṣottama

11 – Subāhu: Uddhārana Datta Ṭhākura

12 – Kusumāsava: Kholāvechā Śrīdhara

List of Cowherd Boys from Sri Govinda-Vṛndāvanam

Listing of cowherd boy names as found in the *Śrī Govinda-Vṛndāvanam*. In Chapter Two and Chapter Five of *Śrī Śrī Preyo-Bhakti-Rasārṇava*, we find the following quote from a portion of the *Bṛhad-Gautamīya-Tantra* called *Śrī Govinda-Vṛndāvanam* (1.149–150):

> *ayutāyuta-gopālāḥ sakhāyo rāma-kṛṣṇayoḥ*
> *teṣāṁ rūpaṁ svarūpaṅ ca guṇa-kannādayo 'pi ca*
> *nahi varṇayituṁ śakyā kalpa-koṭi-śatair api*

> Rāma and Kṛṣṇa have tens of thousands upon tens of thousands of cowherd boyfriends. Even if I had a billion millenniums to do it, I would not be able to describe all their forms, nature, qualities and activities.

This passage comes just after a group of 23 verses in the *Govinda-Vṛndāvanam* listing the names of some 200 eternally liberated cowherd boys. No other scripture gives so many nectarean names of these eternal associates of the Lord. First, Lord Mahā-Viṣṇu affirms to Brahmā in verse 125 that just as Śrī Kṛṣṇa is glorious, just so are Rāma and the other boys; then the names of numerous boys are listed in verses 125–148; and finally, Mahā-Viṣṇu declares in verses 149–150 that even He could never adequately describe these *gopas*. Their names are reproduced below along with our simple definitions. Had space permitted more explanation might have been offered here to illustrate how each boy embodies the particular transcendental jewellike quality that his name represents.

- Subāhu – of powerful arms
- Subala – very strong
- Śrīdāmā – majestic effulgence
- Vasudāmā – sun effulgence
- Sudāmā – exceedingly effulgent
- Mahābala – great strength
- Labaṅga – hairy limbs
- Mahābāhu – powerful arms
- Stoka-Kṛṣṇa – a small Kṛṣṇa
- Arjjuna – foxglove tree
- Angśuka – fine cloth
- Vṛṣabha – like a bull
- Vṛṣala – an outcaste
- Jaya-mālava – glorious tune
- Ūrjasvī – powerfully energetic
- Śubha-prastha – auspicious plateau
- Vinodī – giver of satisfaction
- Varūthapa – leather craftsman
- Rasika – the relisher
- Madāndha – blinded with pride
- Mahendra – great warrior
- Candra-śekhara – moon-crest
- Rasāla – mango-lover
- Rasāndha – blinded with mellow
- Rasāṅga – mellow-limbs

- Suraṅga – wonderful complexion
- Jaya-raṅga – glorious games
- Raṅga – playful one
- Ānanda-kandara – cave of bliss
- Nanda – delightful one
- Sunanda – exquisite delight
- Ānanda – blissful one
- Chanchala – fickle one
- Chapala – restless one
- Bala – of great vitality
- Śyāmala – dark one
- Vimala – faultless one
- Lola – tottering one
- Kamala – lotuslike one
- Kamalekshana – lotus eyes
- Madhura – sweet one
- Mādhava – honey-sweet
- Candra-bāndhava – most excellent friend
- Suratha – having a fine chariot
- Mahānanda – immense bliss
- Gandharva – celestial musician
- Kandarpa – Cupid
- Keli-darpa – amorous pride
- Rasendra – master of mellows
- Sundara – handsome one
- Jaya – victorious one
- Sugandharva – very talented musician
- Sarasendra – emperor of lakes

- Kalālaya–abode of artistry
- Sumukha–princely face
- Yaśasīndra–sovereign of fame
- Sānanda–always glad
- Candra-bhāvana –creator of luminosity
- Rasa-bhṛṅga–bee of mellows
- Rasālānga–luscious limbs
- Vilāsa–playful enjoyment
- Keli-kānana–love-sport forest
- Ananta–limitless one
- Kelivān–frolicsome one
- Kāma–lusty one
- Prema-bhṛṅga–bee of love
- Kalā-nidhī–abode of arts
- Sabala–armed strength
- Nāgara–valiant one
- Śyāma–dark beauty
- Sukāma–extravagantly lusty
- Sarasa–very succulent
- Vidhī –the creator
- Gaurānga–fair complexion
- Stoka-govinda–a small Govinda
- Devendra–lord of the gods
- Candra-mālaya–camphor and sandalwood
- Śyāmāṅga–dark limbs
- Paramānanda–supreme bliss
- Candra-yādava–moon dynasty
- Kṛṣṇāṅga–dark limbs

- Stoka-dāmā – a small Dāmā
- Vibhaṅga – creator of division
- Rasa-mānava – mellow-man
- Premāṅga – limbs of love
- Stoka-bāhu – small arms
- Hemāṅga – golden limbs
- Jaya-yādava – glory of Yadu dynasty
- Raktāṅga – reddish limbs
- Tri-bhaṅga – threefold bent
- Sunāgara – valiant hero
- Pavanendra – ruler of the wind
- Surendra – leader in godliness
- Surathendra – best of charioteers
- Jayadvrata – victorious in vows
- Sukhadā – giver of happiness
- Mohana – enchanting one
- Dāmā – effulgent one
- Keli-dāmā – dalliance-effulgence
- Sumanmatha – exceptional mind, agitator
- Sucandra – lovely moon
- Candramān – luminous like the moon
- Indra – the leader
- Jaya-śekhara – chief of victors
- Upendra – similar to Indra
- Sujaya – great victory
- Stoka-nāgara – little hero
- Vasanta – springtime
- Sumanta – abundantly endowed

- Rasavān – full of mellows
- Rasa-kandara – grotto of mellows
- Kāmendra – king of desire
- Kāmavan – full of desire
- Kāma – pure desire
- Ajitendra – foremost of the unconquerable
- Candra-chanchala – foremost of the fickle
- Dambha – boastful one
- Sudambha – of immense pride
- Dambhika – proud one
- Para-dambha – extreme bragger
- Vidambhaka – especially proud
- Prema-dambha – love-vanity
- Sugandhi – sweet-scented
- Dambha-nāyaka – boastful hero
- Upananda – excessive delight
- Chāru-nanda – lovely, nice
- Rasānanda – mellow-bliss
- Vilocanā – amazing eyes
- Jaya-nanda – glorious delight
- Prema-nanda – love delight
- Darpa-nanda – proud delight
- Sumohana – remarkably enchanting
- Bhadra-nanda – auspicious delight
- Candra-nanda – moon delight
- Vīra-nanda – heroic delight
- Sudhākara – spring of nectar
- Bala-nanda – prowess delight

- Bāhu-nanda–delightful arms
- Stoka-nanda–a small Nanda
- Yaśaskara–acclaimed deeds
- Kṛṣṇa-nanda–delight of Kṛṣṇa
- Gaura-nanda–fair golden delight
- Viśārada–particularly expert
- Śyāma-nanda–delight of Syāma
- Dāma-nanda–delight of Dāma
- Sukha-nanda–happiness delight
- Priyam-vada–speaker of sweet words
- Upakārṣṇa–intimate attractor
- Kalā-krsna–arts of Krsna
- Bāhu-krsna–arms of Krsna
- Sukhākara–abode of happiness
- Upasāmā–resembling everyone
- Rasa-stoka–a drop of mellow
- Prema-dāmā–effulgence of love
- Jaya-prada–bestower of victory
- Madhu-kaṇṭha–honey voice
- Vikuṇṭhā–free from hesitation
- Sudhā-kaṇṭā–nectar voice
- Priya-vrata–beloved vows
- Rasa-kaṇṭā–mellow voice
- Vaikuṇṭha–abode of freedom
- Sukanda–excellent genesis
- Candra-sundara–beautiful moon
- Keli-kaṇṭā–amorous voice
- Prema-kaṇṭā–loving voice

- Vara-kaṇṭā – exquisite voice
- Rasam-vada – luscious speaker
- Jaya-kaṇṭā – victorious voice
- Kalā-kaṇṭā – artful voice
- Amṛta-kaṇṭā – nectar voice
- Kalākara – embodiment of art
- Nṛtya-kendra – dances in the center
- Nṛtya-śakta – able to dance
- Nṛtyamān – always dancing
- Nṛtya-śekhara – crest of dancers
- Nṛtya-raṅga – frolicky dancer
- Nṛtya-tuṅga – exalted dancer
- Nṛtyānanda – dance-bliss
- Suyodhana – master of fighting
- Rasa-candra – mellow moon
- Kāma-candra – moon of desire
- Rūpa-candra – form of the moon
- Vimohana – especially captivating
- Keli-candra – amorous moon
- Sudarpa – explicit pride
- Darpa-nāgara – haughty hero
- Premendra – deity of love
- Prema-candra – love moon
- Prema-raṅga – love play, and many others

Chart of the 40 *Daṇḍas*, comprising a day in the life of the cowherd boys

from *Preyo-Bhakti-Rasārṇava*, chapters 7–10

Prātaḥ-līlā (Morning Pastimes)

(1) 6:00-6:24 – The *priya-sakhās* headed by Śrīdāma are awakened by the sound of Balarāma's buffalo horn; then the *upa-sakhās* (the greater assembly of cowherd boys) come, and all go to the town of Nandīśvar to get the darśana of Kṛṣṇa.

(2) 6:24-6:48 – Nanda-Suta is fast asleep; everyone first watches Him for a while, then His servants step forward and stir Him from His rest. Nanda Rāṇī performs the *maṅgal-ārati*, after which she gives Him benedictions and cleans His face.

(3) 6:48–7:12 – Arising from bed, Hari sits and eats some sweet things given by His mother. Afterwards He ascends a jewelled platform to wash His face and brush His teeth. Then He goes to milk the cows in the company of His boyfriends.

(4) 7:12–7:36 – Śyāma and Rāma gather with the cowherd boys to play different games while joking, dancing, and singing. Nanda-Rāṇī serves sweets to everyone, and then all the boys bid farewell to Kṛṣṇa and return to their own homes.

(5) 7:36–8:00 – Within the inner chambers, Balarāma and Kṛṣṇa are massaged and bathed by servants. Different cowherd boys arrive, and Kṛṣṇa goes inside with them to jubilantly snack on fresh butter and various milk sweets.

(6) 8:00–8:24 – All the boys proceed to the Sporting Arena to engage in mock fighting. Afterwards wandering here and there, they admire the different kinds of animals and birds, listening to parrot recitations and watching dancing peacocks.

Pūrvāhna-līlā (Forenoon Pastimes)

(7) 8:24–8:48 – When Yaśodā calls, Rāma-Kṛṣṇa and the other boys stop playing and go to the dining hall, Śrīmatī Rohinī serves the opulent morning meal, after which the boys wash their mouths and then go to recline on soft couches.

(8) 8:48–9:12 – They arise, rinse their mouths and sit outside to receive their gradually-arriving friends. Discussions about herding the cows cause Yaśomatī some alarm, which is eased by the promise of Balarāma to always protect Kṛṣṇa.

(9) 9:12–9:36 – Mother Yaśodā decorates Rāma and Kṛṣṇa with clothing and ornaments suitable for going to the forest. Overwhelmed with ecstatic bliss, she chants prayers of protection while bathing their bodies with her nectar-tears.

(10) 9:36–10:00 – The cowherd boys drive the cows and calves before them, sounding their buffalo horn bugles. All the townspeople follow the group to the edge of town; after Nanda instructs them in cowherding, they depart for the pastures.

(11) 10:00–10:24 – Rāma and Kṛṣṇa along with countless boys and cows enter the forest of Vṛndāvana and enjoy excellent pastimes of dancing, singing, laughing, and rolling on the ground. Then they proceed to Bhāṇḍīṛavan for a brief rest.

(12) 10:24–10:48 – There Kṛṣṇa and Balarāma begin mock fighting sports; they play arm-wrestling, stick-fighting, hand-boxing, and club-fighting. Next they play a game in which the losers of a contest must carry the winners upon their shoulders.

Madhyāhna-līlā (Midday Pastimes)

(13) 10:48-11:12 – They continue to the forest of Kāmyavan to dance, sing, and make jokes. Wandering to the bank of the Yamunā

river, the boys drink the water and jump in to have a big water fight. Up on the riverbank they put on dry clothes.

(14) 11:12–11:36 – Gathering the cows they all go to the forest of Bahulāvan picking flowers and weaving garlands to adorn themselves. Keeping Kṛṣṇa in the center, the boys sit around in a circle and enjoy partaking of a grand forest feast.

(15) 11:36-12:00 – In Madhuvan, Rāma and the others drink honey, then play a vigorous game of ball, then rest by the Yamunā to eat fresh fruits in the shade. Making royal forest arrangements, the boys perform Kṛṣṇa's coronation ceremony.

(16) 12:00–12:24 – They play numerous games under the trees by the bank of the Yamunā, making jokes, laughing, engaging in mischievous pranks, picking flowers, herding the cows, and energetically frolicking on the bank of the river.

(17) 12:24–12:48 – Nanda-Suta, along with several friends, leaves the assembly of boys on the pretext of searching for some stray cows. Haladhar then takes charge of all the cowherd boys, and they blissfully go to Śrīvan to search for other cows.

(18) 12:48–1:12 – Balarāma and the other boys climb trees, enjoy fresh fruits, dance and sing and clap their hands. They jump here and there tending the cows, and they play on flutes and buffalo horn bugles while wandering throughout Śrīvan.

(19) 1:12–1:36 – Balabhadra accompanied by the others travel to Kumudavan where they begin arm-wrestling and stick-fighting sports. Some boys amusingly imitate the birds, peacocks, swans, maddened elephants, lions, frogs, and snakes.

(20) 1:36–2:00 – Holding hands and forming a circle, the boys dance in the company of Haladhar in great bliss. Cavorting to the beat, they compliment each other's dancing. Beholding this sight, even the animals and the birds become stunned.

(21) 2:00–2:24 – Everyone leaves for Bhadravan, enjoying various mellows with Balabhadra as they wander from forest to forest. Arriving at Śyāma-kunda, they rest briefly at the base of a tree and listen to the charming songs of cuckoos and bees.

(22) 2:24–2:48 – Balarāma comes to Śrīdāma's grove to the south of Śyāma-kunda and rests upon a golden platform in the shade for a brief nap. The followers of Śrīdāma prepare various sweet edibles and fruits and offer them one by one to Rāma.

(23) 2:48–3:12 – Haladhar takes the boys to the sporting-grove of Sudāma to the east. At that time Kṛṣṇa suddenly returns, causing grand jubilation and all enjoy an ecstatic picnic of sweets and fruits served by the friends of Sudāma.

(24) 3:12–3:36 – Various services are rendered to Balarāma and Kṛṣṇa side by side upon the same seat, offering flower garlands, waving whisks, giving betel nuts, pouring cool water, holding an umbrella, gently massaging their limbs and feet.

* * *

Aparāhna-līlā (Afternoon Pastimes)

(25) 3:36–4:00 – Lord Hari and His friends happily play ball and various other games. Rejoicing in the natural splendor of the forest. Rāma takes a few of his friends and visits woodlands, caves, riverbanks, and streams in search of straying cows.

(26) 4:00-4:24 – On the bank of the river by the base of Govardhana Hill, they begin playing the fast-paced sport whereby one runs quickly to grab hold of their opponent's feet. Thus they all enjoy romping in the lush gardens of Govardhana.

(27) 4:24–4:48 – Now it is time to gather the cows and go. Haladhar sounds his buffalo horn bugle. Then Kṛṣṇa vibrates His flute with the sounds of the cow's names, and all the cows immediately come running, and stand mooing before Him.

(28) 4:48–5:12 – Next, the cowherd boys assemble together and drive the cows toward the path back home. Calling the names of their cows and clapping their hands, they bugle, play flutes and sing, settling the cows to graze at the edge of town.

(29) 5:12–5:36 – The cows move forward as the boys of Vraja run behind in the form of a circle; in the center Rāma and Kṛṣṇa are dancing and dancing. The joyous townspeople hear them coming and cease all activities, rushing to see their return.

(30) 5:36–6:00 – The waiting townspeople catch sight, and ecstatic cries of jubilation arise. Individual cowherd boys gradually withdraw and depart for their own homes, while Rāma and Kṛṣṇa move onward to Nandīśvar with their friends.

Sāyāhna-līlā (Dusk Pastimes)

(1) 6:00–6:24 – Nanda-Rāṇī runs out of the palace to tearfully greet and kiss Rāma and Kṛṣṇa. Pouring cool water for them she performs auspicious rituals. Seating them inside upon a jewelled lion-throne, she tends to their fatigue.

(2) 6:24–6:48 – Male servants wash their feet while their limbs are massaged with scented oil and rinsed. Offered fresh clothes, Rāṇī Yaśodā performs their *ārati*. After a snack of sweets and fruits, they go to the *gośālā* for milking the cows.

(3) 6:48–7:12 – After finishing the milking, both Kṛṣṇa and Balarāma then go and recline in the Mohan Mandir, finally resting upon jewelled bedsteads for a nap. Thus they doze peacefully throughout the entire third *daṇḍa* of the nighttime.

(4) 7:12–7:36 – Arising Nanda-Nandana proceeds to a sitting place along with Rāma, and they meet with their boyfriends who gradually arrive. Kṛṣṇa becomes very satisfied by them and even offers them His own seat within that assembly.

(5) 7:36–8:00 – After this, Rāma and Kṛṣṇa don elegant costumes and go to sit upon their throne in the outdoor Royal Assembly Hall for the evening entertainment They behold performances of singing, musical concerts, dance, and comedy.

(6) 8:00–8:24 – Finally rewarding the talented artists, Kṛṣṇa generously lavishes each of them with gifts of opulent cloth and precious gemstones. After this comes a grand finale of dancing and singing, and the artists bid farewell and depart.

Rātri-līlā (Evening Pastimes)

(7) 8:24–8:48 – After Mā calls, Kṛṣṇa says goodbye and enters the inner chambers. Washing His face, He goes to sit with His father. Rohiṇī calls everyone to come to the dining hall for the evening meal. Then all retire to their own quarters.

(8) 8:48–9:12 – Kṛṣṇa and Balarāma again go to the Mohan Mandir, where wonderful flower-couches have been fashioned, and each reclines to rest upon their own. There the fortunate *dāsa* and *dāsī* servants massage their lotus feet.

(9) 9:12–9:36 – The cowherd boys light lamps to proceed home to Vṛṣabhānu-pur. With their friends in the gardens, They amuse themselves with dancing, singing, playing musical instruments, joking, and becoming boisterous in ecstatic bliss.

(10) 9:36-10:00 – Finally the cowherd boys embrace each other and depart for their own resting quarters. All night long in their dreams they behold the pastimes performed that day while tending the cows in the company of Rāma and Kṛṣṇa.

Kṛṣṇa-pāda-padme-prārthanā
Prayer to the Lotus Feet of Lord Kṛṣṇa

This book is offered to Jagat-Guru Śrīla Prabhupāda who wrote the following verse expressing appropriate devotional longing while on board the steamship to America in 1965; who brought pure brilliant knowledge of service to Śrī Śrī Kṛṣṇa-Balarāma and the cowherd boys to the dark and remote corners of the suffering West; and who still guides us onward to the eternal pasturelands.

tomāra milane bhāi ābār se sukha pāi
gocārane ghuri din bhor
kata bane chuṭāchuṭi bane khāi luṭāpuṭi
sei din kabe habe mor

tomdra – Your; *milane* – in the meeting; *bhāi* – dear brother!; *ābā* – once more; *se* – that; *sukha* – happiness; *pāi* – I experience; *go-cārane* – tending the cows; *ghuri* – I wander; *dina* – the day; *bhor* – all through; *koto* – so many; *bane* – in the forests; *chuṭāchuṭi* – familiar joking, energetic frolicking; *bane* – in the forests; *khāi* – I relish; *luṭāpuṭi* – rolling on the ground; *sei* – that; *din* – day; *kabe*? – when?; *habe* – will it be; *mor* – mine.

"O my dear boyfriend! In Your company I will experience great joy once again. Wandering about the pastures and fields, I will pass the entire day with You in tending the grazing cows. Joking with You boisterously and frolicking energetically throughout so many forests of Vraja, I will roll upon the ground in spiritual ecstasy. When, oh when, will that day be mine?

Thankfulness

My heartfelt thanks and praises go to the entire cowherd crew at Murāri Sevaka farm community in Mulberry, Tennessee for tolerating my presence during the first edition production of this translation; whether they know it or not, each of these sweet-hearted devotees inspire us in their own unique ways.

Their Lordships Śrī Śrī Nitāi-Gauracandra for:

Paramparā Prabhu – for merciful invitation and shelter.

Nirguṇa Prabhu (since departed) – for ceaseless and enthusiastic devotional example.

Nandana Āchārya Prabhu and Mother Puṣpakā – for so many years of loyal service (in sun, rain and snow) to Kṛṣṇa's cows, fences, and land of Murāri.

Mother Kamrā – for practical and intense *cow-sevā* example.

Jaya Balarāma Prabhu – for ecstatic singing, *śloka* tweaking and boiled *sabji*.

Jaya Śrī Prabhu – for the wonderful cow graphics and bicycle modifications.

Prāṇa Gaurānga Prabhu – for firewood, holy names, philosophy and smiles.

Jeff, Keśava, cows, peacocks, horses, and Spikey – for blissful association.

Also many thanks to:

Our departed godbrother, Kuśakratha Prabhu – for priceless *phone-sanga*, and especially for the excellent and very rare manuscript copy, without which this presentation would not have been possible at all.

Special thanks to Prāṇadā Devī Dasī for keying this edition – a long and arduous task, and for proofreading. Also thanks to Gāndharvikā-Keli Devī Dasī for proofreading.

And, lastly, to my publisher, Māyāpriyā Devī Dasī, for all the work involved in bringing this book back to life by designing and publishing this new edition.

—Daśaratha-Suta Dāsa